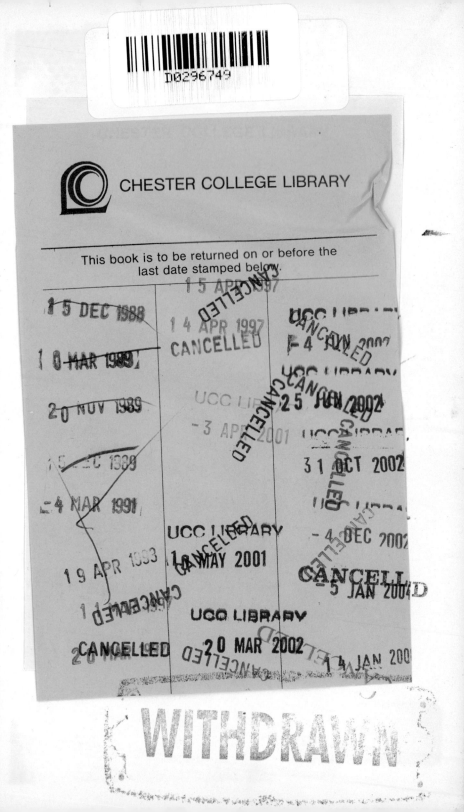

E. M. FORSTER'S INDIA

By the same author

E. M. FORSTER: A HUMAN EXPLORATION
(co-editor with John Beer)

E. M. FORSTER'S INDIA

G. K. Das

Foreword by
John Beer

First edition 1977
Reprinted 1979

Published by
THE MACMILLAN PRESS LTD
London and Basingstoke
Associated companies in Delhi Dublin Hong Kong
Johannesburg Lagos
Melbourne New York
Singapore Tokyo

British Library Cataloguing in Publication Data

Das, G. K.
E. M. Forster's India
I. Forster, Edward Morgan – Criticism and
Interpretation   2. India in literature
I. Title
893'.9'12   PR6011.058Z/

ISBN 0-333-22360-8

Printed in Great Britain by
BILLING AND SONS LTD
Guildford, Worcester and London

To the memory of my father

GURUJEE BISWANATH DAS

Contents

Foreword

A Passage to India remains one of the most widely-read of English novels, appealing both to the general reader and to the student who may find it among his set texts. This is not always a matter simply of content: indeed, some time ago a lecturer in a training college told me that he made the novel central to one of his courses, since he found that its pages offered examples of every kind of English style and usage which he wished to discuss with his students. But the main reason for its success is undoubtedly the quality of thought and reflection displayed in its pages.

Further light has recently been thrown on its origins by the emergence of the original manuscripts and drafts of the novels, along with other papers and diaries. These have been examined perceptively, notably by June Perry Levine and John Colmer.[1] To those who have read and reflected on the novel, however, another question must often arise. How true is the novel to the facts with which it deals? Many of its characters can be attested to from our own experience, for the pettiness and self-importance of small-town officials are always with us. But just how accurate was Forster's picture as a whole? In spite of all the commentary that the novel has attracted, surprisingly little attention has been given to this question. Dr Das's book now assembles the materials that are available—which must mean most that we are ever likely to have—for considering it. He not only brings together the many scattered discussions of Indian affairs that lie scattered through Forster's letters, reviews and diaries, but sets them in a context of contemporary events and reactions to them. His book is of value even to those who simply want a straightforward account of British India in its penultimate phase.

What conclusions emerge? Firstly, one is freshly struck by the liberating effects of Forster's acquaintance with India. In this respect, it stands in a line with a number of such liberations during his early career. It was liberating to reach Cambridge after the enclosed atmosphere of a public school and to discover a world where intellect was valued for its own sake; liberating, also, to spend a year in Italy soon afterwards and encounter a society which was not bound by the conventions of suburban England. In 1907 he visited Figsbury Rings in Wiltshire and had a succession of undramatic experiences which proved enlightening and sparked off a whole section of *The Longest Journey*.[2] Six years later he met Edward Carpenter and his friend George Merrill and experienced a physical revelation which disclosed to him the possibility of accepting his own homosexuality without having to endure the sense of shame decreed by society.[3]

Before this last event, however, he had visited India, and that too proved a liberation. As with many of the other experiences, it first focussed itself in a personal relationship. He has recorded how it was his friend Syed Ross Masood, first met in 1907, who was responsible for awakening an initial interest in the country.

> He woke me up out of my suburban and academic life, showed me new horizons and a new civilization and helped me towards the understanding of a continent. Until I met him, India was a vague jumble of rajahs, sahibs, babus and elephants, and I was not interested in such a jumble: who could be? He made everything real and exciting as soon as he began to talk . . .[4]

Seventeen years later, Forster dedicated *A Passage to India* to Masood.

That novel did not arise out of a single friendship, however. As one comes to know the novel more intimately, in fact, one realises how complex is the intertwining of factors that led up to it. At the time of his first visit, as P. N. Furbank has recorded,[5] he was in a state of some uncertainty about his literary future. After the success of *Howards End*, published in 1910, he had begun to fear that he might be drifting into creative sterility. He had begun a new novel, *Arctic Summer*, but had not been able to finish it.

India broadened his horizons beyond all expectation. Cambridge, Wiltshire, even Italy itself, were dwarfed by its vastness. It was also artistically forbidding in a new kind of way, however: he began a novel based upon it, but found it impossible to carry on. Not until many years later, after another visit, did he finally find a form for what needed to be said.

His difficulties were not surprising when one considers his early aspirations towards wholeness of achievement. Writing to Forrest Reid early in 1915 about his novel *Maurice*, he said,

> My defence at any Last Judgment would be 'I was trying to connect up and use all the fragments I was born with'—well you had it exhaustingly in *Howards End*, and Maurice, though his fragments are more scanty and more bizarre than Margaret's, is working at the same job.[6]

But how to connect up and use everything that he experienced in India? That was a much greater problem. He could not do it at the time when he produced *Maurice*, nor could he do it when he took out the early part of his first attempt on his second visit to India, in 1921. Only when he returned and was reflecting on his experiences did the whole come together.[7]

In certain respects, world events seem to have assisted the process of gestation in an unexpected manner. The First World War came, with all

its horrors, but Forster spent the later war years in Alexandria: as a result
he missed the years during which the war pressed hardest on the
consciousness of those who remained in England. And eventually this fact
brought an unexpected literary bonus. For many writers the experiences of
the years 1914–18 proved so traumatic that they could not handle them
adequately at the time. Forster, whose outlook belonged primarily with
the outgoing liberalism of the pre-war generation, shared something of this
malaise but was not quite so radically affected. And having missed the
worst years in England, he was eventually able to use his Indian
experiences to provide a form for the change in consciousness which he,
like others, had necessarily experienced.

In one sense he had found a form for it before the war began. In the
'Hymn to Action' which he wrote in 1912, he records how Arjuna finds, in
spite of his misgivings, good reasons for going into battle and eventually
wins a great victory:

> But it is necessarily and rightly followed by disillusionment and remorse.
> The fall of his enemies leads to his own, for the fortunes of men are all
> bound up together, and it is impossible to inflict damage without
> receiving it.[8]

The man who had written these words two years before the war was not
likely to fall victim to the disenchantment that overtook many of his
contemporaries.

In *A Passage to India*, however, he found a much larger and more
complex form for what had happened. The richness of this novel is such, in
fact, that it can be read in three quite differing ways, according to the
character whose experience is made central. Those who seek in the novel
primarily a statement about British rule in India, are likely to see Fielding
as the hero, as he tries to make sense and organisation from what is
essentially a chaotic situation. For them, the point of the novel lies with the
dearth of Fieldings in India; it is primarily a statement of scepticism and
disillusion.

For those who concern themselves with the emotional impact of India
upon a sensitive person, on the other hand, Mrs Moore moves to the centre
of the scene. Her nightmare experience in the Marabar Caves and her
subsequent breakdown become the crucial events in the novel, as
demonstrating the impotence of Western values against the great and
unorganisable facts of the sub-continent. Her experience becomes, in fact,
allegorical of the breakdown of nineteenth-century reliance upon culti-
vation of human affection when faced with the horror of the First World
War.

For those who share Forster's deep-rooted and abiding Romanticism,
finally, the true heroine of the novel is Adela. Her desire to see something of
'the real India' is perhaps callow; but it is she who, by her response to the

beauty of the naked punka-wallah in the court-room and by her truth to that response, breaks into the unrealities of the trial and points the way (if only temporarily and fleetingly) to a more genuine relationship between English and Indians than any that is actively rendered in the book. For a moment we see Forster still grasping for an over-arching perfection, however much that dream must subsequently be dwarfed.

If Adela's naive romanticism is inadequate except at such a moment, moreover, there are suggestions in the novel that a more developed romanticism provides the attitude best fitted to cope with experience of India. John Colmer has recently shown how a chief failure of the English attitude lies in its insistence on categorising and cataloguing everything.[9] Events and sights in the novel consistently resist such categorisation. A bird seen by two characters is neither bee-eater nor parrot; but it has flown away before it can be identified. The creature that hits the Nawab Bahadur's car is similarly mysterious. 'Nothing embraces the whole of India, nothing, nothing'; and we come to realise that for a mind that is resilient enough the fact is not defeating but exciting. The jaded twentieth-century consciousness is offered a new way forward.

These are the ways in which Forster 'connects up and uses' all the fragments of his Indian experience: not attempting a final Wagnerian harmony but allowing the various strands of his consciousness to live side by side in different characters. And this helps to explain why Indian nationalism, though more of a presence in the novel than some critics have admitted, does not occupy a central position. It is not true that the novel 'depicts a pre-1914 India', but it does draw heavily on material from the more settled time of the earlier visit.

It is important to remember, for instance, that that visit was undertaken in the company of Goldsworthy Lowes Dickinson. Dickinson's interest in India was partly that of a philosopher. As an enthusiastic Platonist who had studied Plotinus from cover to cover as a young man, he was able to strike up an instant rapport with the Maharajah at Chhatarpur and discuss philosophy with him endlessly.[10] At the same time he found his own brand of idealism challenged deeply by what he saw in the East: there is a letter, for example, in which he records how he has been watching a wasp depositing paralysed spiders in a hole in one of the tables, laying her eggs and sealing them up with wax. 'I think perhaps, after all, the Hindus took in more of the facts in their religion than most people have done', he writes.[11]

Dickinson was rather jaded during the journey, however, and did not respond to the sights and sounds of India with the same eagerness as Forster. Hindu architecture repelled him, in fact: Forster later wrote 'I remember how he used to cower away from those huge architectural masses, those pullulating forms, as if a wind blew off them which might wither the soul . . .'[12] One suspects that a good deal of his experience may have found its way into the conception of Mrs Moore.

It is important that all these factors in the novel should be accurately understood, since it is otherwise easy to assume that Forster was attempting a fuller and more accurate estimate of India under British rule than was actually the case. Some critics, as Dr Das mentions, have shown impatience with the novel on precisely these grounds. Nirad Chaudhuri, for instance, has pointed out that India during the period of its westernisation contained great Indians, of a stature to rank with the greatest European intellectuals, who are not represented at all in Forster's novel, while George Orwell pointed to the practical achievements of the British, such as the building of the railways, and maintained that these would have been impossible if those who undertook them had been men of Forster's outlook.[13] There is room for considerable disagreement here, of course. Chaudhuri maintains that Forster's Godbole is not an exponent of Hinduism but a clown, for instance, and Forster himself said in his interview with Dr Das that he was a created character; yet other Indians to whom I have spoken have found Godbole utterly credible. The fact still remains, however, that *A Passage to India* is essentially a novel which looks out on India from a backwater of British rule, and that by concentrating on a princely state it offers no chance of examining the problems of British rule as conducted from the great metropolitan centres of the country. To believe otherwise would be rather like taking D. H. Lawrence's *Women in Love* as one's central guide to the condition of the mining industry in England earlier this century.

Dr Das's book helps place all this in a proper perspective: it enables us to see something of the background to the events of the novel, whilst also showing how minutely accurate Forster is in his references to particular events of the time. But it also goes a great deal further by demonstrating the full range of Forster's thought about India as a whole. When his other writings are examined we discover a Forster who was concerning himself with Indian affairs for half a century, and continually revising his judgements in the light of new evidence.

How good was Forster's political sense? In certain respects he was very shrewd indeed. He understood, as few have done, the kind of tone needed in dealing with members of a civilisation which while 'backward' in terms of administration and technological achievements, was far in advance of the West in other respects.

Lionel Trilling, pursuing a similar point, retails an exemplary story from H. N. Brailsford:[14]

Here and there mildness and good-temper disarmed the local agitation. I heard of one magistrate, very popular with the people, who successfully treated the defiance of the Salt Monopoly as a joke. The local Congress leaders made salt openly in front of his bungalow. He came out: bought some of the contraband salt: laughed at its bad quality: chaffed the bystanders, and went quietly back to his house. The

crowd melted away, and no second attempt was made to defy this genial
bureaucrat. On the other hand, any exceptional severity, especially if
physical brutality accompanied it, usually raised the temper of the local
movement and roused it to fresh daring and further sacrifices.

Trilling's further comment, 'For want of a smile the Empire was lost', is less
perceptive, however. The Empire was going to be lost whatever happened,
and most people on the spot had grasped that long before. Forster's point
was that with a different kind of attitude the loss might have been
transformed into a greater gain for both sides. The British Empire could
not have been retained, but it might have been (to quote his words in the
novel) 'a different institution'. His comments about the insularity of the
English, confined as they were to the narrow society of Anglo-India, were
later to be supported by Nehru in his *Autobiography*:[15]

> Usually the Englishman meets the same set of Indians, those connected
> with the official world, and he seldom reaches really interesting people,
> and if he reached them he would not easily draw them out.

Nehru goes on to discuss the 'deterioration of mind' which he observed in
many Anglo-Indian administrators. Such an individual might blame
many factors, 'not realising that the cause of intellectual and cultural
decay lies in the hide-bound bureaucratic and despotic system of
government which flourishes in India and of which he is a tiny part'.

The fact still remains, of course, that the domination of an entire sub-
continent by such a small group of people was an extraordinary feat and
that total relaxation of grip might well have meant that the British would
have been forced to leave the country much earlier. Forster himself
recognised by 1921 that the position had deteriorated beyond hope of
recovery on that score, and could only hope for a change of mind that
might 'minimise' its effects. And it is likely that in this, at least, he himself
achieved some success—that his attitudes, as conveyed not only through
his novel but through his journalism of subsequent years, helped to prepare
the ground for the final cession of English power as it took place, by
revealing to many politicians in England the shaky kinds of foundation on
which that power had been built and exercised, and the need for a graceful
retreat.

Dr Das's account, by integrating Forster's creative achievement with his
lifelong engagement with India, provides a unique record of the times,
which is interesting in its own right. His account of Forster's dealings with
Hinduism rounds the account impressively. We are led to see how an
Englishman whose basic presuppositions were those of a sceptical Western
intellectual could, without ever being drawn to a full commitment, find in
Hinduism a way of life which was deeply sympathetic to him. It is a
beautifully delicate and poised position, which Forster's own summarising

phrase, 'Call me a Non-Believer', typically understates. After Dr Das's close analysis of his dealings with British India, his long account of the matter recalls us to the fact that Forster's basic preoccupations always extended far beyond politics.

Peterhouse   John Beer
Cambridge

Notes

1 June Perry Levine, *Creation and Criticism: A Passage to India*, 1971; John Colmer, *E. M. Forster: The Personal Voice*, 1975.

2 See his introduction to *The Longest Journey* (World's Classics ed.), 1960, pp. x–xi.

3 *Maurice*, 1971, p. 235.

4 *Two Cheers for Democracy*, 1951, p. 299.

5 P. N. Furbank, Preface to *Maurice*, 1971, p. v.

6 Ibid., viii.

7 *The Hill of Devi*, 1953, p. 155.

8 *Abinger Harvest*, 1936, p. 334.

9 Op. cit., 170–2.

10 Forster, *Goldsworthy Lowes Dickinson*, 1973, p. 115.

11 Ibid., 116.

12 *The Listener*, 10 September 1953, p. 420 (Cf. G. L. Dickinson, *Appearances*, 1914, p. 32).

13 N. Chaudhuri, 'Passage to and from India', *Encounter*, June 1954, pp. 15–24; George Orwell, 'Rudyard Kipling' (1942) in *Critical Essays*, 1946, pp. 103–4.

14 Lionel Trilling, *E. M. Forster*, 1951, p. 129n, quoting from H. N. Brailsford, *Rebel India*, 1931.

15 Jawaharlal Nehru, *An Autobiography*, 1936, pp. 28–9. Quoted by K. Natwar-Singh, in *Aspects of E. M. Forster*, ed. O. Stallybrass, 1969, p. 47.

Preface

E. M. Forster wrote that his Indian friend Syed Ross Masood 'woke me
out of my suburban and academic life, showed me new horizons and a new
civilization'. Like the European experience of Henry James or T. S. Eliot,
Forster's India is a pre-eminently vital part of his life and work, and an
essential factor behind his eminence. In *A Passage to India* (the novel which
alone would secure his fame) we have the real tests, as also the fulfilment of
his many-sided personality: as an internationalist, a democrat, an
individualist, a sceptic, and a visionary. His numerous other writings
about India, though less commonly known, were all significant for his
purpose. One motive which prompted me to study all these works in
conjunction with *A Passage to India* and *The Hill of Devi* was the urge to
attempt a comprehensive picture of an aspect of Forster which is familiar to
his readers without being fully known, admired (or disliked) without being
fully understood.

Some of his earliest writings, the two major works, and certain later
writings about India, all pursue some common themes, and are essentially
exploratory and interpretative in nature. Taking these as the basis of my
study, I have been concerned to collect and examine the mass of his
writings, published as well as unpublished, including the accounts in his
personal letters and diaries, some of which have not hitherto been
examined in this larger context, in order to project what might be called
Forster's image of India.

His writings between 1912 and 1920, i.e. during the period between his
first and his second visit to India, are marked by disenchanted and realistic
observations on contemporary Indian society, and also by an enquiry into
certain aspects of the Indian heritage, with the purpose of finding terms of
continuity between India's past traditions and her posterity. His second
visit to India (1921–2) provided him with a unique variety of experiences.
A 'resident Voltaire' at the court of the central Indian state of Dewas
Senior, he had such varied duties as looking after the palace tennis courts,
motors and electric house, and dispatching cows to the pound from His
Highness's garden. At the same time he was also a keen observer of the
changing social and political scene of British India outside Dewas, listening
to reports: 'the disciples of Gandhi . . . shout subversive slogans at us over
the border'. The writings based on his experiences of this period are more
concentrated and complex studies on the contemporary situation in
Imperial India. They reveal, among his varied reactions, his misgivings

concerning Princely India, and a deep sympathy with India's democratic aspirations after the First World War as expressed in the revolutionary ideas of Gandhi's Non-cooperation movement. His own ideological conflict with Imperialism, reflected only partially in his early work, is fully defined in these writings, which I have studied in relation to certain actual historical and official records of the period. In other writings of the time he looks beyond the political situation, at certain more permanent aspects of India.

A Passage to India shows the whole range of Forster's Indian interests. He described it on one occasion as 'the best documented of my work because I did get to know a little about the country from the inside'. Read along with some other relevant works of the period, such as those of Edmund Candler, Hilton Brown and Edward Thompson, it stands out as the most distinguished achievement among contemporary literature about India. Forster's search for an India in the traditions of her humanity, her religions, her cultural and artistic achievements, and for more meaningful bonds than the Imperial between India and Britain, based on an essentially humanistic and cultural understanding between the two peoples, distinguishes his novel from others of the period. Examined as an original study based on actual contacts with India and Indians, it demonstrates Forster's realism, and a totally serious concern for history and fact.

With *A Passage to India* Forster's interpretation of India is not complete; some of his later writings (apart from *The Hill of Devi*, which substantially belongs to an earlier period) continue the investigation and present new insights. For example, his enquiry into the spiritual element of the Hindu tradition, as expressed in the Hindu consciousness in general, and in Hindu ideas of God and of the temple in particular, is pursued in several articles written after *A Passage to India*. Evidence from these writings and certain other sources suggests that he recognised a significant value and modern relevance in the fusion of spiritual and human elements in the Hindu tradition.

Based on my doctoral thesis for the University of Cambridge, and on subsequent research into the private papers and manuscripts of Forster released after his death, this book has gained from assistance received in various ways. I express my indebtedness to the late E. M. Forster for giving me the opportunity to meet and talk with him on several occasions. I am also indebted to: the late Sir Malcolm Darling for answering some queries about the Maharajah of Dewas, and also for giving a very kind personal interview; the late T. R. Henn for his many appreciative comments and criticisms; J. B. Beer, for his invaluable supervisory guidance during the period of my research as a graduate student and his unfailing support and encouragement ever since; P. N. Furbank, for giving, in the course of our numerous conversations and in letters, various factual details from Forster's diaries and private papers relating to his first two visits to India, and for reading the manuscript and offering several helpful suggestions; Oliver Stallybrass, for answering queries on the manuscripts of *A Passage to India* and for giving some valuable comments on the typescript; F. R. Leavis, for answering a letter I had written to Mrs Q. D. Leavis on the question of the reception of *A Passage to India*; B. J. Kirkpatrick, Forster's bibliographer, for answering a query about one of Forster's earliest publications; Frederick P. W. McDowell, of the Department of English, University of Iowa, and John H. Stape, for supplying some useful reference materials; the Editor of the *New Statesman*, for identifying the author of an anonymous Indian contribution on Forster, which appeared in that paper; the librarians of Cambridge University Library, the libraries of the English and Oriental Faculties at Cambridge, the libraries of the British Museum; the Provost, Scholars, and library staff (and in particular, Penelope Bulloch, archivist of twentieth-century papers) of King's College, Cambridge, for giving me access and all facilities to study various Forster papers, including the Indian Diary, the Commonplace Book, and the MSS. (copyflow) of *A Passage to India*; Karen Stringer and Sarah Polyviou for preparing the typescript with care and interest; and Bulbul, my wife, for reading and offering many helpful comments on the draft versions at various stages.

I should like to express my gratitude to the Association of Commonwealth Universities, London, and to the British Council, for giving me a Fellowship for the period of my research. I am thankful also to the Executive Council of the University of Delhi for granting me leave, and to the President and Fellows of Queens' College, Cambridge, for their support and encouragement during the whole period.

Queens' College   G. K. Das
University of Cambridge, 1976

Textual Note

The particular editions of Forster's books used for the purposes of references and citations in the book are:

> *The Longest Journey*, World's Classics edition (London, 1960)
> *Howards End* (London: Edward Arnold, 1965)
> *A Passage to India*(London: Edward Arnold, 1971)
> *Goldsworthy Lowes Dickinson* (London: Edward Arnold, 1962)
> *Collected Short Stories* (London: Sidgwick and Jackson, 1948)
> *Abinger Harvest* (London: Edward Arnold, 1953)
> *Two Cheers for Democracy* (London: Edward Arnold, 1951)
> *The Hill of Devi* (London: Edward Arnold, 1953)
> *Marianne Thornton: A Domestic Biography* (London: Edward Arnold, 1956)

The author and publisher wish to thank Edward Arnold (Publishers) Ltd and Harcourt Brace, Jovanovich, Inc. for permission to quote from the works of E. M. Forster in which they hold the copyright.

The passages cited from the manuscripts of *A Passage to India* have been kept in their original form as found in the MSS. (copyflow) in the possession of King's College, Cambridge, showing signs of corrections etc., which have not been altered.

Spelling variations will be found in the following Indian and Oriental words and names, which, occurring in quotations cited from various sources, have been kept in the forms in which they occur:

(i) Khajuraho: Khajraho: Khajraha (ii) Khilafat: Caliphate (iii) Moghul: Mogul (iv) Moslem: Muslim (v) Mohammedan: Mohamedan: Muhammedan: Muhamedan (iv) Swarajya: Swaraj (vii) Upanishad: Upanisad

The term 'Anglo-Indian' is used in the first of the senses defined in the *Shorter Oxford English Dictionary*, as referring to persons 'of British birth, now or formerly resident in India'.

1 India 'in Legend and Fact': Forster's Writings about India between 1912 and 1921

One main engagement of E. M. Forster's mature years of authorship has been his search for an interpretation of India. According to evidence available from his early pieces on India, this seems to have been a clear purpose for him, which he has pursued through all his fictional and non-fictional writings about India. In an early article about India he looks at the subject in perspective, and writes:

India has reached the English imagination by different routes. To the stay-at-home of the eighteenth century 'India' meant southern India, a land of coal-black heathen, and tropical vegetation, wherein elephants trumpeted and Little Henry converted his Bearer. Becky Sharp dreamt of such an India when Jos Sedley first met her virgin gaze, but Jos came from Bengal really; the centre of interest had already shifted from the extreme south. During the nineteenth century it moved up to the Imperial cities of Delhi and Agra, and another India, less fantastic but more interesting, dawned upon the stay-at-home. Sleeman – that noble and fascinating writer! – rambled with him through the States of Bundelkhund and the Kingdom of Dudh [Oudh]: Tod led him into the chivalrous deserts of Rajputana . . .

After the Mutiny and the transference from John Company to the Crown . . . the new type of official . . . was harder worked, less independent, and less in touch with the Indian socially . . . Such a man was not likely to waste his time in interpreting India to the stay-at-home . . . So it followed that our conceptions of the land grew more sterile. The glamour of the old nabobs and missionaries had gone, the kindly light of Tod and Sleeman had gone also. Our guides now were often Anglo-Indian ladies, and their theme the disaster of inter-marriage; that disaster obsessed and obsesses them, and the novels that exhibit it read as though written on an elephant's back, high above the actualities of the bazaar. We were assured that there was no real religion in the country, no literature, no architecture except the Taj, and that was built by an Italian. Official enthusiasm had petered out.

With the twentieth century begins a new interpretation. It comes from many sources which have only this in common: they are unofficial. In religion Mrs. Besant has shown us that Hinduism has a meaning, even for the West. In music, Mrs. Mann has unlocked a subtle and exquisite spirit. In art, Dr. Coomaraswamy has revealed the beauty of Rajput miniatures, Mrs. Herringham has worked among the frescoes of Ajanta, Mr. Havell has celebrated forgotten sculptures and buildings, many of them admirable. And in literature India has told her own heart, through the mouth of Rabindranath Tagore. A new conception of the country has come to us in consequence. She may be puzzling, but we cannot now ignore her . . .[1]

This passage is of central importance to an understanding of Forster's approach and his attitude to India. It shows not only his deep enthusiasm about the emergence of a new vision of India but also the full range of his own interests in the country. His writings about India between 1912 and 1920, i.e. the period between his brief first visit and his more consequential second visit to the country, reflect these many-sided interests. These writings, which comprise the letters and diaries of the period of his first visit and a number of periodical essays which he published after this are of a greatly varied quality, and although they appear as disconnected pieces, they give, when looked at in one group, a brief yet comprehensive introduction to Forster's total picture of India.

There is a wide variety of subjects in these writings. There are some light-hearted and delightful descriptions of his travels in India, as well as some sombre thoughts on certain aspects of the contemporary Indian society. There are some imaginative and sympathetic accounts of certain elements in India's past heritage and culture (there is, for example, a beautiful rendering of the conversation in the *Bhagvad-Gita* between Krishna and Arjuna,[2] and there are two charming notes on the themes of Kalidas's *Meghaduta* and *Sakuntala*), and also some intriguing observations on the tradition of Indian temple art and architecture.[3] There are investigations into certain traditional aspects of Indian religion, and there are also comments on the actual states of the Hindu and Muslim societies in contemporary India. All these subjects are dealt with more seriously and more intensively in the later stages of Forster's writings about India, but their treatment in the earlier stage is neither conventional nor vague.

Two principal themes define the scope of Forster's range of interests in India: (i) his awareness of the general legend about India's past greatness and splendour, and (ii) his actual observations of facts of life and society in contemporary India. Between these two themes Forster sees a gulf: he sees that the past achievements of India appear enchanting, but they are largely a matter of legend and history; he finds the actual condition of contemporary India deeply disenchanting in many ways, but it is the reality he has to grapple with. He tries in his early approaches to India to look for the links and the terms of continuity between these two themes, and although he is mainly baffled in the attempt he pursues his enquiry with a sustained curiosity and interest.

An example which shows him confronted by the two themes together is the brief account of his visit to Ujjain in the present Indian state of Madhya Pradesh. During his travel in central India he visits the city, situated on the bank of the river Sipra, which was once famous as the capital of the legendary Hindu king Vikramaditya, and for its famous poet Kalidas and the eight other men of learning who belonged to the Court.[4] He thinks of the city's great past history; of the legendary charm of Vikramaditya's palace, of Kalidas's poetic description in his *Meghaduta (The Cloud Messenger)* and *Sakuntala*, of the beauty and joys of the city in the past, and he sees, in contrast to that past, contemporary Ujjain's empty and desolate plains, its few scattered villages, and its quaint modern buildings on the bank of the Sipra. He knows that Ujjain is famous in modern India also, for its religious fairs, when Hindu pilgrims visit the city in large numbers for a holy bathe in the river; but he is intrigued by his thoughts of the contrast between the city's past and its contemporary orders, and writes:

> I want the ruins of which the stationmaster spoke; the palace that King Vikramaditya built, and adorned with Kalidas, and the other eight. Where is it? Where are they? . . .
>
> Ujjain is famous in legend and fact, and as sacred as Benares, and surely there should have been steps, and temples, and the holy river Sipra. Where are they? . . .
>
> Was that really Vikramaditya's palace? Had Kalidas and the other eight ever prayed in those radiant waters? . . .
>
> But it is only in books that the past can glow, and Kalidas faded as soon as I felt the waters of the Sipra round my ankle. I thought not of Sakuntala's ornaments, but of my own, now spread on the splashboard, and I wondered whether they would dry before we reached the railway station.[5]

The feelings of disenchantment and deep curiosity which are present in this account of Ujjain are present in Forster's other accounts of India at this period – whether they are of other Indian places,[6] of Indian society in general, or of Indian religions in their actual visual forms. He sees that the contemporary Indian society, despite its high traditions of humanity and gracious hospitality, is greatly backward. He is worried at the sight of economic poverty, and the social differences between Indians and Indians – 'The richer sat [at a public wedding] on chairs, the poorer on a long carpet against the wall'[7] – and he is bewildered by the extravagance and splendour of the Courts in the Native States. He sees that, although occasionally a single Muslim family has broken the purdah system and changed a particular old social custom, assuming itself to be 'rationalistic' and advanced in outlook, and although the Muslims in general think that the Hindus are more advanced than they, social backwardness is, in fact, widespread. 'It was depressing, almost heartrending', he writes, thinking of the problem: 'How could this jumble end?'[8]

In the general context of this social picture Forster looks at the contemporary political developments in Anglo-India. The period of his first visit was not marked by the amount of political unrest which was present in India during the period of his second visit in the 1920s; yet he found it in the aftermath of the political crisis which had been caused by the partition of Bengal in 1905 and by the launching of the Swadeshi and boycott movement by the Indian National Congress.[9] The Congress had been pressing its demand for self-government for India on the model of the self-governing British colonies, and also for the introduction of national education in place of the prevalent British system of education, since 1906. Forster looked at the political situation with sympathy and with deep scepticism: he was disturbed to think that India's road to political freedom was going to be long and difficult – 'the unlovely chaos that lies between obedience and freedom – and that seems, alas! the immediate future of India'[10] – and yet he considered that the social and economic problems of India were far more important than the political problems. 'They yearn for political freedom and don't care about economic', he remarks, and comments in his private journal:

> Poor Indians'll do nothing yet: no constructive policy except vague 'education': but it is character not knowledge they need, and they will get this best by building up a framework of social intercourse. At present the educated class has created no conventions . . .[11]

From this disenchanting social scene he turns again to look at certain features of the Hindu society in the past, and sees in them evidence of the greatness of the Hindu character and the Hindu vision of life. He sees that the past traditions of Hindu civilisation were based on certain profound conceptions of human life and society. The past society was based on caste, and was divided, and the people belonged to various communities and worshipped many gods and goddesses in various forms, but in these levels of social and communal divisions in the past Forster sees an inner significance which he does not see behind the barriers of contemporary Hindu society. He points out that the Hindu caste system was based on the conception that human nature is varied, and that Hindu religion, which truly reflected Hindu society, emphasised variety, yet emphasised also the idea of the oneness of all men despite that variety. He sees that the old Hindu tradition of polytheistic worship was also based on the same complex conceptions of the unity and the variety of life. While looking into this feature of traditional Indian thought he seems (having already 'lost' his own faith in Christianity) to find in Hinduism a more compelling attraction:

> It is true that Hinduism emphasizes the fact that we are all different. But it also emphasizes the other side of the human paradox – the fact that we are all the same . . . Stripped of its local trappings, of its hundred handed gods, and monkeys and bulls and snakes, and Twice-born, it preaches with intense conviction and passion the doctrine of unity. It believes in caste, it believes in Pantheism also, and these two contradictory beliefs do really correspond to two contradictory emotions that each of us can feel, namely, 'I am different from everybody else,' and 'I am the same as everybody else' . . . Hinduism . . . does reveal a conception of Man's nature, and in consequence always has appealed and will appeal to souls who are technically outside its pale. It may not intend to proselytise, or may proselytise with its tongue in one of its hundred cheeks. But it gains proselytes whatever its intentions, because it can give certain types of people what they want.[12]

Forster's later writings about India, from the date of his second visit, show him still more drawn towards the country – attracted by the 'unlovely chaos' of its social and political situation as well as by the wide heritage of its civilisation. His later writings also explore, at a deeper level, the two main themes of India's past and present. His early writings about India may not show the depth of his later writings, but they are the foundations on which the later interpretations are built. These early writings show a mind that is truly and deeply interested in India, and yet not prepared to accept any aspect of India in reverence, or reject any other in prejudice, without questioning and learning for himself.

2 'Unrealities' in Dewas: A View of Princely India

Forster's Indian writings between 1921 and 1924, prior to the publication of *A Passage to India*, constitute a more definitive phase in his interpretation of India. They consist of his letters and accounts of Dewas and other Indian Native States, written in 1921 and later published in *The Hill of Devi*, and his four main articles about India, published in *The Nation and the Athenaeum* in 1922.[1] They are essentially social and political writings concerning the situation of the Indian Empire after the First World War, and they are important because they show Forster in an entirely new and public role, as in interpreter of modern India. They give a realistic account of a critical time of India's history, as seen through the eyes of a private individual who had also made his mark among the modern English novelists, and their special significance may well lie in the background and equipment they were to provide for *A Passage to India*.

These private and journalistic writings reflect upon the post-war situation both in British India and in the Princely States. Although Forster lived and worked in Dewas for the most part of his stay, his observations extended beyond the limits of Princely India. He wrote with equal understanding and penetration about the humane tradition as well as the backwardness and obscurantism of some of the Native States and also about the enlightened struggles and aspirations of British India. His interpretations of these two units of the Indian Empire form two distinct sides of one picture, and have to be studied separately.

When Forster went to India in the spring of 1921, he did not go merely to 'sightsee', but to work for the Maharajah of Dewas, as his private secretary, on a salary of three hundred rupees a month.[2] That he should have chosen to come and work in what he himself knew to be a remote and sleepy Princely State may seem surprising, for in 1921 much was happening outside the Native States, in British India – it was the year when Gandhi's Non-cooperation movement,[3] under which Indian nationalism had thrown an extraordinary challenge to the British Government, was at its height, and British India was vibrant with activity and interest. Yet in choosing to live in Dewas, Forster, like Fielding in *A Passage to India*, may well have secretly wished to remain in an unofficial capacity outside the territories of British India and be among Indians, 'maintained directly' by them – not indirectly through taxes paid by them to the British Government. A cancelled passage from the manuscripts of *A Passage to India* gives a clue to Fielding's unfulfilled wish and, possibly, to Forster's own intentions:

> ~~Still he~~ [Fielding] ~~was out not to worry, like most of his compatriots, and unlike them he had a good sound racial conscience~~, for it was a pleasure to him to ~~work~~ be in India and among Indians, and this ought to leak through. It was a pity he had to work – that was a great mistake, for no one knows how nice Indians are until he has spunged on them, ~~in a race~~ with a race supreme for its hospitality how could it be otherwise? Indians paid for him indirectly, through taxes, and consequently he maintained official pomp; he wished they maintained him directly.[4]

In Dewas Forster could live and work among Indians without official pomp. He also toured other Central Indian States and Hyderabad, and thus acquired close and extensive knowledge of the affairs of the Princely States. These states extended in territory over one-third of India's total area and sustained more than one-fifth of her population. An understanding of pre-Republic India could not have been complete without taking them into account. Forster's portrayal of Dewas was an essential part of his whole Indian picture. His accounts of 1921–2 also show that he visited Nagpur and Simla, the nerve-centres of British India at that time, and was thus in a position to write about both sections of India from personal knowledge.

The letters from Dewas, written in 1921, and the two parts of the article 'The Mind of the Indian Native States', in *The Nation and the Athenaeum*, contain Forster's experiences and reflections in native India. In 1921 his experiences, unlike those of his earlier visit, were critical and intense. His thoughts about Dewas and the Native States in general were deep and more objective. Although the Maharajah's affections and the magical religion of a few people around the court held much charm for him, Forster was constantly oppressed in his mind by the stark backwardness and 'unrealities' of Dewas. In the letters of 1921, more critical than those of 1912–13, the tone of the curious and sensitive travelogue of the earlier period continues, but they are dominated by a searching attention given to the banalities of life in a Native State, which 'The Mind of the Indian Native State' had attempted to expose long before the letters were published. Dewas seemed to bore Forster in some ways, and during his short stay he often felt attracted to look out to the changing face of British India, to its enlightened struggle and spirit of Independence. Frequently his letters show this, and his impatience with Dewas:

> I don't see, nor am I likely to see, anything of present movements in India, except indirectly . . . There are said to be new ideas, even in Dewas, but they are not perceptible to a western eye.

Politically—though not socially—we are still living in the fourteenth century.[5]

Simla sounds imminent . . . It will be curious to see something of the India that is changing. There is no perceptible change here, indeed the atmosphere is in some ways less western than it was nine years ago.[6]

The National Congress meets in December at Ahmedabad, and it will certainly carry through its resolution in favour of Civil Disobedience . . . I have been with pro-Govt. and pro-English Indians all this time, so cannot realize the feeling of the other party . . .[7]

If in 1912–13 Dewas had only surprised Forster by its court intrigues and 'petty treacheries', in 1921 he found it 'an untidy ant-hill', a 'slackly administered', politically backward, and 'bankrupt' state.[8] Forster's account of its maladministration and its gross economic disproportions was substantially true of the situation in the Native States in general. The material condition of the Central India Agency as a whole, whose many states Forster came to be better acquainted with in 1921, had not very much improved since his previous visit to that part of the country. The 1921 Census of India, describing the years between Forster's two visits, paints a gloomy picture of these states, and shades of this gloom appear in Forster's own accounts and explain his deeper disappointments with 'native' India.

The Census[9] reports that the years between 1911 and 1921 had disclosed 'an abnormal state of things' in the Central India Agency. Plague and influenza epidemics had caused numerous deaths. Agriculture had been impoverished. Prices had risen, and there had been a general rise of about 100 per cent in the cost of living. The farmer had had to pay enhanced wages to his labourers, but did not get the full benefit of enhanced prices which should have balanced this, because of his indebtedness to the local money-lender. According to the Report the pensioner, the Government employee and the salaried servants, whose earnings were fixed, suffered most. The rise in the cost of living had proved a serious blow to the small states in particular, and the gradual rise in the cost of administration had been telling upon them, as a result of which it had become extremely difficult for these small states to obtain officials, on such pay as they could afford.

The misery must have been realised by Forster immediately when he arrived at Dewas as a stop-gap for the Maharajah's ex-private secretary, Colonel William Leslie ('Colonel Wilson' of *The Hill of Devi*), whom the state had owed Rs1500, His Highness's cheque having been dishonoured by a Bombay bank.[10] The financial debts of Dewas and its unseemly courtly splendour had often worried Forster. It was one of the poorest and administratively most muddled states of the Central India Agency. The *Imperial Gazetteer of India*[11] records that Tukoji Rao III's predecessor was 'a bad administrator' and had 'plunged the State in debt'. When Tukoji Rao III succeeded, and was still a 'junior', the state's financial allocations showed no sense of proportions. The main heads of expenditure out of a total of Rs350,000 were: Chief's Establishment, Rs76,000; Collection of Revenue, Rs69,000; General Administration, Rs24,000. Against these figures the Gazetteer records that the total expenditure on education for both the senior and junior branches of the state amounted to Rs16,000. A state which spent on the ruler's establishment five times more money than on education obviously took little interest in its people. The result of this was that the Court shone in splendour and extravagance, while the people were neglected and continued to suffer.

Malcolm Darling, Forster's friend and the Maharajah's erstwhile tutor, describes the situation in Dewas between 1907 and 1909. Of the stricken and debt-ridden peasantry he writes:

Looking into a village one day I came upon a peasant sitting idly and hugging a blanket thrown over his shoulders. Fever had laid him low. I told him to come and see me on the morrow and I would give him medicine. When he failed to appear, I went in search of him, but in vain. A neighbour however promised to give him the quinine I had brought for him. 'And now here he is at my door with five others', all wanting to be doctored. As we saw at Rajanpur, malaria could have devastating effects.

A propos of what I was to write many years later, I was already beginning to enquire into the conditions of the peasantry round me. For example, in both Dewas and Kolhapur they were said to be in the clutches of the money-lender and to borrow for their weddings at 25 per cent, and the women were thought to be wearing less jewellery, whether from increasing poverty or good sense was not clear. Village industries, too, were decaying and prices rising.[12]

In view of the widespread want and destitution in the state the wasteful and extravagant court feasts had 'puzzled' Malcolm Darling. Within fifteen days of his arrival at Dewas, he had been treated to a dinner consisting of thirty-seven dishes.

'Why so many dishes?' [he wondered]. The answer was simple: it was the limit of the cook's inventiveness. When the Maharajah of Kolhapur, the Raja's father-in-law to be, came here on a visit, he was given fifty dishes, but all the master-cooks of Dewas had to be summoned for the purpose. For a dinner with no guests six or seven dishes sufficed, and for a formal dinner-party twenty-five. Only a special occasion demanded as many as thirty-seven.[13]

Forster's letters home in 1912–13 described these elaborate, wasteful banquets in the palace and also the Maharajah's sixty-five attendants who 'have come to attend a Chiefs' Conference' in Delhi.[14] His accounts show his bewilderment and a feeling of ill-ease about the extravagance. In 1921, when, as the Maharajah's private secretary, he had looked at the palace finances and administration, he wrote almost immediately to Malcolm Darling, in the nature of a report: 'I have been here for a fortnight, happy and worried at once . . . To check the idleness, incompetence, and extravagance is quite beyond me.'[15] Another letter, written two months later, relates the same situation: 'I cannot grasp the finances of the State. I am told they are admirable. They may be, but they do not look it.'[16] Forster was embittered by the huge waste of state funds on useless royal ceremonies, when there was so much unalleviated misery around. On the occasion of the visit to Dewas by the Maharajah of Gwalior, Scindia, he wrote in a letter:

> We have had much expensive and uninspiriting nonsense to do honour to the Maharajah of Gwalior, who has paid us a twelve hours' visit, which I did not find too short. Since he likes singing, H.H. would order singers from Bombay . . . though warned it was risky. Sure enough, the singers caught too late a train, and are arriving now, when the whole Gwalior party has left. They are at the top of their tree (i.e. it is like ordering Tarnini, etc. to come to Weybridge from Berlin), and they will wear jewels worth thousands of pounds, with none but my drooping eyes to regard them. Partly through fatigue, partly through thoughts of the misery in England and elsewhere, I feel glum and disapproving. One can go too far down the 'primrose path' and we have done so on this occasion. Moreover, Maharajah Gwalior was a bounder, so there has been no satisfaction in any direction, at least from my point of view. It is poor work at the best of times, spending money on rich men.[17]

On a later occasion, when the Prince of Wales was visiting India and the Maharajah of Dewas was hoping for the honour of a royal visit to his own state, Forster wrote anxiously about the expenses this might involve: 'I have suggested leaving in September, after the Simla visit, but I fear H.H. will want me to see him through the Prince of Wales too. Which means I shall see about 50,000 Rupees spent.'[18] Forster's anxiety over the state's bankruptcy is seen equally plainly when he writes about the kind of treats which he himself was accorded by the Maharajah:

> He is in for a bad time, merely because he has an exaggerated estimate of the claims of friendship. It is a sweet fault and he is one of the sweetest characters on this earth. Fearing that I may feel flat, his one thought is to give me pleasure. I have only just returned from Chhatarpur, but he has sent me off at once in the best of his cars to Dhar and wired to its Maharajah who is his cousin. I arrived last night. H.H. (of Dhar) was

very polite and called me to his birthday party, which happened to be in progress . . . Dhar itself is not interesting . . . I came in order to go to Mandu . . . Mandu is 20 miles from Dhar which is 33 from Indore which is 23 from Dewas – 76 miles there and the same back. A pretty penny this treat must have cost H.H. and his bankrupt state.[19]

The biggest drain on the state's money, however, was the New Palace and the gardens which had been begun years ago under Colonel Leslie's plans and had not been completed for lack of funds. 'It is an appalling tragedy', Forster wrote from Dewas,

rooted in the folly of ten years ago. The works should never have been begun. Properly administered they might have come through, but as it is, they have drained the life of the State. H.H. will certainly reign for the rest of his life in a ruin, and how he is to pay the interest on the loan without overtaxing the cultivator I don't see, and if he overtaxes the cultivator in these days, it means trouble.[20]

The financial muddle in Dewas followed the pattern of Forster's prognostications. Shortly before he was to leave the state he observed that the Maharajah was borrowing from the merchants of Indore to carry on his administration. Dewas became bankrupt and an open scandal in the early thirties. Forster wrote later, in *The Hill of Devi*, about the tragedy and about the Maharajah's role in it:

The final blow to his fortunes, however, was economic. His financial position had been bad even in my day, it had got worse, he had spent immense sums on the Yuvraj's marriage and on the birth of a son to Bai Saheba and on secret-service agents at Delhi and elsewhere. And then came the slump of agricultural prices. It came in 1930 and lasted four years. All the agrarian areas suffered. Dewas, being already insecure, went bankrupt. In one year the Land Revenue of the state was halved and its total income fell from about ten lakhs to six, officials were not paid, cultivators were over-taxed, land alienated. By 1933 the position was so grave that the Government of India was obliged to intervene.[21]

The Maharajah fled his bankrupt state and went to Pondicherry, then in the territory of French India, hoping to 'elude the Government and negotiate with it from safety'. But his negotiations failed, and the Maharajah never returned from Pondicherry. There 'he dug himself in and died' in 1937 in penitence and in want. An obituary notice of him, published in *The Times*, described the faults of the Maharajah's public and private life. Forster considered it as 'a model of ungenerosity and prim indignation',[22] and wrote a personal 'tribute of affection' which *The Times* published on 28 December 1937. In it Forster described the Maharajah's

'incomparable qualities as an individual, whatever his weaknesses as a
ruler'.

Forster's generous compliments to the Maharajah – more of them
appeared in *The Hill of Devi* – have led to the supposition in some quarters
that he was unaware of or wished to condone the Maharajah's misrule. A
noted Indian historian has criticised *The Hill of Devi* for seeking 'to enlist
our sympathy on the Maharajah's side in the catastrophe which engulfed
him.'[23] 'What cannot be hidden', the critic adds, 'is the misgovernance,
corruption and obscurantism.' Along with Dewas and the State of Alwar,
cited as 'characteristic examples', the case of the deposition of the Holkar is
also told; it is forgotten however that Forster in turn has written
disapprovingly of these very states. He criticised the 'archaic pomp' of
Dewas and its 'faery budgets, such as might occur in the parliaments of
Gilbert and Sullivan'.[24] He mocked the Native Princes' 'taste for
unrealities', and the 'grotesque pride which imprisons some of the shyer
rulers in their own jungles', which reportedly had once led the Maharajah
of Alwar 'to promenade the deck of a P. & O. with a crown upon his head,
under the belief that it was expected from him'.[25] The story is also
recounted by Forster of the abject Holkar of Indore 'rolling in the dust' in
Hyderabad so that the Nizam descended 'from his carriage to greet' him.[26]
As for Scindia, the Maharajah of Gwalior, one of Forster's letters from
Dewas described him as 'in private life an insolent and surly buffoon and in
public a militarist and an obscurantist'.[27]

Forster's criticism of Princely India is indeed fundamental. His points in
'The Mind of the Indian Native State', all derived from close personal
observation and experience, are basic and indisputable. The system was
feudal, Forster writes, and gave the princes extensive powers with which
'they can exalt and depress their own subjects at will, regard the State
revenue as their private property, promulgate a constitution one day and
ignore it the next'.[28] The mentality of the princes 'was anything but
modern':

> It is neither in their tradition nor to their interests that India should
> become a nation . . . However cleverly they may discuss democratic
> Europe or revolutionary Russia with a visitor, they do not in their heart
> of hearts regard anything but Royalty as permanent, or the movements
> against it as more than domestic mutinies. They cannot understand,
> because they cannot experience, the modern world.[29]

At a time when Indian nationalists were contemplating a federated self-
governing union of the states and British India, the princes, with the
exception of one or two enlightened ones like the Gaekwar of Baroda or the
Maharajah of Bikanir, were doing everything to protect and proclaim
their separatism. Forster was aware of his own Maharajah's secret dreams
about 'a Maratha confederacy perhaps with himself as leader',[30] and he

once wrote from Simla pitying the Maharajah's schemes to restore to power 'two preposterous creatures called Rajahs' of Nagpur: 'H.H. – misguided creature – moved by patriotism and pity, is scheming to set them on their feet again, and to get them, not indeed Nagpur itself, but certain districts round it which will be re-created into a Native State and abundantly misgoverned in consequence.'[31] Indeed the separatism of the princes, and the Government of India's policy supporting it in exchange for the princes' loyalty to the British Dominion, had been a feature of history. It had been the main factor behind the states' backwardness, but in maintaining it the princes as well as the Government of India had pursued their own peculiar interests, though with uncertain results. Percival Spear sums up the situation in the following words:

> In general, it may be said that the states, with certain marked exceptions, were well behind the rest of India in all-round development. By maintaining the princes after 1858, the British secured their steady support, but the failure to modernize and develop them, or to integrate them into the British Indian system as a whole, rendered that support passive instead of active. The policy of segregation and *laisser-faire* meant that the chance of modernizing India within a traditional framework was missed and that traditional institutions themselves became the objects of neglect and contempt. The princely order was an imposing but increasingly feeble prop of the British Dominion.[32]

The princes and the Government of India desired to strengthen their positions by closer alliances with each other when, at the end of the First World War, national unrest had reappeared in British India and was widespread. Forster observed how the situation in the early twenties had stood peculiarly to the princes' advantage:

> Whether the Princes of India are safer now than they were ten years ago is questionable, but they are certainly having a pleasanter time. Both socially and politically they receive from the British authorities increased civility . . . There are two reasons for the change. The Native Princes have shared in the increased consideration accorded to Indians generally, and they are also encouraged because of their usefulness as counter-weights against the new Nationalism.[33]

A 'Chamber of Princes' had been set up, along with the introduction of constitutional reforms into British India in 1919, their main purpose being that 'if the control of matters common to India as a whole is shared with some popular element in the government, it must be anticipated that these Rulers may wish to take a share in such control also'.[34] The Chamber was composed of the princes of the larger states who were members of it in their own right, and also a group of the lesser princes, who became members by election. At the opening conference of the Chamber, the Viceroy, Lord Chelmsford, had spoken in Simla 'of the advantage such a gathering offered to exchange ideas with the Princes who shared the burden of ruling India'. The princes might 'lend valuable assistance' to the British Government in their difficulty, Lord Chelmsford had said:

> The British Empire was at peace in Europe and the East, and tranquillity reigned in India, but the difficulties and dangers of peace were less patent than those of war, and accordingly were more difficult to cope with. The new after-the-war spirit was the greatest danger that ever faced mankind, and the Princes and Chiefs could lend valuable assistance by guarding their States against a lawless and malicious spirit and by refusing to tolerate lying stories as to the motives of the British Government.[35]

Another idea that Montagu and Chelmsford, the joint-architects of the Chamber of Princes, apparently had in mind was that in addition to making a stronger force against political disaffection, the Chamber might also provide 'ideas' and enlightenment to many a prince. In effect, the Chamber became nothing but a forum for anti-nationalist resolutions and also a house for the princes' own bickerings, and those between the Government of India and them. Forster reported how the princes particularly disliked 'being criticized by British India newspapers, and have begged the Government of India to strengthen the Press Act in their favour'.[36] They were demanding greater autonomy for the states, and the issues that occupied their minds were 'the disregard of their treaty rights by Government, and the injuries which the existing fiscal system of British India inflicts upon them'.[37] Forster's criticism of the Chamber of Princes was remarkably perceptive and unequivocal:

> The Chamber of Princes, one of the many stillborn children of Lord Chelmsford, attempted to give them a meeting-place where they could discuss matters affecting their class. The smaller rulers, who had nothing to lose, repaired to it in shoals. Not so the larger fish. The Nizam, for instance, with dominions as large as France and as populous as Egypt, does not want to hobnob with chieftains who may be far less powerful than his own vassals. The little Rajput chiefs alone are so numerous that they can outvote any combination that can be brought against them, and do outvote, since they are organized under an able leader, the Maharajah of Bikanir. Until the Rajput block is broken by some device – e.g. by the introduction of a system of group-votes – the leading Mohammedans and Marathas do not care to attend. Thus history and mythology intervene at every turn. The hand of the past divides the rulers whenever they attempt to discuss the present. They forget the common enemy as soon as they see one another, and waste their time in

discussing the form of their organization, in exchanging insincere courtesies, in cracking jokes of a symbolic nature, and in being photographed either officially or semi-officially or informally. The Maharajah of K——, for instance, always likes to stand in the back row of a photograph, but modesty is not suspected as the cause, his Highness being of a bulky build, and dominating from his high position such Princes as are perched on chairs. The Nawab of L—— pushes for the front; serve him right when the humorous Maharajah of M—— obscures him, quite by accident, during the exposure of the plate. The Rajah of N—— takes a side seat himself, but brings in his children at the last moment and spreads them along the carpet, so that they lean against their Highnesses' legs, and appear to be heirs of the whole continent of India. Fortunately the Viceroy says: 'Who are these children?' And so on and so forth . . . While the New Spirit knocks with increasing irritability upon the door. The Chamber of Princes, and all that it connotes, seems absurd not only to the politically minded Indian, but to him who pursues the more elusive goals of science and art. 'For what reason are such people important?' asks the Bengali painter or the Punjabi poet. 'What are they doing, what have they ever done, that is either beautiful or interesting?'[38]

Forster knew that even when the princes showed an interest in democratising their administration it was only for the sake of appearance: 'Today their loyalty to the Crown is sincere and passionate, and they welcomed the Prince of Wales, although his measured constitutionalisms puzzled and chilled them. Why did he not take his liegemen aside and ask in his father's name, for the head of Gandhi upon a charger?'[39] The princes were by their temperament and tradition opposed to constitutional changes in British India, which they feared might disturb their own despotic rule. About their pattern of despotism Forster wrote: 'Trained in Western history, we tend to assume that a Prince is a lonely despot whose word is law, and our knowledge of the particular acts of Princes seems to confirm this: they can make or break an individual subject.'[40] When, therefore, a prince talked about or produced a constitution for his state, Forster knew what it really was. The tendency towards a show of popular and responsible government had appeared in some Native States since expanded representation had been introduced into the Councils in British India, under the Morley–Minto Reforms of 1909. But the concrete results of this 'show' in Dewas were personally known to Forster.

During his earlier visit to Dewas Forster had written about the state's feudal Durbar, where the 'Rajah made a long dull speech about the constitutional changes that he is making; a new advisory council; I believe it is important. No one was much pleased'.[41] In 1921 he observed that the ruler had remained loyal to the British and enthusiastically loyal to the King-Emperor, whom he regarded as his feudatory chief, and he had done all he could to assist the allies during the first world war. Consequently he was highly esteemed in official circles, and Sir Valentine Chirol, a travelling journalist of repute, had signalized him as one of the most enlightened of the younger princes, and had made his name known to a wider public.[42]

That the Maharajah was opposed to the introduction of popular government in India is clear from Sir Valentine Chirol's account[43] of him.

Following the wave of liberalisation that appeared in British India after the constitutional changes of 1919, however, it became fashionable among the princes to talk of constitutions and liberalisation in their own states. Many states promulgated constitutions providing for so-called advisory and legislative councils, to consist of popular representatives, so that the Viceroy, or a visiting representative of the British monarch, would call them modern and be pleased with their progressiveness. But in actuality the provisions of the constitutions were such that the councils were all dominated by the hereditary nobles and the rulers' nominees, while the elected members were few and insignificant. Forster wrote from Dewas about its own long preparation for a constitution: 'A new constitution is to be drafted, so that the people may be educated gradually, but a new constitution was being drafted when I was here ten years ago.'[44] Later, when the constitution was ready, he wrote from Simla that Lord Reading 'will probably come and open the absurd constitution that is being inaugurated at Dewas next year'.[45] When the constitution was actually promulgated, Forster had already left Dewas. 'When I returned to England the first news I had about Dewas concerned its new constitution. Not a success. Lord Reading had after all not come.'[46]

'The Mind of the Indian Native State' gives in detail Forster's views on the constitution of Dewas: 'a sample of the crop' that 'had burst into sudden bloom' in Princely India, on the occasion of the visit of the Prince of Wales. The preamble to the constitution had boastfully recorded that there was no demand for reforms in the state, but the ruler thought fit to anticipate the wishes of his subjects in the matter. The constitution was tripartite, consisting of the ruler, a state council of six, and a representative assembly of about sixty. The ruler was to remain 'the fountain of all power in the State', and the officials of the council were all to be nominated. The council could legislate, but the ruler had a veto. The composition of the representative assembly was 'more remarkable than its powers'. It included one representative of the ruler, one member of the ruling house, twenty nobles of various grades (total number of nobles in the state being eighty), twenty-one officials, eight members elected by the towns (each representing two thousand electors), and fifteen village members (each representing four thousand electors). It had no executive or legislative power, and though it 'may send up suggestions to the State Council, that body is not obliged to discuss them'.[47]

'Such are the chief provisions of our sample constitution', which in its climactic final clause enacts that 'for the first five years all the members of both the Assembly and the Council shall be nominated, not elected, since the population is not yet sufficiently educated to work the constitution!' 'We are not told', Forster comments, 'what steps will be taken to educate it. The whole document is from the Western and British Indian point of view as unreal as a Dessera Budget.'[48] The show of democratisation in Dewas was thus a mockery. Even in the big and well-to-do states the situation was the same and remained so till after Indian independence. 'All of them are autocracies', Jawaharlal Nehru wrote years after Forster's report, in 1946,

> though some have started elected councils whose powers are strictly limited. Hyderabad, the premier state, still carries on with a typical feudal regime supported by an almost complete denial of civil liberties. So also most of the states in Rajputana and the Punjab. A lack of civil liberties is a common feature of the states. . . . Some of the princes are good, some are bad; even the good ones are thwarted and checked at every turn. As a class they are of necessity backward, feudal in outlook, and authoritarian in methods, except in their dealings with the British Government, when they show a becoming subservience. Shelvanker has rightly called the Indian states 'Britain's fifth column in India'.[49]

With the British policy of protection and separatism in regard to the Native States, Forster had no sympathy. He criticised the 'curious alliances' between the Government of India and the princes in their efforts to suppress nationalist aspirations, and denounced imperialists like Frederick Lugard, who were advocating that 'we should apportion British India among the loyaller rulers, and control the whole peninsula through them'.[50] 'An alliance between the British and the Princes against the rest of India could only lead to universal disaster', Forster wrote, 'yet there are people on both sides who are foolish enough to want it.'[51]

Forster wished the states and the rest of India to come closer: 'any change, however trifling, is to be welcomed which lessens the gulf between the States and the rest of India – a gulf which sometimes seems even more menacing than that which divides Indians from Europeans.'[52] He wanted the uneducated peasant subjects of a prince to be educated, to be conscious of their duties and rights so that 'they begin to question'. His sympathy was with the subjects of the Maharana of Udaipur when, wearied by the 'extortions of his officials', they besieged the ruler, 'a semi-sacred figure', who 'fled to one of his island-palaces in disarray, and was obliged to delegate his powers to his son'.[53]

The political awakening that was coming in Princely India was for the most part slow and ineffectual. The princes remained hostile to British

India's aspirations for independence. Forster's picture of Princely India remained remarkably true, at least until the states came to be merged in independent India under its federal constitution, and the 'gulf' between the states and British India that had dismayed him was on its way to disappearing. The extent to which his experiences in Princely India coloured his vision in *A Passage to India* will be examined in a later chapter.

3 'The Great Blunder of the Past': Forster's Concept of a 'Democratic Empire'

Unlike the Princely States, the situation in British India at the time of Forster's second visit was a subject which he could approach with interest and sympathy. With the social and political problems of British India, linked primarily with India's post-war democratic aspirations, he felt more familiar, and they appealed to him directly. His own democratic thinking had long been in an ideological conflict with British imperialism in general, and in British India, ruled directly by the Imperial Government, he could observe the peculiar results of imperialist policy, and thus write about them even out of a personal conviction and concern. In his writings about British India his view of imperialism assumed a clearer and more trenchant definition than before.

His account appeared mainly in the form of his three factual reports in *The Nation and the Athenaeum*,[1] that is 'Reflections in India I and II' and 'India and the Turk', and the essence of this picture later percolated into *A Passage to India*. These reports have remained obscure to those who see Forster's India as limited only to Princely India,[2] but given due attention they stand as an important and integral part of a more complete and extensive picture which, in fact, Forster intended to present.

Following his repudiation of Princely India, Forster took a close look in these reports at some aspects of the imperialistic structure of society and politics in British India, and in doing so, he was able firmly to criticise its unequal foundation and also to visualise a different base on which a more meaningful and enduring Indo-British relationship might have been constructed. Two main considerations emerge from these writings: first, Forster's information about the social and political situation in British India at the end of the First World War was extensive; and second, his interpretation of the situation, being unofficial, was neither pro-Indian nor pro-British, and as such, it had the positive value of an impartial personal account. Forster's main conclusion in these writings is also equally worth remarking. In his opinion, the Indian Empire could have been made a 'democratic' and enduring institution had it been founded on the basis of

social equality between the British and the Indians, but having been raised
upon a 'pedestal of race' it was bound to collapse.[3] The political reforms,
conciliation and official courtesies advanced by the British in the twenties
were too late, he thought; British India had been led by 'past mistakes'[4] to
a point beyond salvage, and was in a crisis from which it was impossible to
recover.

Forster was in India from March 1921 until January 1922. This was a
particularly crucial period in the history of British India. The nationalist
agitation, revived after the war and precipitated by repression and the
massacre in the Punjab,[5] had reached a climax in 1920. Gandhi's Non-
cooperation movement, protesting chiefly against the Punjab massacre,
and the British injustice to the Moslem sentiment in India over the
Khilafat issue,[6] had begun during this year, aiming to achieve 'swaraj'
within one year,[7] and was at its height of success during the months Forster
was in India. Forster's own views about the Non-cooperation and Khilafat
movements will be discussed in the next chapter. What is however
important to note here is that he had no misgivings about the wide
effectiveness of these movements. On 12 November 1921 he wrote from
Hyderabad that the Congress in its session at Ahmedabad in December
'will certainly carry through its resolution in favour of Civil Disobedience'.[8] This the Congress did, and during the last two weeks before
Forster's departure, the policy of civil disobedience was implemented in
many parts of Andhra, in the vicinity of Hyderabad where Forster was
staying after leaving Dewas, and the movement was not suspended by
Gandhi until 12 February 1922 when Forster had already left India.

Having watched the Non-cooperation movement thus in its months of
triumph Forster had observed how the crisis had greatly compromised
Britain's imperial posture. The British Government's policies in relation to
Indian nationalism had undergone a remarkable change. The British
officials had been subdued and had become courteous, and some were even
respectful towards the Indians. All over the country they had been
instructed by firm official circulars to abstain as far as possible from
interfering with the non-cooperators and to avoid precipitating disorders.
From London too it had been pointed out that in the interest of amity 'it is
the plain duty of every Englishman and woman, official and non-official, in
India to avoid the offence and the blunder of discourtesy.'[9] 'Orders had
come down from Headquarters enjoining courtesy', Forster wrote,
remarking about the plight of the Anglo-Indian official:

> This hasty and ungraceful change of position is typical of Anglo-India
> today. Something like a stampede can be observed. Some officials have
> changed out of policy; they know that they can no longer trust their
> superiors to back them up if they are rude or overbearing . . . Others
> have undergone a genuine change of heart. They respect the Indian
> because he has proved himself a man.[10]

Indeed the challenge of the period of non-cooperation, epitomising all events of 1920–1 and charged with Indian ideas of moral power and independence, had drawn the sympathy of the enlightened British liberal and had undermined the morale of the authorities of government. They were realising the unalterable fact that they were losing India: ' "Yes, it's all up with us", is their attitude. "Sooner or later the Indians will tell us to go. I hope they'll tell us nicely." ' [11] To explain these results and his own thoughts about the future of Indo-British relations Forster examined some of the questions which were mainly underlying the conflicts between the two communities.

The major factor responsible for the conflicts was, in Forster's view, the social gulf which the Empire had created between the Indians and the European communities living in India. 'The decent Anglo-Indian of today realizes', he remarked, 'that the great blunder of the past is neither political nor economic nor educational, but social; that he was associated with a system that supported rudeness in railway carriages and is paying the penalty.' [12] The unequal 'system' had been built up in the past, he thought, by the Englishman's racial prejudices and operated in many ways at different levels of society. He described incidents in railway carriages, and in Anglo-Indian clubs, which had commonly and almost traditionally shown the Englishman's racial arrogance. A show of overbearing temper towards an Indian fellow-traveller on a railway journey had been 'instinctive' with the Englishman, 'or what would happen to the British Raj?' 'Excluded from our clubs, [the Indian] has never been introduced to the West in the social sense, as to a possible friend. We have thrown grammar and neckties at him, and smiled when he put them on wrongly – that is all.' [13]

Unlike Lowes Dickinson, who used to blame the Indians as being responsible for the gulf that existed in Anglo-Indian society, [14] Forster wished to draw attention to the social apartheid practised by the Englishman himself, and he thought that the Englishwoman too had played her own part in this. He wrote about the lady who had warned him at the time of his first visit to India, 'Never forget that you're superior to every native in India except the Rajas, and they're on an equality', as an example of her 'species'. [15] He criticised Anglo-Indian women as a class for their insensitivity, lack of understanding and racial arrogance. Defending their case, a sympathiser, writing anonymously in the *Cornhill Magazine* some time before Forster's article appeared in *The Nation and the Athenaeum*, had described the charges against the Ango-Indian women as 'conventional' and blamed the legendary tales by Thackeray and the satires of Kipling for their origin. [16] The 'unsympathetic' charges were summed up in this article thus: the Anglo-Indian woman (1) 'is given to the cult of the *Tertium Quid*, (2) or, at best, she is overfond of pleasure, and (3) she, who might do much, does painfully little to bring about an *entente cordiale*: her attitude towards India is aloof, stupid, unsympathetic'. In her defence the article pointed out her difficulties, sacrifices and dangers in the days of the nationalist and seditious disturbances, and pleaded for 'sympathy and understanding'. Forster's comments, however, which may have been read as a direct answer to this article, referred mainly to the social follies of the Anglo-Indian woman of the past that had made her class partly the cause rather than the victim of Indian disaffection. 'She has lived her life and she has done her work', wrote Forster emphatically. 'If the Englishman might have helped the Indian socially, how much more might the Englishwoman have helped!' he continued, picking up, as it were, the words of the *Cornhill Magazine*;

> But she has done nothing, or worse than nothing. She deserves, as a class, all that the satirists have said about her, for she has instigated the follies of her male when she might have calmed them and set him on the sane course. There has been an English as well as an Indian *purdah*, and it has done greater harm because it was aggressive. Instead of retiring quietly behind the curtain it flaunted itself as a necessity, and proclaimed racial purity across a live wire.[17]

Forster's criticism of the way in which the Anglo-Indian's racial prejudices caused social friction was no superficial or mere journalistic criticism. Citing his own experience he wrote that, free from such prejudices, it was possible to live on terms of social equality with the Indians, 'that *purdah* in India is not impenetrable, that the Parsis do not observe it, and the Marattas only in a modified form; that even Islam moves towards a change'; but the Anglo-Indian, blinded by his prejudices, had not made the effort: 'If one said that one had actually shared in Indian family life, both Mohammedan and Hindu, been on motor drives, sat on chairs or the floor as the case might be, the eyes grew incredulous, and the voice changed the conversation as improper.'[18]

Forster knew that the Anglo-Indian's blind superiority had been supported by an age-old imperialist system and policies, and although the situation was beginning to change as a result of the reforms of 1919,[19] and the attempts by high British officials and dignitaries to create an atmosphere of cordiality,[20] he was firmly sceptical about their real achievement. He observed that the British officials working in India were not all very happy with the reforms: 'They dread the reforms, but propose to work them . . . Though friendships between individuals will continue and courtesies between high officials increase, there is little hope now of spontaneous intercourse between the two races.'[21]

The acuteness of Forster's view of the crisis and his understanding of the prevalent Indian feeling may be realised by referring to two other accounts of the contemporary situation. One is by Surendranath Banerjea,[22] the liberal Indian leader, who welcomed the reforms, and himself became a minister in Bengal advocating co-operation with the British, and the other is by Gandhi, who had also at first accepted the reforms, but later pleading for complete racial equality became the pioneer of the Non-cooperation movement. Surendranath Banerjea wrote that in the era of reforms, 'largely instrumental in establishing better relations between Europeans and Indians than existed before', a 'wholesome change is observable in our social relations', and he described as evidence of this his own cordial relations with his secretary who was an Irishman, and with his chief engineer in charge of sanitary works and the surgeon-general in the medical department, who were both Englishmen.[23] This however was only one aspect of the whole complex position.

Forster's report, while admitting the possibilities of 'friendships between individuals' and 'courtesies between high officials', nevertheless registered and sympathised with the dominant Indian opinion which in the days of non-cooperation believed, with Gandhi, that

> although we are not at war with the individual Englishman . . . we do desire to destroy the system that has emasculated our country . . . We consider it inconsistent with our self-respect any longer to brook the spirit of superiority and dominance which has systematically ignored and disregarded the sentiments of thirty crores of innocent people of India . . . We desire to live on terms of friendship with Englishmen, but that friendship must be friendship of equals both in theory and practice, and we must continue to non-co-operate till . . . the goal is achieved.[24]

Like Gandhi and the mass of Indian non-cooperators, Forster believed that British imperialism had dug its own grave in the Indian Empire. Its failure in the past to create an integrated society by recognising the Indians and Europeans as equals had made the dissolution of British India inevitable.

Forster's scepticism about the British Empire had been deepening ever since he had remarked in *The Longest Journey* about the imperialistic vainglory in the English public school tradition, pointing his finger to the portraits of empire builders in Sawston's Dunwood House, and at the housemaster, Herbert Pembroke, who quoted imperial poets in his opening address;[25] but his most direct and forceful indictment came as a result of his view of the events of British India. The liberal sceptical outlook on the Empire that was developed through *Howards End* and subsequently through Forster's exposition of the case of Egypt[26] achieved its culminating strength and justification in his writings about British India.

Forster's view about the Indian case, however, was unlike that of Wilfrid Blunt, the impulsive 'anti-British' friend of India, whom Forster called 'the *enfant terrible* in politics'[27] and who had once advised the 'moderate' Indian nationalist leader, Gokhale, to carry a couple of bombs in his pocket when he went to the India Office.[28] Forster looked at the issue between India and British Imperialism dispassionately, and although ideologically he disliked an empire, he was not carried away by his ideological differences to condemn the British Empire outright. Analysing his own conflicts with imperialism he had even seen that there could be something appreciable in an empire: 'An Empire bores me, so far, but I can appreciate the heroism that builds it up. London bores me, but what thousands of splendid people are labouring to make London', says Margaret Schlegel in *Howards End*.[29] The same spirit is seen in Forster when he admires 'Anglo-Indian officials of the fine old type' like Alfred Lyall, for example, who, 'cultivated, leisured, and sympathetic to the country they had made their home',[30] achieved all that an imperialism at its best could achieve. Forster saw these possibilities, and indeed he would have valued, for a more important reason than that pursued by English politicians (including the Liberals), Britain's imperial connection with India, but his enquiry into the prevalent doctrines of imperialism and its modes of operation confirmed his own disbelief in it as a tenable policy in international relations.

In a paper entitled 'Utilitarianism and all that: the political theory of British imperialism in India'[31] Raghavan Iyer has analysed four main doctrines on which the imperialist theory and work in India had been supported. They are: the Burkean doctrine of imperial trusteeship, the utilitarian doctrine of state activity propounded mainly by Bentham and the two Mills, the Platonic idea of a ruling élite to act as wise guardians, and the Evangelical belief in the spread of the gospel for the benefit of all heathens. All four doctrines derived from one main common assumption: that Britain was superior to India and had power over her to work for her own well-being in one way or another. This assumption, which the imperialist used as an argument to justify despotism in India and which was at the root of social friction between Englishmen and Indians, was fundamentally unacceptable to Forster. It led to disasters in Indo-British relations and precipitated the decay of British India, he thought. 'Behind all the failures and successes of the political theories of British imperialism', Raghavan Iyer writes,

> lay the fact that the system they justified was a despotism and that the men who administered it were alien. Had the British settled down in the country and played the part of the Manchus in China, many of their theories and doings would have lasted longer and taken deeper root in Indian life, with the Indian genius for assimilation . . . By the very application of their doctrines, the trustees, the guardians, the utilitarians and the evangelicals brought about their own downfall, leaving behind them scattered traces of their thought and vocabulary.[32]

Forster's own account came to the same conclusions about the four classes of imperialists and their doctrines; his own vision of British India as it might have been constructed stood outside their limits.

The ideal which Forster would have liked to see imperial Britain fulfil in

India was the creation of a 'democratic Empire', not in the mere political sense of introducing representative self-government, which British Liberal opinion was in favour of providing as against the Conservative idea of despotic rule, but in the wider sense of constructing an equal, multiracial, and integrated society in which it would have been possible for the Indians and Englishmen living in India to enjoy equal rights and privileges and to live unrestricted by racial differences as individuals and as friends. But the possibilities of such an India had been frustrated by the imperialist doctrines, and the Liberals woke up to grasp them too feebly and too late, Forster thought, so that they achieved little more than the granting of political concessions and constitutional reforms. Forster did not believe that a political solution could undo the damage that had been done by the imposition in India of the imperialist system and doctrines in the past.

The foremost imperialist doctrine of trusteeship, which, as will be seen, is challenged in *Howards End*, had derived from Burke's famous speech on Fox's East India Bill at the time when the British Parliament was assuming control of the actions of the East India Company, and Burke expounded his theory supporting Parliament's responsibility as the ultimate trustee of power in India. 'The rights of *men*, that is to say, the natural rights of mankind', Burke said, 'are indeed sacred things.' The rights which some men exercised over others are only 'chartered rights . . . all political power which is set over men . . . all privilege claimed or exercised in exclusion of them, being wholly artificial, and for so much a derogation from the natural equality of mankind at large – ought to be some way or other exercised ultimately for their own benefit.'[33] He thought that a guarantee of this position could be obtained for India by placing the ultimate control over the exercise of power, rights and privileges, which are 'in the strictest sense a *trust*', in the hands of the British Parliament.

This principle of trusteeship, underlying Britain's ultimate right over India, was, in the words of Burke, 'the *magna charta* of Hindoostan'; it was extended a step further in the actual wielding of imperial power to mean that Britain had been ordained by Providence in the sacred authority of establishing power in India for India's own good. Even the most aggressive forward-looting policies which were pursued during the governor-generalship of Wellesley, and were decisive in establishing British power in India, were apparently inspired by this imperialist faith in the will of Providence. 'We feel that it would not only be impolitic, but highly immoral to suppose', Wellesley wrote in a despatch to the Court of Directors of the East India Company, 'that Providence has admitted of the establishment of the British power over the finest provinces of India, with any other view than that of its being conducive to the happiness of the people, as well as to our national advantage.'[34] The belief in the Empire as a divine trust provided the highest sanction for the British assumption of complete sovereignty, and it was upheld in the twentieth century by the great imperialists such as Curzon:

I would describe the Empire . . . as the result, not of an accident or a series of accidents, but of an instinct – that ineradicable and divinely planned impulse, which has sent the Englishman forth into the uttermost parts of the earth, and made him there the parent of new societies and the architect of unpremeditated creations . . . Count it no shame to acknowledge our Imperial mission, but, on the contrary, the greatest disgrace to be untrue to it, and even if God no longer thunders from Sinai, and His oracles are sometimes reported dumb, cling humbly but fervently to the belief that so long as we are worthy we may still remain one of the instruments through whom He chooses to speak to mankind.[35]

True to his faith, Curzon opposed the idea of introducing self-government in India, for 'it would mean ruin to India and treason to our trust'.

The position of the imperialist as the divine trustee is questioned by Forster in *Howards End*. The Schlegel family, who have lived in both imperial Germany and imperial Britain, raise the question in their family discussions. Margaret Schlegel is puzzled by a dilemma: if her cousin and his wife would speak one day for imperial Germany, 'both convinced that Germany was appointed by God to govern the world . . . Aunt Juley would come the next day, convinced that Great Britain had been appointed to the same post by the same authority. Were both these loud-voiced parties right?'[36]

Asked about this, Margaret's father, 'surveying the parties grimly, replied that he did not know'. Ernst Schlegel had been saddened by his own past experience in imperialist Germany. He was an idealist – 'the countryman of Hegel and Kant . . . whose imperialism was the imperialism of the air' – but, believing in action, he had nevertheless fought, 'without visualizing the results of victory', to make Germany an empire, and the victory had made him unhappy in the end:

A hint of the truth broke on him after Sedan, when he saw the dyed moustaches of Napoleon going grey; another when he entered Paris, and saw the smashed windows of the Tuileries. Peace came – it was all very immense, one had turned into an Empire – but he knew that some quality had vanished for which not all Alsace-Lorraine could compensate him. Germany, a commercial Power, Germany a naval Power, Germany with colonies here and a Forward Policy there, and legitimate aspirations in the other place, might appeal to others, and be fitly served by them; for his own part, he abstained from the fruits of victory, and naturalized himself in England.[37]

The younger Schlegels, brought up in the freer atmosphere of England, were indifferent to imperialist Germany, but although they appreciated many liberal British doctrines they did not sympathise with Britain's own imperialist policies. 'Temperance, tolerance, and sexual equality were intelligible cries to them; whereas they did not follow our Forward Policy in Thibet with the keen attention that it merits, and would at times dismiss the whole British Empire with a puzzled, if reverent, sigh.'[38] Margaret Schlegel saw the absurdity in the theory of the divine origin of imperialism, whether German or British. 'To me one of the two things is very clear', she remarked; 'either God does not know His own mind about England and Germany, or else these do not know the mind of God.'[39] Her own conclusion was that any individual human being is really higher than an empire. 'A hateful little girl', Forster writes about her, 'but at thirteen she had grasped a dilemma that most people travel through life without perceiving. Her brain darted up and down; it grew pliant and strong. Her conclusion was, that any human being lies nearer to the unseen than any organization, and from this she never varied.'[40] Margaret's conclusion is Forster's own conclusion on the 'trusteeship' doctrine of Empire. Not sure about God or His wishes about the world, she uses the word 'unseen', which is Forster's word for the divine,[41] and in saying that 'any human being lies nearer to the unseen than any organization', she in fact had spoken for Forster; 'I have no mystic faith in the people. I have in the individual. He seems to me a divine achievement and I mistrust any view which belittles him'.[42]

The organisation of British power into its supreme imperial position in India was complete at the end of the eighteenth century. The orthodox believer in the imperial destiny of Britain saw its triumph in the conquests and annexations of Wellesley, which expanded British territorial possessions over the whole peninsula. It was now left to the Utilitarians and the Evangelicals, who followed the 'trustees' in India, to carry out the mission of improving and civilising the Indians economically and morally by westernising them and their public institutions, and by evangelising their faith. Forster describes the situation and the 'British deportment' in India at this period:

> To the student of British deportment overseas, the end of the eighteenth century in Calcutta is an interesting period. A change is at hand. The English are no longer merely traders, soldiers, adventurers, who may take up what attitude suits them towards the aborigines; they are acquiring racial consciousness and the sense of imperial responsibility . . . A Supreme Council and a High Court brought solemn social consequences in their train. Viceregal airs begin, the King's birthday is already a religious event although he was George the Third, Lady Governess and Chief Justice hold their state, and apart from them, with a pride exceeding their own, Charles Grant lays the foundation of Protestant Missions in Bengal.[43]

In the beginning of the nineteenth century, when the Mahrattas, the last

independent power, were conquered, Sir John Malcolm of the East India
Company thought that 'The task of conquest was slight in comparison with
that which awaits us, the preservation of the empire acquired'.[44] The
Utilitarians and the Evangelicals by their work in India attempted to fulfil
this task. The Utilitarians wanted the feudal, primitive order under native
Indian rule to be transformed by the establishment of enlightened Western
institutions of administration and legislation. Bentham took a direct
interest in introducing English laws into India, and his influence on the
organisation of reforms and legislation was considerable.[45] James Mill was
in the East India Company's service for many years. As one who was an
assistant examiner for a long period and later appointed to the chief
executive post of Examiner, he was 'at the very centre of power', Eric
Stokes observes, 'and was in a position to carry out into practice the
principle of utility as he had expounded it in his *History of British India*'.[46]
His view of the natives in India was that they were in 'a hideous state . . .
tainted with the vices of insincerity; dissembling, treacherous, mendacious,
to an excess which surpasses even the usual measure of uncultivated
society', and he denounced the caste system, despotism and priestcraft, on
account of which 'the Hindus, in mind and body, were the most enslaved
portion of the human race'.[47] The poverty and ignorance, according to
James Mill, were 'the effect of bad laws, and bad government . . . never a
characteristic of any people who are governed well. It is necessary,
therefore, before education can operate to any great result, that the
poverty of the people should be redressed; that their laws and government
should operate beneficently'.[48] John Stuart Mill exercised less direct
influence on Indian government policy; a believer in the principles of self-
government, he disapproved of direct British rule in India, but while he
remained for long years in the Company's service, he shared his father's
desire for the 'good government of India' and his 'real opinions on Indian
subjects . . . and many of the true principles of Indian administration'.[49]
The influence of the Utilitarians on the British administrators and law-
makers in India led to a progress throughout the nineteenth century
towards a general security of life, economic welfare, education and the
well-being of the educated class, but under the impact of this development
India was set on the road to anglicisation and lost the distinctions and
variety of her native traditions. Together with the Evangelical movement,
the Utilitarian movement 'formed intellectual pressure-groups for reform
and influence in India along Western lines', comments Percival Spear:

> They were, each in their own ways, westernizing influences, tending to
> replace Indian customs, values, and ways of thought by European. They
> did not control the Government of India, but their influence ensured
> that when the Government moved at all, it would move along the lines
> which they had laid down. Together they constituted the Western
> challenge not merely to Hindu or Muslim power, but to Hindu and

Muslim thought and culture also. Wellesley's victories meant no more to the Hindu or Muslim than Babur's or Timur's, but the new ideologies were daggers pointed at the heart of both.[50]

Forster's comment on the utilitarian side of the imperialist's belief and work was reflected in *Howards End*. Leonard Bast, stepping out of Hilton into the country, noticed that 'a motor passed him' at the chalk pit:

> In it was another type, whom Nature favours—the Imperial. Healthy, ever in motion, it hopes to inherit the earth. It breeds as quickly as the yeoman, and as soundly; strong is the temptation to acclaim it as a super-yeoman, who carries his country's virtue overseas. But the Imperialist is not what he thinks or seems. He is a destroyer. He prepares the way for cosmopolitanism, and though his ambitions may be fulfilled, the earth that he inherits will be grey.[51]

Forster criticised the outlook of the champion of utilitarianism and the chief architect of anglicisation in India in the nineteenth century, Lord Macaulay, and also the later upholders of the same spirit like Cromer, Milner and Curzon.[52]

Believing in 'the intrinsic superiority' of Western literature and science, Macaulay had said that 'a single shelf of a good European library was worth the whole native literature of India and Arabia',[53] and he had, as the President of the Committee of Public Instruction in 1835, laid the foundation of English education in India. 'Macaulay was a great man', Forster says, but 'he never thought of learning from India, he only thought of improving her . . .'[54] Cromer made Egypt 'solvent, and he introduced useful and humane reforms . . . But he had a profound distrust of Orientals; his sympathy with Nationalism was purely academic; he started the flood of British officials who now deluge the administration, and his aim was a contented but torpid Egypt who would never criticize the Occupying Power.'[55] About Milner, whom Curzon during his foreign secretaryship sent to Egypt in May 1919 as Head of the Imperial Mission, 'encircled by machine-guns and aircraft' and boycotted by all 'with the exception of the European communities', Forster remarks that he was 'known as a militant Imperialist, who sincerely believed that the world would be happier if it were ruled by the British upper-middle classes.'[56] Milner had wanted 'a better organization of the dependent Empire as a whole', and he visualised a future in which Britain, remaining 'a Power of the very first rank', might continue to work for 'the welfare of many generations, millions upon millions of human beings', and 'every white man of British birth . . . [could] be at home in every state of the Empire.'[57] The Wilcoxes in *Howards End* embodied a kindred spirit and were the object of Forster's indignation: 'They had the colonial spirit, and were always making for some spot where the white man might carry his burden unobserved'.[58]

Forster's criticism of the 'utilitarian' approach to the Indian Empire is that it ignored the importance of Indian native traditions, and aimed to achieve a transformation of India in the wrong way. Westernisation, imposed as India's 'inevitable destiny',[59] was introduced into her without sympathy and a broader vision, he thought; the utilitarian outlook inclined to treat the Indian as socially inferior and his culture as unimportant, was blind to much that India, her native character and potentialities, given the right attention, would have contributed to the achievement of the Empire. Forster regrets that the task of promoting Indian cultures and introducing them to Britain was ignored by the imperialists of the utilitarian English middle-class. Commenting on this aspect of the failure of the Indian Empire, he wrote:

After two hundred years of political connexion with India, we in England know next to nothing about the Indian cultures. Our ignorance is disgraceful and is indeed an indictment of our Empire. We have sent our soldiers and administrators and money-makers to the East, but few scholars, and fewer artists . . . It is unwise to suppose that culture is unimportant and that distance in space and differences in idiom are a sufficient excuse for superciliousness and obtuseness. Our record here is poor. What attempt has been made by our rulers to promote Oriental scholarship and carry on the tradition of Sir William Jones? What attempt have they made to familiarize Britishers with the Indian arts and literatures or with Indian music? The answer to such a question is 'Wembley'; those who remember Wembley will know what the answer means, and those who have forgotten Wembley are to be congratulated.[60]

Forster's indictment of the Utilitarian aspect of imperialism has to be seen alongside his equally strong views about its Evangelical side. The work of evangelisation was begun in India by men (including his own forebears) who had formed the Clapham Sect and believed that the blessing of the Gospel was to be carried to all heathens. Henry Thornton, Forster's great-grandfather, and his close associates Charles Grant, William Wilberforce and Thomas Babington, were the leading members of the Church Missionary Society, and were responsible for obtaining Parliament's authority for establishing Evangelical Missions in India. Henry Thornton believed that it was not his wish 'to show intolerance to the religion of any of my fellow creatures', but as in India 'barbarous and immoral' practices were given 'the name of religion' and worship, and as the Indians were 'sunk in a low and deplorable state of ignorance and superation . . . it is the bounden duty of this Christian country not to exclude that light from its Indian subjects, which shall tend to the suppression of such horrible evils, and to the general melioration of their character'.[61] Charles Grant, who had served the East India Company in Bengal and later became its chairman, was more vehement in his condemnation of native Indian society and about the task of improving it. 'We cannot avoid recognizing in the people of Hindostan', he wrote,

> a race of men lamentably degenerate and base; retaining but a feeble sense of moral obligation; yet obstinate in their disregard of what they know to be right, governed by malevolent and licentious passions, strongly exemplifying the effects produced on society by a great and general corruption of manners, and sunk in misery by their vices, in a country peculiarly calculated by its natural advantages, to promote the prosperity of its inhabitants.[62]

Grant believed that to improve the character of the native his moral environment had to be transformed by abolishing Hindu despotism and priestcraft and by spreading the enlightenment of the Gospel. Wilberforce was Clapham's chief exponent in Parliament. In his speech on the East India Company's Charter Bill in 1813, which authorised the Company to issue licences to Christian missions in India, he had pleaded for spreading Christianity in India as vigorously as British laws and institutions of government:

> Are we so little aware of the vast superiority even of European laws and institutions, and far more of British laws and institutions, over those of Asia, as not to be prepared to predict with confidence, that the Indian community which should have exchanged its dark and bloody super- stitions for the genial influence of Christian light and truth, would have experienced such an increase of civil order and security; of social pleasures and domestic comforts, as to be desirous of preserving the blessings it should have acquired; and can we doubt that it would be bound even by the ties of gratitude to those who had been the honoured instruments of communicating them?[63]

The impact of Wilberforce's oratory in Parliament was matched by the strength of private petitions and subscriptions organised by Henry Thornton, and by Thomas Babington and Zachary Macaulay – Lord Macaulay's maternal uncle and father respectively – and the work of the Clapham Sect, pursued with invincible sincerity and dedication, ul- timately succeeded in stamping Christian missionary action in India as an important part of the imperialist effort. Other missions followed the Evangelicals, and missionary work was backed by its supporters in the government. Lord Macaulay wrote to his father from Bengal in 1836 that 'if our plans are followed, there will not be a single idolater among the respectable classes of Bengal, thirty years hence'.[64] The missions did considerable work towards social reforms, education and general welfare, but their subversive effect on the native religion and cultures roused acute discontent and reaction in the tradition-bound Indian society. It was manifested publicly in the mutiny of 1857, and later became a main factor in the nationalist grievance.

Forster's comment on the Christian missionary aspect of British imperialism is objective, clear and forceful. Himself a non-believer, he strongly condemned the proselytising outlook of Christianity which caused disaffection in India and the 'fanaticism' of wars elsewhere,[65] although his criticism of the missionary enterprise did not exclude sympathy with the human idealism, sincerity, and understanding of many individual missionaries. 'Missionaries have their faults . . . and there are bad missionaries', he writes,

> but for the most part they are Christians of integrity, and fine fellows, too, who try not merely to alter the heathen, but to understand him. It is the missionary rather than the Government official who is in touch with native opinion. The official need only learn how people can be governed. The missionary, since he wants to alter them, must learn what they are. He seems to be, and sometimes he is, the ideal student of human nature, passionate after facts, and moving through analysis towards sympathy . . . He has largely abandoned 'direct preaching' and tries to win converts by showing Christ in his life.[66]

An example of such individual missionaries Foster sees in S. Pollard, the author of *In Unknown China*, who worked among the tribes of Western China; he admires Pollard's 'most charming and sympathetic personality', and his love and understanding of the people he lived and worked with.[67] But when it comes to the question of avowed missionary proselytisation, and when Forster looks at the history of its alliance with imperialism, his criticism of it is expressed with unequivocal disapproval.

He shared both Samuel Butler's distrust of organised evangelisation and his scorn for the church missionary establishment; he gives an account of its bourgeois origin and motives in his own plain words:

> Missions in England began with the industrial revolution. Thanks to the development of machinery, a pious and leisured middle class came into existence who, mindful of the Gospel injunction, prepared to evangelize the heathen. There had been missionaries before their day, but they had been isolated idealists like St. Francis, or had held the sword like Cortes and Pizarro. Middle-class Englishmen shunned either alternative. They did not want to be murdered nor to murder, but to convert, and being business men, they knew that nothing can be done without money. Subscription lists swelled; and in particular did elderly and childless women find comfort in the movement and would sometimes leave it all

their wealth. Much unselfishness and heroism went to the growth of Missions, but they also met a home need. There was surplus money in England, seeking a sentimental outlet. Some societies would have endowed art and literature with the surplus: our middle class spent theirs in trying to alter the opinions and habits of people whom they had not seen.[68]

While denouncing the organised missionary movements generally, Forster condemns sharply those individual missionaries who carried out missionary work in the Empire fanatically. Living among the native people, for whom they had no sympathy, these missionaries wanted only to improve their character in their own way. In India, they maintained a position of imperial superiority and exercised their authority over the native people blindly. Forster assails their type when he writes about the Rev. C. E. Tyndale-Biscoe, headmaster of the C. M. S. school at Srinagar, and 'the deeds for the Empire and Christianity that he has wrought in that city'. He finds Tyndale-Biscoe and his 'heartless' work in Kashmir a complete contrast to Pollard and his admirable work in Western China. 'There is no rubbish about sympathy now', he writes, commenting on Tyndale-Biscoe's missionary principles, and work in Kashmir:

> Take the Kashmiri by the scruff of his neck; that is the only way you can strengthen his backbone. Kick him about until he has learned Boy Scout methods. Srinagar was a cesspool, moral and physical, when Mr. Tyndale-Biscoe arrived – Brahmanism and corruption, early marriages, cruelty to animals, nor did the population wash. Not 'boys' were his pupils, but 'jelly-fish': he can only call them 'jelly-fish', bundles of dirty linen; and he started their education by throwing them into the river Jhelum, then he caned and fined them and bullied them into breaking caste and mocked their religious observances, also thwarting and insulting their parents whenever an opportunity occurred, for he knew that whatever Indians think right is bound to be wrong, and that the British Raj exists in order that missionaries may drive this home.[69]

Forster condemns Tyndale-Biscoe's book, *Character Building in Kashmir*, as 'noisy, meddlesome and self-righteous, so heartless and brainless, so full of racial and religious "swank"'. It was valuable, he remarked, 'for it indicates the sort of person who is still trotting about in India'.[70] This observation, made in 1920, may well explain the unfavourable light in which the missionaries were to be portrayed in *A Passage to India*.

With the general collapse of the spirit of Christendom in the First World War, however, Forster knew that the imperialism of the Christian missionaries was inevitably declining, and consequently he shows the missionaries in *A Passage to India* as playing a limited and conspicuously harmless role. They are 'brainless' like Tyndale-Biscoe, but they do not

possess Tyndale-Biscoe's brutality or his imperial authority. In portraying
Graysford and Sorley in *A Passage to India*,[71] Forster actually portrays the
missionaries in their state of decline, and also the decay of the missionary
movement as a whole. As he wrote about this in 1920:

> The industrial revolution, which created it [the surplus British money
> that went into foreign missions], also created the abyss that has
> swallowed it up. The factories, as the century progressed produced more
> and more guns and ammunition. The Gospel of Peace was preached to
> all nations, but the countries that preached it most meanwhile perfected
> the sinews of war. In 1914 there was an explosion at the heart of
> Christendom whose effects are incalculable; but among them we may
> predict the decay of foreign Missions. It is not only that the heathen have
> shown themselves puzzled and cynical, so that the Chinese who have
> served in France raise eyebrows when cargoes of Bibles arrive in China.
> It is that there is less money to pay for the Bibles. Missions must mainly
> depend on private enterprise. No Imperial Government dare subsidize
> them in its own territories, or it risks a religious mutiny. And private
> enterprise, taxed without, and ravaged by agnosticism within, grows less
> and less inclined to foot the bill.[72]

After looking at Forster's thoughts on the Evangelical, the Utilitarian
and the 'trusteeship' doctrines of British imperialism, it is necessary finally
to examine his view of the one other school of thought which lay behind the
British Empire, deriving its origin from the Platonic conception of
government, and supporting the theory that the British ruled in India as
her 'guardians'. The idea that the British officers forming the Indian Civil
Service were rulers on the Platonic model was popularised by Platonists
like Benjamin Jowett who taught the young probationer officers at Balliol
College and inspired them in the Platonic ideal of government. By a
Parliamentary Act of 1853 the old system of arbitrary nomination of civil
servants by the East India Company's directors was abolished and
selection to the Indian Civil Service was to be made through competitive
examination, so that only men with the highest ability could enter its
service. Also, on the recommendation of a committee of which Lord
Macaulay was the chairman and Benjamin Jowett a member, the selected
candidates were to be on probation for a period to ensure that they
acquired the highest standard of education before going to India. Philip
Woodruff in the second volume of his book *The Men Who Ruled India*,
subtitled *The Guardians*, describes them as 'chosen and trained on Plato's
principles as Guardians who would rule in the light of their own vision of
the Good and the Beautiful – or, at least, on an English compromise with
Plato',[73] and he writes that the condition of the traditional and conservative society in India was peculiarly suitable for the introduction of the

Platonic ideal of rule by the 'guardians'. 'That was the Platonic ideal', he explains,

> a state in which property does not change hands, in which anything new, even in music or poetry, is prohibited, in which a rigid caste system keeps each man to his own function. In India, the caste system was there ready-made and it is odd that the four original castes of the Hindus, sages, warriors, traders, and menials, correspond with Plato's. The Indian Brahmans of the nineteenth century however were not at all like Plato's guardians: a new caste was needed to complete the state and the English supplied it. The English Guardians certainly believed there was something in their composition that distinguished them from the people they ruled; they were forbidden to own land in India or to take part in trade; they were governed by their elders on exactly Plato's principles. Plato had called the warriors who defended the state auxiliaries and from their number some were chosen to become guardians. In India, too, the military power was made subordinate to the civil, but military officers were chosen for the Political Department and thus joined the ranks of the Guardians.[74]

Philip Woodruff argues that the English 'guardians' supplied a needful part of the Indian society. As sub-divisional officers, as specialists in various branches of administration, and as district officers, they did hard and at times impossible work to secure welfare and justice for Indians, which it was assumed that the Indians, left to themselves, were incapable of achieving. The Indian Civil Service had remained exclusively British so long as it was under the East India Company. Indians were admitted in a limited number only to subordinate posts in the judicial and revenue departments, but they were excluded from the covenanted posts in the Civil Service because the directors of the East India Company 'believed that owing to defective education Indians had not yet attained a level which would make them fit for membership of the Service'.[75] Under the Imperial Government the situation remained practically the same, for although the Act of 1853 threw open the Service to Indians, they were debarred from entering it in any significant number by the peculiarly stringent conditions of the examination which, until 1922, despite protests from India, was held only in London, so that the Indian candidates in order to qualify had to travel to London to appear for the examination. Indian demands for more places in the Service for Indians and for the holding of simultaneous examinations in England and India to facilitate this move were repeatedly ignored by the Imperial Government, and when steps towards 'Indianisation' were taken under the Reforms Act of 1919, strong disagreement was expressed by British conservative opinion and also by the members of the Indian Civil Service themselves.[76] Philip Woodruff writes that

By the end of the century, contrast was at its clearest between on the one
hand the ideal of a liberal empire, an India held in trust, and on the
other the reality of despotic power wielded by Platonic Guardians in the
interest of order and tranquillity. It was an odd kind of despotism, for
which there is no parallel anywhere else, because its distinguishing
principle was the delegation of power. Almost from the day he arrived in
India, a member of the Guardian caste was given authority which
anywhere else he could hardly have attained with less than twenty years'
experience; he felt confident that he would be supported and that what
he did would be understood. And he too must learn to delegate if he was
to get through the day's work.[77]

The system in effect became a bureaucracy which, by concentrating a lot
of power under individual British officers and by virtually excluding the
Indians from high authority, perpetuated a type of imperialism which the
Indians resented fiercely. For them the system meant their perpetual
subjugation under the British through an authoritarian official rule, and
they considered it as one more proof that the ruling class regarded them as
their inferiors. Forster looked at this situation as an important question
affecting the character of British India, and his reflections on it form an
important part of his total comment on the role British imperialism played
in India.

The crux of the question from the Indian point of view is raised by
Forster when in *A Passage to India* Hamidullah tells Fielding that 'Well-
qualified Indians also need jobs', and asks: 'is it fair an Englishman should
occupy one when Indians are available?'[78] The British answer to this
question, which the Imperial Government had dodged for many years,
came in the form of 'Indianisation' of the Civil Service in the 1920s, and *A
Passage to India* looks at some important aspects of Indianisation as will be
seen in a later discussion. But it is relevant at this point to remember what
Forster actually thought about the general attitude of British civil servants
in India and about their Platonic 'guardianship' – a subject which he was
to treat as an important theme in his novel. Of Plato he says that he 'never
particularly appealed to me',[79] and as to forms of government, he declares
himself a believer in democracy, in parliamentary government, and in the
public's right to criticise abuse of power, and thus, ideologically, his
position is opposed to the Platonic ideal of rule by the 'guardians'.
Reflecting on its actual application in the Indian situation also, he finds
that the Platonic idealism was hardly realised in practice. He observes that
there were among the English civil servants in India some very great men
of the type of Alfred Lyall, for example, whose outlook and work reflected
the true spirit of the guardians, but the general character of the Civil
Service did not remain true to the ideal of these individual great men. 'If all
Englishmen had been like Lyall', writes Philip Woodruff, 'we should
perhaps never have been in India at all; empires are not made by men who

see both sides of a question. But our presence would have been less of an irritant; there would have been fewer who wanted us to go.'[80] 'Alfred Lyall was the last . . . and perhaps the greatest' of his type, says Forster, and he comments on the decline of men of Lyall's type:

After the Mutiny and the transference from John Company to the Crown, a change began. The new type of official may have been as fine as the old, but he was harder worked, less independent, and less in touch with the Indian socially. He could get back more easily to England for his leave, owing to improved steamer service, and his womenfolk could come out more easily to him. Such a man was not likely to waste his time in interpreting India to the stay-at-home; indeed, he would gruffly imply that there was nothing to interpret: 'India's a hole in which you've got to do your job, that's all'.[81]

Under the imperial system, the officials who came to India in large numbers through competitive examination from the English public schools[82] and from Oxford and Cambridge were in reality normally required to 'govern' Indians rather than be interested in them personally or socially. 'Do you feel fitted to govern Rajanpur?'[83] Malcolm Darling had been asked by the assistant commissioner when he was appointed sub-divisional officer of Rajanpur: incidentally, it is interesting to note from Malcolm Darling's account that he had been introduced to Plato by his assistant commissioner, and he himself too had been lending his sub-ordinate Indian pleader Benjamin Jowett's translation of *The Republic*. 'I was now Vice-President of two small Municipalities', Malcolm Darling says, describing the power and authority that were vested in him, 'chief magistrate and civil judge, head of the local Land Revenue staff, Superintendent of the Jail, and, above all, the representative of the British Raj standing on the lowest step of the long stairway leading through the Deputy Commissioner, Commissioner, and Lieutenant-Governor to the Viceroy himself.'[84] If he wanted to look beyond his official position and to take a social interest in the Indians, he says, he was prevented by the gulf that existed between them and the British officials. 'Such were the social conditions in India sixty years ago' — Malcolm Darling is referring to the period of his apprenticeship during 1904–8 – 'that it was a full year before I had my first talk with an educated Indian who was not an official, and even then it came by chance.'[85] He writes how senior British officers told him not to trust the native:

I find myself opposed to everyone I meet, and as they always insist upon their experience I can say nothing, though in fact I do say a great deal! You can't trust the native, they say, as if you could trust nine Englishmen out of ten. Then there is 'sedition' and 'disloyalty': and finally 'they want to shoulder us out'.[86]

One might expect Forster to be indirectly acquainted with the lapses of British officials in India from his intimacy with Malcolm Darling. But he had his own personal experience of the situation too. In Egypt he came across the 'racial arrogance' of the Anglo-Indian officials and their women-folk, who had gone there from India.[87] In India, working at Dewas, he actually had to deal with the officials of the Political Department who were in charge of the affairs of the Native States, and he records his observations about them in *The Hill of Devi*. In a report to Malcolm Darling he wrote about the political agent who was a 'bully' – 'a cow has to be milked in person before the person of Political Agent Adams, otherwise he will feel uneasy about his tea'. 'I hear that *his* superior', he wrote in another letter, 'also a "Colonel" at Indore – is even his inferior in deportment. It is strange that the Political Department, which has to deal with Princes, should specialize in bad manners.'[88] One officer's 'impudence' towards the Maharajah of Chhatarpur even vexed him to write in a letter to Lowes Dickinson: 'He need not tolerate such impudence now that the Government of India has changed its policy. Dewas doesn't, and I am urging this monarch to kick too. He won't of course. He has even been bullied into dismissing all his actors and dancers and there are no more of those lovely Krishna performances at the Palace.'[89]

Forster knew that under the imperial system the spirit of the 'guardians' of the civil service in India had degenerated into authoritarianism and even tyranny. The repression in the Punjab and Bengal around the years of his second visit showed this. In 1919, the year of the massacre at Amritsar and governmental repression in Egypt, he wrote, commenting about the general situation of the Empire, 'it seems improbable that a rule which now rests avowedly upon force can endure',[90] and he condemned the Amritsar massacre in his 'Notes on the English Character', written in the following year, as an 'example of public infamy'.[91] He criticised the repressive action of Lord Ronaldshay's Government in Bengal when on the occasion of the visit of the Prince of Wales it declared the non-cooperationist volunteer organisations in Calcutta illegal, and ordered extensive arrests. 'It is sad', he wrote, 'that the pleasure of a young man [the Prince] should be spoilt, but it is sadder that hundreds of other young men should be in prison on account of his visit to their country.'[92] He observed that during the days of heightened national movement in India the British civil servant, whose spirit had previously remained indifferent, callous and racially arrogant, tended more and more to assert himself in his own position of official power and authority when he came face to face with the nationalist agitators. It was now the spirit of a Reginald Dyer or a Michael O'Dwyer,[93] who thought that he was to hold India by force and that the British Raj existed for India's own good. When Ronny Heaslop announces in *A Passage to India* – 'I am out here to work, mind, to hold this wretched country by force. I'm not a missionary or a Labour Member or a vague sentimental sympathetic literary man. I'm just a servant of the

Government . . . We're not pleasant in India, and we don't intend to be pleasant. We've something more important to do'.[94] – he speaks for the spirit of the callous, authoritarian, so-called 'guardian' of British India.

Lord Ronaldshay, the Marquess of Zetland, who was the Governor of Bengal, writes in his foreword to L. S. S. O'Malley's *The Indian Civil Service* that 'a paramount part has been played by a body of men known as the "Indian Civil Service"' in fashioning British India. Describing British India as 'a miracle of organization' he says:

> To the 'factors' and 'writers' of the East India Company, brought into contact with a jumble of races separated by language, by religion, by social custom and by the standards of their civilization into innumerable entities great and small, existing fortuitously within the confines of a sub-continent itself vast in area and infinitely diverse in its physical characteristics, the evolution of an India such as we know today can have been neither calculated nor, indeed, even dimly imagined. How, and by whom, has the miracle been accomplished? How, and by whom, has the quite remarkable measure of political and administrative uniformity which characterizes British India today, been imposed upon a continent presenting in all other respects so great a medley of diversities, contrasts and contradictions?[95]

The Marquess of Zetland's answer to this question is that a 'paramount part' was played in this achievement by the Indian Civil Service. Such a claim cannot altogether be refuted. There is no evidence anywhere in Forster's writings about British India to suggest that he would deny the useful role played by the Civil Service in the organisation of British India. Reviewing the first volume of Philip Woodruff's book *The Men Who Ruled India*, subtitled *The Founders*, he wrote: 'Mr. Woodruff believes British rule has been good . . . And his eulogy of the British Raj is not fulsome',[96] and, indeed, Forster knew that the Indian Civil Service included men like Alfred Lyall, and Malcolm Darling, his own personal friend, who had in them the spirit required of a true 'guardian' of the Empire, the spirit which he partly embodies in *A Passage to India* in the character of Fielding.[97] But what seemed to Forster important was that the mere organisation of British India into a part of the Empire linked with Britain by only a system of official rule was not a great achievement. He sympathised with the Indian criticism of the British civil servant as 'the sun-dried bureaucrat',[98] and himself believed that the generally limited and narrow outlook of the civil service was partly responsible for the decay of British connection with India. If the spirit of the civil service had also been accompanied and inspired by an inner core of personal feeling for the Indians in the mind of the Englishman who went out to serve in India, he might have helped in making a greater achievement possible and turned the Empire into a happier and more enduring institution. Forster believed in Mrs Moore's thoughts about her son, Ronny Heaslop – 'One touch of regret – not the canny substitute but the true regret from the heart – would have made him a different man, and the British Empire a different institution'[99] – and the portrayal of Ronny, and the Turtons, the 'little gods' of Chandrapore, in *A Passage to India*, is intended to show what Forster thought to be the essential weakness of the Indian Civil Service and why it had made itself unpopular with the Indians and a failure in his own eyes.

The substance of Forster's criticism of the British officials, that is their lack of a personal approach towards the people of India, was reflected also in the account Edwin Montagu wrote of the Indian Civil Service after his visit to India as parliamentary under-secretary of state in 1912–13. 'Up to the present I do not see anything very alarming with regard to the rift between the I.C.S. and the people', Montagu wrote, 'but what I do think I see is, that I.C.S. men ignore the existence of the people and pursue a machine-made path.' 'The Civil Servants', he commented further, 'seem to me to live in great state. They are, of course, conventional and none of them can break through except at the cost of a reputation for lowering prestige or being misers.'[100] Montagu became Secretary of State for India in 1917 and was chiefly responsible for introducing the reforms of 1919 which enabled Indians to enter the Civil Service in large numbers as equals with the British. Following the reforms and the generally conciliatory policy adopted by the Imperial Government after the Amritsar massacre, there was apparent heart-searching among British official circles, and Forster wrote about the change he noticed in their general manner towards the Indians; many of the officials found it expedient to give up their rude and overbearing ways, though in other cases, there was a genuine change of heart.[101] But the softening of the official attitude happened too late, Forster thought, to influence the rebelling Indians and to prevent them from wanting to see the end of Britain's connection with them. The repression in the Punjab had shown that the tyranny of British rule by the alliance of officialism with militarism had reached its highest watermark, and the Indians were determined not to co-operate with the Government under which such repression had been made possible. One main issue for the non-cooperationists, as Gandhi wrote in a letter to the Duke of Connaught, was 'to battle with all our might against that in English nature which had made O'Dwyerism and Dyerism possible in the Punjab'.[102] The tragic failure of the policy of imperial guardianship was no doubt a root cause of the Indian grievance: campaigning to achieve Swaraj within a year Gandhi wrote after the Nagpur Congress, in January 1921:

The new aim is the achievement of Swaraj in the form of our choice, that [is], Swaraj with the British connection kept up, if possible, or severed if it is not to our liking. If this connection is to continue, it can do so only in such form as will permit the aim of the Congress to be fully realized. That is to say, the British should give up behaving as our superiors. The

British connection ought to be intolerable to us so long as we feel that a handful of Englishmen are ruling over us.[103]

During the period of the Non-cooperation movement the Duke of Connaught and the Prince of Wales were announcing in India that they were friends of Indians, and were appealing to them to live in friendship with the British,[104] but it was then too late to plead for friendship between the two communities in the Empire, from which the scope for such a relationship had been excluded in the past. The Prince of Wales was disillusioned in his hopes by the strong anti-British feeling he noticed in India, and he returned from his visit convinced that 'India is no longer a place for a white man to live in'.[105] Forster, reflecting on the deep conflicts of the situation, came to the same sad conclusion, and wrote,

> though friendship between individuals will continue and courtesies between high officials increase, there is little hope now of spontaneous intercourse between the two races. The Indian has taken up a new attitude . . . Responsible Englishmen are far politer to Indians now than they were ten years ago, but it is too late because Indians no longer require their social support.

Forster was certain that Britain had lost her chances in the Indian Empire, and, blaming the 'rude', 'overbearing' officialism of the British Raj chiefly for this failure, he affirmed in his report: 'never in history did ill-breeding contribute so much towards the dissolution of an Empire'.[106]

A critic of all forms of imperialist doctrines that sought to establish Britain's supremacy over India, Forster conceived his own ideal of the Indian Empire in the image of a 'democratic Empire'. It may seem that his conception merely echoed the democratic idealism which inspired the Liberals when they were in power in Britain to provide for self-government in India at an ultimate stage, but Forster's idea sprang from a distinctively personal vision and outlook, which distinguishes it from the limited political goal pursued by the Liberals in India. A liberal by his own description, he is an 'individualist'[107] uncommitted to a political creed, and it will be seen that he criticised some aspects of official Liberal policy towards India.

The British Liberal party's policy towards India was broadly based on the intention to prepare India for self-government, but in actual practice this policy, involving conflicts and divisions among groups of Liberals themselves, was followed by much confusion, inconsistency and delay, and the realisation of the real goal of self-government remained outside its reach. This curious history of British Liberalism in relation to imperial policies and achievement in India has been surveyed by R. J. Moore in his book *Liberalism and Indian Politics 1872–1922*. Reflecting on the circumstances in which self-government was finally established in India when the

Liberals were out of power in Britain and therefore no longer in control of the Empire, Moore writes:

> After the eclipse of the Liberals the pace of India's advance towards Independence lay at issue between home governments that were generally Conservative and nationalists whose methods were character-istically non-constitutional . . . The last quarter of the *Raj* was a period of non-co-operation, communal bitterness and violence, official re-pression and nationalist frustration, from which release came through the knife of Partition and Britain's departure in indecent haste. It was a mockery of the ideal of a united India's steady progression towards self-government through successive constitutional adjustments. Why, one wonders, were the builders of the *Raj* so ineffective in dismantling it? Why did fifty years of liberal influence upon Indian politics fail to produce the constitutional machinery for that transfer of authority and responsibility which Whigs, Gladstonians and radicals had always accepted as the object of British rule?[108]

Moore explains that the peculiar conflicts, uncertainties and conditions inhering in British liberal policies towards India were chiefly responsible for this failure. For many years the Whig–Liberals, believing that 'the subject peoples of the Queen-Empress would have the greatest freedom to develop under the *pax Britannica*', opposed the democratic liberalism of Gladstone, 'who favoured self-determination not only at home but also in Ireland and, as soon as possible, in the foreign parts of the Empire',[109] and after Gladstone's retirement official Liberal policy towards India, under the leadership of the 'Liberal Imperialists', Lord Rosebery and Lord Fowler, came nearer the Tory ideal, looking at the Empire as 'a vast inheritance which we will not dishonour or abandon'.[110] Actually, imperial control passed into the hands of the Tories with the defeat of the Liberal party at the elections of 1895, and thus, until the next stage when the party was back in power, the Liberals had not been able to follow a coherent policy or implement an effectual change in the direction of democratising India.

The Indian Councils Act of 1909 which introduced nominal con-stitutional reforms, known as the Morley–Minto Reforms,[111] was the Liberals' first achievement, and with the rise of Indian dissatisfaction and demand for a self-governing status in the post-war years, this Act was followed by the Government of India Act of 1919, introducing more reforms. In response to the insistent Indian demand for a definitive declaration of Britain's policy, and in appreciation of India's loyal support during the war, the Liberal Secretary of State, Edwin Montagu, declared in the British Parliament on 20 August 1917, that

> The Policy of His Majesty's Government, with which the Government

of India are in complete accord, is that of the increasing association of Indians in every branch of the administration and the gradual development of self-governing institutions with a view to the progressive realization of responsible government in India as an integral part of the British Empire.[112]

The Montagu–Chelmsford Reforms were introduced in pursuance of this declaration, providing for 'diarchy', that is for Indians to participate in the government, sharing political and legislative powers with the British within prescribed limits, and also for a progressive Indianisation of the Civil Service. These reforms were an inadequate answer to the Indian demand for a fully self-governing colonial status, and their introduction did not even clarify that Britain's aim in India was the establishment of full self-government; yet these reforms were the British Liberal party's sum of achievement in India in the beginning of the 1920s, and were to remain its final achievement. In March 1922 Montagu resigned as the last Liberal Secretary of State for India, under Conservative pressure, and in October of the same year, with the resignation of Lloyd George as the leader of the Liberal – Conservative coalition, the Liberals fell, never to recover power in Britain again nor to play a part in the crucial imperial politics which in the next twenty-five years led to the actual establishment of self-government in India.

In contrast to the narrow and confused Liberal political ideal of India, Forster's own ideal was a sincere, personal ideal, the ideal of a liberal individualist, believing in the conception of India as a 'democratic Empire' in a deeper and essentially personal sense. If Liberal politics centred its aim and attention around the form of the government of India and its relationship with the British Government, Forster based his own considerations on individual and social life in India and on the relationship between individual Indians and Englishmen, and between their two communities. He knew that if Indian nationalism was turning wholly anti-British after the First World War, it was because the Government of India, under an imperialist system, whether Tory or Liberal, had failed to create the conditions in which Indians and Englishmen could live together in an atmosphere of social equality and friendship. 'Here is the Sepoy, back from France', he observed, 'failing to see why the Tommy should have servants and *punkhas* when he has none. And here is the European chauffeur who drives through the streets shouting at the pedestrians and scattering them; the looks of hatred they cast back at him show how deep the trouble goes.'[113] He criticised the sense of the superiority of the British race, religion and intellectual and political wisdom on which imperialist outlook and policies on India had been based, and he also attacked the impersonal machinery of officialdom through which the imperial government of India was carried on. He thought that the imperial system was wrong and was based on wrong assumptions, and he believed that the liberal reforms

could not make it right. On his first visit to India, soon after the
Morley–Minto Reforms had been put into effect, he noticed their
insignificance in the context of the acute failures of consideration from
which the Indians suffered: by giving them a political concession in terms
of places in the Councils of Government, the reforms did not affect the
deeper social inequalities that existed between Englishmen and Indians. If
in a part of Jodhpur, in the present state of Rajasthan, Forster came across
an English community living with the native people in good fellow-feeling,
he observed that it was 'rare', and for other, exceptional reasons and not
the result of political reforms:

> They loved the city and the people living in it, and an outsider's
> enthusiasm instead of boring them, appeared to give pleasure. Men and
> women, they shared the same club as the Indians, and under its gracious
> roof the 'racial questions' had been solved – not by reformers, who only
> accent the evils they define, but by the genius of the city, which gave
> everyone something to work for and think about. I had heard of this
> loyalty at the other end of the peninsula – it was avowedly rare.[114]

Of the meagre consequence of the reforms of 1919 also Forster wrote
with insight and from personal observation. These reforms, designed to
conciliate the nationalists, provided for 'responsible government' to be
introduced in India in the long run, through a period of experiment by
placing partial control over local government under elected Indian
ministers responsible to the legislative councils. They were unsatisfactory
from the Indian point of view because they failed to give India a status fully
equal to that of the 'white' dominions like Canada, Australia and New
Zealand, and they did not remove all the racial distinctions existing at
various levels in British India. In a cancelled passage in the manuscripts of
A Passage to India Fielding is seen pondering over the disappointment in
India in the aftermath of the reforms: 'India is officially supposed to be like
nothing else in the world', he reflects on his first arrival, . . . Place in the
comity of nations * * * * * was denied to her.'[115] The irrelevance of the
reforms, as they were seen by Indians, is conveyed by Forster in another
passage where Aziz says to Fielding, in *A Passage to India,* 'What is the use of
all these reforms, and Conciliation Committees . . . and Councils of
Notables and official parties where the English sneer at our skins?'[116]

   The reforms of 1919 were accepted by the Indian Congress reluctantly,
under Gandhi's moderate influence, with much opposition from C. R. Das
and his followers who were later to leave the Congress and form the
Swarajist party.[117] 'So far as may be possible, the people will so work the
Reforms as to secure an early establishment of full Responsible Government. . . .'[118] resolved the Congress at Amritsar in 1919, and co-operation
was offered by the Muslim League too, but the spirit of co-operation was
short-lived. Following the massacre at Amritsar and the vindication of

General Dyer in the House of Lords, the Indians had grown determined to reject the assumption that in the Empire they were treated equally and without racial prejudice. The Muslims took the proposed terms of the Treaty of Sèvres, published in May 1920, as imperial discrimination against Islam, and harboured the same grievance. In 1920 the Congress and the Muslim League jointly launched the Non-cooperation movement, totally repudiating the reforms and their own obligation to the British Raj.

The Non-cooperation movement was a culminating manifestation of India's fundamental discontent with British imperialism. It was a moral protest against the British assumption of superiority and against the humiliation from which the Indians suffered in the unequal, racially divided society of Anglo-India. In his public letter to the Duke of Connaught Gandhi wrote: 'The non-co-operationists have come to the conclusion that they must not be deceived by the reforms that tinker with the problem of India's distress and humiliation . . . We desire to live on terms of friendship with Englishmen, but that friendship must be on terms of equals both in theory and practice.'[119] Gandhi's ideal of India was also the substance of Forster's conception of a 'democratic Empire'. During the Non-cooperation movement, when Gandhi published his open letter to the Duke of Connaught, Forster also wrote, concerning the visit of the Prince of Wales:

> If it crowned another work, if the subordinate Englishmen in the country had also been *naif* and genial, if the subalterns and Tommies and European engineers and schoolmasters and policemen and magistrates had likewise taken their stand upon a common humanity instead of the pedestal of race – then the foundation of a democratic Empire might have been well and truly laid. But the good-fellowship cannot begin at the top; there it will neither impress the old-fashioned Indian who thinks a Prince should not be a fellow, nor conciliate the Oxford-educated Indian who is excluded from the local Club. It will be interpreted as a device of the Government to gain time, and as an evidence of fear. Until the unimportant Englishmen here condescend to hold out their hands to 'natives', it is waste of money to display the affabilities of the House of Windsor.[120]

Like Gandhi, Forster contemplated an India in which Indians and Englishmen might have lived in equality, as friends. Both men valued personal relations above politics, and criticised imperialist policies under which the consideration of personal relations had been ignored. Gandhi had hoped that by launching the Non-cooperation movement, India might transform British imperialism, and remain within a happier British Empire,[121] but for Forster the Non-cooperation movement had spelt the 'dissolution' of British India altogether. History has proved that Forster's judgement was right.

4 'Towards the Dissolution of an Empire': Forster's Thoughts on the Indian Non-cooperation and Khilafat movements

Two specific causes lay behind the Indian Non-cooperation movement: to seek redress for the massacre at Amritsar, and to protest against Britain's hostility towards Turkey as demonstrated by the peace terms announced under the Treaty of Sèvres in 1920.[1] Forster was in full sympathy with both these causes. It has been mentioned in the foregoing chapter that he condemned the Amritsar massacre and also the British complicity in the situation concerning Turkey. His whole approach to the Non-cooperation movement is scrutinised in the present chapter to establish one important point: that when this major movement in the history of the Indian Empire had completely baffled the British official mind, and hostile attempts were being made to misrepresent it, Forster looked at it not only with a remarkably accurate insight, but also with sincere interest and sympathy.

Forster's full reaction to the situation surrounding the Amritsar massacre may be looked at first. The massacre, and the authoritarian repression, martial law and terrorism that were associated with it, had roused bitterness throughout India as well as much public controversy in Britain.[2] General Dyer's action turned Indian national politics firmly anti-British. In Britain it was officially censured by the government and by the Army Council, and the liberal section of British public opinion also condemned it. Describing 'The reign of terror in the Punjab' *The Nation* commented that 'this province, a vital element in the British government of India and the recruitment of its army, was simply trodden under foot'.[3] On the other hand, a large section of the British public, and the House of Lords, vindicated General Dyer and, like the Anglo-Indians and other Europeans living in India who also stood by him, they proclaimed him as the 'Hero of the Hour', and the 'Saviour of India'. In the midst of the excitement of public controversy, Forster's castigation of the Amritsar massacre as an example of 'public infamy' may not have signified his own strong view about it clearly; one has to look closely at *A Passage to India* to realise his full reaction to the events of Amritsar and what, in his view, they signified for the fate of the Empire.

The actual events surrounding the Amritsar massacre have been absorbed centrally into the story of *A Passage to India*. Forster uses them to portray an important part of the historical truth about the decline of British India. He believed that if in the past British policies of racial and social discrimination had weakened the structure of British India, the use of force and repression as a means of imperial governance had precipitated the collapse of that structure. Ideologically Forster disbelieved in force. He accepts that society and government have to depend upon it to some extent, but he rejects force when it is oppressive and exercised to coerce public opinion or in acts of repression of the kind that occurred at Amritsar. He would place such force outside civilised society and human relations. 'Does not all society rest upon force?' is an 'unpleasant question' for him to answer: 'If a government cannot count upon the police and army, how can it hope to rule? And if an individual gets knocked on the head or sent to a labour camp, of what significance are his opinions?' But 'this dilemma does not worry me', he says, 'as much as it does some. I realise that all society rests upon force. But all the great creative actions, all the decent human relations, occur during the intervals when force has not managed to come to the front.'[4] At Amritsar force had been used and exhibited in a gross and naked manner – in the massacre of an unarmed crowd, in making human beings crawl on all fours in a public street, flogging them publicly, compelling them by law to salute the 'superiors', and in various other inhuman ways. Forster exposes these attrocities in *A Passage to India* not with partisan or journalistic excitement but within the bounds of creative and artistic restraint, and also with an uncompromising candour.

The troubled situation at Chandrapore following the alleged insult to Adela Quested and the arrest of Dr Aziz telescopically focuses attention on the actual situation surrounding the Amritsar massacre. The connections between Forster's story and the actual situation are clear, although Forster seems to have deliberately avoided introducing the sensitive name 'Amritsar'. In the prelude to the central episode of the novel which commences with the incident in the Marabar Caves, Calcutta and Lahore (places which, like Amritsar, were also full of unrest and tense political interest) are mentioned significantly as 'important towns . . . where interesting events occur, and personalities are developed'.[5] The source of the trouble at Chandrapore, the alleged attempt made by an Indian to molest an English girl,[6] has a connection with actual events also. Fear of rape by angry Indians threatening to revenge General Dyer's action was actually haunting the English women and their community living at Amritsar.[7] Their fear and anxious condition formed the actual back-

ground to the imaginary scene among the English community at
Chandrapore on the day of Dr Aziz's alleged offence and his arrest.
Forster's description of the meeting at the club has a curious resemblance
with an actual description of Amritsar by 'An Englishwoman', which had
been published in *Blackwood's Magazine* in April 1920.[8] The author of this
article, like Adela Quested, had arrived in India, new to the country.
Amritsar was her first 'station', and she was living there 'in one of a group of
houses called Canal Bungalows' at the time of wide nationalist demonstrations held in the Punjab and many other parts of India in protest
against the Rowlatt Acts.[9] This English authoress had personally seen the
disturbances in Lahore, which had made her nervous. Amritsar was
seething with unrest, and was unsafe. The bungalow in which she was
staying had been chosen as a 'rallying-post for European women and
children in the event of trouble'. She describes the scene that actually took
place there and at the Amritsar fort:

> My suspicions were quickly confirmed when I came into a drawing
> room full of people I had never seen before, who paid no attention
> whatever to my entry. Fresh arrivals poured in every minute, and from
> one or two acquaintances among them I elicited the little that they knew
> of what had happened. A few minutes earlier a wild crowd had burst
> over the Hall bridge (which connects the city with the Civil Lines),
> driving back and stoning the small picket which was posted there. No
> shots had then been fired, but the howl of the mob could be heard a
> quarter of a mile away, and the residents in the main thoroughfare were
> rapidly warned to leave their bungalows for the rallying-posts. The
> crowd was close at hand, and a moment's delay might prove fatal; but at
> this somnolent hour it was no small task to persuade the women to move,
> and one of them persistently refused to quit her house because her baby
> was asleep. As people left their bungalows a few shots were heard from
> the direction of the bridge but nothing was known of the course of
> events.
>
> From men passing on horseback we gradually learned a few details,
> and before long we saw smoke and flames arising from the city and heard
> that Europeans were being murdered . . . About half an hour before
> sunset, news came that the Fort of Gobindgarh was ready to receive
> us . . . We set forth with some trepidation; but the arrival of some
> Gurkha troops about this time enabled the road to be picketed, and the
> way was safe. Men from the Central Followers' Depôt armed with staves
> accompanied us, and it was not long before we were driving through the
> winding entrances to the Fort . . . Dusk was now falling, and we had to
> make haste to prepare for the night. We found places where we could,
> and most of us packed into the centre of a great quadrangle . . . A roll-
> call revealed 130 women and children, besides babies . . . The outlook
> was not pleasant for women who had never known a day's real hardship

before: they found themselves suddenly stripped of all the decencies and comforts they had come to look upon as necessities, and surrounded by the miseries of dirt, heat and overcrowding . . .

The days were monotonous and we had to keep very quiet for the sake of Miss Sherwood, who was lying between life and death. Seizing her as she was bicycling from house to house in the city, the crowd had beaten her down with iron-bound sticks and left her for dead in the gutter, and for many days her life was in danger. After about a week it was considered safe for us to travel and arrangements were made to remove all the women and children to the hills. Special trains were run, packed with refugees from Lahore and Amritsar. It was considered better by the authorities that no women should be left behind, and they decided that Eurasians as well as Europeans should reside in hill stations for a time.[10]

Read alongside the above description, Forster's own portrayal of the scene at Chandrapore club shows a close parallel to the real situation at Amritsar. Here is Forster's account:

People drove into the club with studious calm – the jog-trot of country gentlefolk between green hedgerows, for the natives must not suspect that they were agitated. They exchanged the usual drinks, but everything tasted different, and then they looked out at the palisade of cactuses stabbing the purple throat of the sky; they realized that they were thousands of miles away from any scenery that they understood. The club was fuller than usual, and several parents had brought their children into the rooms reserved for adults, which gave the air of the residency at Lucknow. One young mother – a brainless, but most beautiful girl – sat on a low ottoman in the smoking room with a baby in her arms; her husband was away in the district and she dared not return to her bungalow in case the 'niggers attacked'. The wife of a small railway official, she was generally snubbed . . . They had started speaking of 'women and children' – that phrase that exempts the male from sanity when it had been repeated a few times . . . 'But it's the women and children', they repeated, and the Collector knew he ought to stop them intoxicating themselves but he hadn't the heart. 'They ought to be compelled to give hostages,' etc. Many of the said women and children were leaving for the hill stations in a few days, and the suggestion was made that they should be packed off at once in a special train.

'And a jolly suggestion', the subaltern cried. 'The army's got to come in sooner or later. (A special train was in his mind inseparable from troops.) . . . Station a bunch of Gurkhas at the entrance of the cave was all that was wanted.' . . . 'English no good,' he cried, getting his loyalties mixed. 'Native troops for this country. Give me the sporting type of native, give me Gurkhas . . .' The Collector nodded at him pleasantly, and said to his own people: 'Don't start carrying arms about. I want everything to go on precisely as usual, until there's cause for the contrary. Get the womenfolk off to the hills, but do it quietly, and for Heaven's sake no more talk of special trains' . . .

The smoking-room door opened, and let in a feminine buzz. Mrs. Turton called out: 'She's better', and from both sections of the community a sigh of joy and relief rose . . . Miss Quested was only a victim, but young Heaslop was a martyr; he was the recipient of all the evil intended against them by the country they had tried to serve; he was bearing the sahib's cross . . . The conversation turned to women and children again . . .[11]

Forster's account reflects the general atmosphere and many details of the actual occurrences. The communal isolation of the small English colony at Chandrapore, the hysteria about the safety of the English women and children (Forster's story of the alleged insult on Adela remotely echoes the actual incident of the assault on Miss Sherwood), the civil administration's dependence on troops, especially the Gurkhas, and the nervous dispatch of English families to hill stations – all these details unmistakably refer to the events of Amritsar.

Forster's picture has also some more crucial references to the particular tragedies suffered by the Indians at Amritsar, of which the massacre was the climax. An important clue to the real nature of these tragedies is provided by his reference to the actual instance of General Dyer's 'crawling order'. When, in *A Passage to India*, the English community at Chandrapore is gathered in Ronny's private room adjacent to the Court to observe the trial of Dr Aziz, Mrs Turton, the Collector's wife, remarks (upon Major Callendar saying that 'nothing is too bad for these people . . . there's not such a thing as cruelty after a thing like this'): 'Exactly, and remember it afterwards, you men. You're weak, weak, weak. Why, they ought to crawl from here to the caves on their hands and knees whenever an Englishwoman's in sight, they oughtn't to be spoken to, ought to be spat at, they ought to be ground into the dust . . .'[12] One may read this detailed list of punishments for Indians suggested by an English District Collector's wife as comical exaggerations, but it will be seen that Forster's details are indeed a reminder of some of the most sordid punishments that had actually been inflicted on the people of Amritsar and other parts of the Punjab in 1919.

The full variety of punishments that had been imposed by the military authorities in the Punjab were reported by the Hunter Committee.[13] They were made familiar to the British public through discussion in Parliament and through detailed reports in some newspapers, especially in the columns of *The Nation*,[14] through which Forster could have been well acquainted with all the particulars. The 'crawling order' was the most flagrant of these punishments. This order was imposed by General Dyer on account of an incident which involved the English girl, Miss Sherwood, referred to above. Miss F. Marcella Sherwood had been living in Amritsar, and during the disturbances she had been brutally assaulted by a group of Indians. General Dyer had military control over the city. He ruled that all Indians passing through Kucha Kaurhianwala Lane, where Miss Sherwood had been attacked, must go on all fours. According to the Hunter Committee's Report the 'crawling order' was issued on 19 April, i.e. nine days after the assault had been committed on Miss Sherwood, and continued in force until 26 April, when it was withdrawn on the instructions of the Punjab Government, who disapproved of it. During the period the order was in force about fifty Indians had been made to crawl through the lane. On the release in Britain of the Hunter Committee's Report and the details of the 'crawling order', it was condemned by some newspapers, and also by the British Government as an offence 'against every canon of civilized Government'.[15] It nonetheless remained as an irrevocable act in the vast tragedy of Amritsar, and in subtly drawing attention to it *A Passage to India* underlines the full depth of that tragedy.

In addition to the 'crawling order', reference to public flogging, as had actually been carried out at Amritsar in the case of six Indians implicated in the assault of Miss Sherwood, is also seen in *A Passage to India*. We see the Collector of Chandrapore, sitting in the smoking room on the day of Dr Aziz's arrest, shown as feeling the impulses 'to avenge Miss Quested . . . to flog every native that he saw'.[16] Another purely humiliating punishment that had been inflicted in the Punjab, the 'salaaming order', is also cited by Forster in a more elaborate way. The 'salaaming order' had been enforced by the military authorities so that Indians would, by law, show European officers respect by saluting them. The order proclaimed by General Campbell on 22 April 1919 was stated in these terms:

> Whereas it has come to my notice that certain inhabitants of the Gujranwala District are habitually exhibiting a lack of respect for gazetted or commissioned European Civil and Military Officers of His Majesty's Service, thereby failing to maintain the dignity of that Government, I hereby order that the inhabitants of the Gujranwala District shall accord to all such officers, wherever met, the salutation usually accorded to Indian gentlemen of high social position in accordance with the customs of India. That is to say, persons riding on animals or in a wheeled conveyance will alight, persons carrying opened and raised umbrellas shall lower them, and all persons shall salute or 'salaam' with the hands.[17]

The order had been enforced at Amritsar also with General Dyer's concurrence, and Indians who refused to salute Europeans were severely punished.[18] Fantastic attempts such as this to enforce subjugation on disgruntled Indians and to demand respect for the British Raj are exposed in the peculiar relationship that is shown between Major Callendar, the civil surgeon at Chandrapore, and his subordinate, Dr Aziz. Summoned by the major to see him at his bungalow, Dr Aziz is irritated. Reluctantly he cleans his pan-tinted teeth and rides in a tonga to meet the civil surgeon. He feels inclined to approach the major's bungalow riding in the carriage, but stops himself from doing so as that would have meant lack of respect for his superior. Forster describes the intriguing scene:

> When he turned into Major Callendar's compound he could with difficulty restrain himself from getting down from the tonga and approaching the bungalow on foot, and this not because his soul was servile but because his feelings – the sensitive edges of him – feared a gross snub. There had been a 'case' last year – an Indian gentleman had driven up to an official's house and been turned back by the servants and been told to approach more suitably – only one case among thousands of visits to hundreds of officials, but its fame spread wide. The young man shrank from a repetition of it. He compromised, and stopped the driver just outside the flood of light that fell across the veranda.[19]

Insubordinate habits of Indians, like those of Dr Aziz in relation to Major Callendar, are also talked of later in the story by English officers: 'It's the educated native's latest dodge. They used to cringe', remarks Ronny Heaslop to Mrs Moore, 'but the younger generation believe in a show of manly independence. They think it will pay better with the itinerant M.P.'; in Major Callendar's view, the Indians did so for 'increasing the izzat'.[20] Still later, when Aziz has moved to the Native State of Mau he feels free from the shackles of the enforced servility under the British, and on one occasion he is seen mocking the rules of British India such as the 'salaaming order': seeing Fielding, who is on official tour in Mau, 'Aziz sketched a comic salaam', remarks the author. 'Like all Indians, he was skilful in the slighter impertinences. "I tremble, I obey", the gesture said, and it was not lost upon Fielding.'[21]

Forster cites some of these grotesque tyrannies, repeatedly hitting also at the whole apparatus of military control in the Punjab which was the main background to the tragedies of 1919. One sees that troops are wanted at Chandrapore time and again – whether it is because of a 'religious riot' between the Hindus and the Mohammedans during the Moharrum, or simply because the English community fears that on account of the case against Dr Aziz 'there's supposed to be a riot on'. At the meeting in the club the subaltern cries for 'native troops', and suggests that 'Barabas Hill' should have been 'under military control'. 'Call in the troops and clear the bazaars', says Major Callendar, remarking that 'It's not the time for sitting down. It's the time for action.'[22] There is a particularly sharp comment in one significant passage in *A Passage to India* on military repression in the Punjab and on the fantastic attempts by the Anglo-Indian community in

India and their supporters in Britain to justify it. The passage as it appears
in the printed version of the story is without the obvious reference, present
in an earlier version in the manuscripts, to General Dyer's shooting and his
argument that he had fired in order to 'produce the necessary moral and
widespread effect'. But its allusion is unmistakable, and Forster's intention
to condemn the massacre and all the brutal ideas behind it cannot be
missed. This passage, in the printed version, describes a part of the scene at
Chandrapore club, showing the English official reaction towards Indians
following the alleged offence of Dr Aziz:

> One soldier was in the room this evening – a stray subaltern from a
> Gurkha regiment; he was a little drunk, and regarded his presence as
> providential. The Collector sighed. There seemed nothing for it but the
> old weary business of compromise and moderation. He longed for the
> good old days when an Englishman could satisfy his own honour and no
> questions asked afterwards. Poor young Heaslop had taken a step in this
> direction, by refusing bail, but the Collector couldn't feel this was wise of
> poor young Heaslop. Not only would the Nawab Bahadur and others be
> angry, but the Government of India itself also watches – and behind it is
> that caucus of cranks and cravens, the British Parliament.[23]

The remark about the presence of the soldier as being 'providential' is an
allusion to the acclaim General Dyer had received from his supporters in
India and Britain.[24] 'The good old days when an Englishman could satisfy
his own honour and no questions asked afterwards' could allude to the
grotesque acts and ideas of General Dyer's regime generally; memories of
the massacre are evoked in an earlier version of the passage which reads
thus:

> in the ^vacated^ smoking room about a dozen men ~~sat informally and
> jerked~~ began to jerk little sentences at each other . . . "Oh, one knows
> all that," was a frequent comment. They knew that the natives could not
> be trusted and outnumbered them by thousands to one, and that though
> nothing ~~as bad~~ black as this had occurred before, it was the type of thing
> that ^always^ might occur. They wanted revenge and 'examples', but
> did not ask for them openly. Even their hatred ^wrath^ was tinged with
> disillusionment, for the good old days were over when ~~a man could ride~~
> an Englishman who was wronged could go out and shoot right and left
> until his honour ~~was~~ felt satisfied, ^can satisfy himself^ and no questions
> be asked ~~in Parliament~~ afterwards.[25]

The shootings at Amritsar were not only questioned in the House of
Commons and censured, they were also the subject of bitter debate in the
Indian Parliament during which the Home Member in the Government of
India, Sir William Vincent, leading the debate from the Government

benches expressed 'the deep regret of the administration at the improper conduct and improper orders of certain individual officers; and their determination that so far as human foresight could avail, any repetition would be for ever impossible'.[26] 'The shadow of Amritsar', said the Duke of Connaught in his inaugural speech to the House, 'has lengthened over the fair face of India. I know how deep is the concern felt by His Majesty the King Emperor at the terrible chapter of events in the Punjab. No one can deplore those events more intensely than I do myself.'[27] The Indian Parliament debates on the events of Amritsar took place in February 1921. Forster arrived in India in the following month. The authorities of the Imperial Government were then in a state of subdued power. They were exercising great restraint in dealing with current popular agitations to avoid a repetition of the happening at Amritsar. Although there were demonstrations throughout the country by the non-cooperators, and fierce riots on the Malabar coast in southern India by the Moplahs – a sect of Muslims of mixed Arab and Indian descent who rose in anarchic revolt against the British, killing numerous Europeans and Hindus – local authorities under the lenient policy of Lord Reading's Government were forced to treat the rebels mildly. 'The unfortunate Government', Forster wrote, looking at the situation at that time, 'afflicted with Moplahs and the Diarchy and other genuine difficulties, has in addition to persuade hundreds of millions of people not to be rude.'[28] The Government's leniency was strongly criticised by the Anglo-Indians, who (like their counterparts in *A Passage to India*) were actually recalling the power and strength shown by the authorities in the past in dealing with the disturbances at Amritsar – 'the good old days', already mentioned, 'when an Englishman . . . could go out and shoot right and left until his honour felt satisfied . . .'. In their view the situation caused by the Non-co-operation movement and the Malabar riots required the firm and drastic action used to deal with the situation at Amritsar.[29] The Anglo-Indian district officer, whose primary duty was to maintain law and order, found himself in a difficult position during the period following the Amritsar massacre. He was required as far as possible to avoid force, and use methods of conciliation to get the co-operation of Indians in running the administration. Some officers found this situation odd, precisely as in Forster's story the Collector feels amidst the crisis at Chandrapore: 'There seemed nothing for it but the old weary business of compromise and moderation . . . The dread of having to call in the troops was vivid to him.' Forster's portrayal of the position of the British administration at Chandrapore, faced by conflicts within the city, and the situation precipitated by the incident at the Marabar caves clearly reflects his close observation of the crisis of the Imperial Government of India which had been caused by the Non-cooperation movement and sharpened by the Moplah riots in Malabar. His account also conveys his full reactions to the Amritsar massacre, which was the background to this crisis. The other important factor responsible for the crisis was the Khilafat agitation. Forster's views on this agitation were equally forthright and acute.

At the root of the Khilafat agitation in India was the issue of Britain's prolonged hostility against Turkey. Indian Muslims considered Turkey as the sovereign land of the spiritual head of Islam, the Khalif, and their religious sentiments were intertwined with the destiny of the Khilafat (the kingdom of the Khalif). Conflicts between the Christian powers of Europe and Turkey, therefore, had always had repercussions in India and had produced expressions of Muslim resentment against the British authorities. Before the period of the actual Khilafat agitation in India, which began after the First World War, the attacks on Turkey by Italy, the Balkan League and Greece during the years 1911–13 had roused waves of anti-British feeling among Indian Muslims protesting against Britain's neutrality. Of the situation in 1913 Lord Hardinge, then Viceroy of India, wrote: 'During the whole year there had been a certain effervescence amongst the Mohamedan population owing to the Turco-Italian war in Tripoli and the war in the Balkans.'[30] And it will also be remembered that at this time Saeed, Forster's host at Aurangabad during his first Indian visit, had 'burst out against the English: "It may be 50 or 500 years but we shall turn you out." ' 'He hates us far more than his brother does', Forster noted in his diary.[31] These periodic outbursts of Muslim resentments against the British thickened as Britain and Turkey became enemies during the First World War, and after the war, with fighting still continuing in Turkey, Muslim politics in India became firmly anti-British and agitated in support of the Khilafat. In August 1920 the Treaty of Sèvres was signed, and large parts of Turkish territory were apportioned by the Allies. Indian Muslims, pursuing the cause of the Khilafat, were fiercely agitated by the treaty; protesting against the British participation in it they joined the Hindus, already embittered by the events of Amritsar, to campaign for non-cooperation against the British Government in India. The Khilafat movement thus became a part of the Non-cooperation movement. In 1920–1 the political union between the Hindus and Muslims, known by the name of the 'Hindu–Muslim entente', was complete. Gandhi and the Khilafat leaders, Mohammed and Shaukat Ali, were campaigning together for a common cause, against a common adversary. Protesting against the Treaty of Sèvres Gandhi[32] campaigned for 'swaraj' to be achieved through complete non-cooperation against the British. Mohammed Ali demanded aggressively (his words echoing in the anti-British outbursts of Dr Aziz at the conclusion of *A Passage to India*) that the British must be driven out of India.[33]

Forster had personally met Mohammed Ali in Delhi, and was well acquainted with the growth of the Khilafat movement in India and its conflicts with the British Government,[34] and its ultimate results. Although he did not wish to support the Khilafat as an institution, he was strongly opposed to Britain's continued conflicts with Turkey after the First World

War, and sympathised with the embittered agitation it had roused in India. His thoughts on the Indian Khilafat movement and his criticism of the British Government's hostile policy towards Turkey were publicly expressed in three pieces which he wrote on the subject in 1922, namely: 'India and the Turk' in *The Nation and the Athenaeum* of 30 September (pp. 844–5), 'Another Little War', letter in the *Daily News* of 9 October (p. 6) and 'Our Graves in Gallipoli: A Dialogue' in the *New Leader* of 20 October (p. 8). In the first of these pieces, 'India and the Turk', the main aspects of the Indian Khilafat movement are examined. Writing about its origins Forster points to the pioneering part played by the Pan-Islamic propaganda of the Ali brothers. 'Why have the Indian Mohammedans acquired this strong feeling for Turkey? Is it aritificial?' he asks, and goes on to say:

> In a sense it is. It did not exist under the Moguls, where a vague respect for the Sultan as guardian of the Holy Places of Arabia was all that was accorded. It mainly dates from the present century and from the propaganda of the Ali brothers among the students of Aligarh. Aligarh was founded by a great Mohammedan of a past generation and a vanished outlook, Sir Syed Ahmed Khan, who hoped to combine there the moral regeneration of his people with political enthusiasm for the British Raj. Until about twelve years ago the College could be described as pro-British, and the authorities smiled upon it. Then a change took place, and under the influence of Mohammed and Shaukat Ali, Aligarh took to Nationalism and Pan-Islamism (two diverse yet not incompatible aims), and its students, the ablest young men of this generation, have spread these ideas throughout India. Thus much must be admitted; except for the conscious efforts of clever men, the sentiment about the Khilafat would not have crystallized into its present form.[35]

The propaganda of the Ali brothers, as Forster observes, developed in the mind of the Indian Muslim a natural feeling of kinship with the Turk based on thoughts of the oneness of their Islamic faith and the greatness of their common Islamic culture in the past. 'Even if the pro-Turkish movement was "artificial" in its origin', Forster says,

> it is natural now, that is to say, it is part of the Mohammedan's mental outfit. He (also, she, for the Purdah is equally vehement) instinctively connects the future of Constantinople with that of his own religion. History may not support him, and may throw doubts upon the procedure of Sultan Selim who returned from Egypt in 1518 with the standard and cloak of the Prophet, and claimed to have inherited the spiritual power of the Abbassides. And he may not be clear as to what that spiritual power is, or what connection it has with the tangled trinity of Constantinople, the Straits, and Thrace. But his emotion – that exists,

and all his neighbours in India respect it, and would not affront it without good reason. Moreover – the Khilafat apart – Turkey has a special appeal to him as the one power surviving from a great past, the appeal of pathos, so overwhelmingly to an Oriental, as a glance at his literature will show. Islam is more than a religion, and both its opponents and its supporters have wronged it by their hard legalistic insistence on the Faith. It is an attitude towards life which has produced durable and exquisite civilizations, an attitude threatened by Europe's remorseless crusade today.[36]

Looking objectively at the situation created by the wars of the European powers against the Islamic peoples of North Africa and Central Asia, Forster remarks that although

Europe is not really Christian, either in theory or fact . . . to the Mohammedan, continually vexed by her aggressions, she does seem Christian, and for him the Crusades did not end with St. Louis, but are still in progress. He need not go back to the Middle Ages, he can observe what he has lost in North Africa and in Central Asia during the last twenty years. France, Spain, Italy, Germany, Russia have carried on their old warfare.[37]

The result of the First World War in which Turkey fought against the Allies was disastrous for Turkey. The Muslims in India saw that the Turkish territory was partitioned despite the assurances to the contrary which they received from the British Government while they fought the war on the side of the Empire. Their reactions are looked at by Forster with an objective eye also:

When the Great War broke out, and Turkey took to the German side, he [the Indian Muslim] still listened to our assurances, he ignored the Jehad that was proclaimed at Constantinople, and died by the thousand in France. Place yourself in his position. Peace comes. The Holy Places of Mecca and Medina are entrusted to a man whose ancestors have swindled his ancestors for generations when they made pilgrimage, Egypt becomes a protectorate, Palestine Brito-Jewish, Mesopotamia Brito-Sherifian, Syria French, Greece must have Thrace and a kingdom in Asia Minor, Italy must have something too, Constantinople must be occupied. It is hard; but [he is told] it is war; Turkey has lost, and Great Britain must compensate herself and her allies.[38]

Forster condemns the part played by Britain when, following the Treaty of Sèvres, the Turkish nationalist party under Mustapha Kemal rejecting the treaty fought the Greeks out of Smyrna, and the British Government supported the Greeks against Mustapha Kemal. 'And now the saviour arises', he observes,

> Mustapha Kemal, in the restricted area that is left to the Ottomans. He attacks not Great Britain, but the ally whom Great Britain has had least reason to love – King Constantine of Greece. He drives the Greeks out of Smyrna, and then turns northward. France and Italy, the other Christian powers, do not hinder him. It is Great Britain, the protector of Islam, who appears as a solitary crusader, whose troops remain in Chanak, whose fleet holds the Straits, and whose Ministers assert that the British Empire stands behind them.[39]

Criticising the British Government's support for the Greeks in this war Forster also wrote his forceful letter in the *Daily News* referred to above. The letter in question, written in connection with an article on the same subject by A. A. Milne,[40] published previously in the *Daily News*, is reproduced below:

'Another Little War'

Sir, – Mr. A. A. Milne's brilliant article deserves special thanks for its scathing analysis of 'the sanctity of our graves in Gallipoli'. Our rulers knew that their policy would not be popular, and in the hope of stampeding us into it they permitted this vile appeal – the viler because the sentiment that it tries to pervert is a noble one and purifies the life of a nation when directed rightly. The bodies of the young men who are buried out there have become spirit; whether they were British or Turk, they have no quarrel with one another now, no part in our quarrels or interest in our patronage, no craving for holocausts of more young men. Anyone who has himself entered, however feebly, into the life of the spirit, can realise this.

It is only the elderly ghouls of Whitehall who exhume the dead for the purpose of party propaganda and employ them as a bait to catch the living.

> Peace would do wrong to our undying dead –
> The sons we offered might regret they died
> If we got nothing lasting in their stead
> We must be solidly indemnified.

Thus wrote Wilfred Owen, a month before he was killed on the Sambre Canal. The men about whom he wrote it are still in office, still pleasantly busied in their task of finding graves for heroes. At the next election can we not provide them with a quiet retreat of their own? Its sanctity should be inviolable.

E. M. Forster

Forster's tone in this letter shows how strongly he felt against the anti-

Turkish policies of war of Lloyd George's Government. He continued his attack on the Government in a third piece which he published in the *New Leader* under the title 'Our Graves in Gallipoli'.[41] This piece is in the form of an imaginary dialogue which takes place on the summit of Achi Baba – the scene of Britain's disastrous war in Gallipoli in 1915 – between an English and a Turkish grave. 'Churchill planned this expedition to Gallipoli', says the English grave,

> where I was killed. He planned the expedition to Antwerp, where my brother was killed. Then he said that Labour is not fit to govern. Rolling his eyes for fresh worlds, he saw Egypt and fearing that peace might be established there, he intervened and prevented it. Whatever he undertakes is a success. He is Churchill the fortunate, ever in office, and clouds of dead heroes attend him.[42]

Having been a victim of the Gallipoli war the English grave ridicules Lloyd George's fresh call for war against Turkey in support of the Greeks and says:

> Lloyd George, fertile in counsels, has decreed. He has tried to enter Asia by means of the Greeks. It was the Greeks who, seven years ago, failed to join England after they had promised to do so, and our graves in Gallipoli are the result of this. But Churchill the fortunate, ever in office, ever magnanimous, bore the Greeks no grudge, and he and Lloyd George persuaded their young men to enter Asia. They have mostly been killed there so English young men must be persuaded instead . . . and Chanak receives them.[43]

Forster felt that Britain's support for Greece provided a justification for the Khilafat agitation in India. 'We may argue that the Khilafat agitation was factitious in its origin and is historically incorrect; but it is not factitious now', he wrote,

> it is intertwined deep with his [the Indian Muslim's] faith. He observes that under God's will the guardianship of Holy places has passed to the Turks, and that Constantinople itself has become half-holy. Sentiment, no doubt, but it is part of his spiritual life; it is not like the 'sacred peninsula' of Gallipoli which the elderly ghouls of Whitehall suddenly dragged into their manifestoes.[44]

'Indian sentiment about Turkey', he continues

> is decent, it is human, and even if it cannot be furthered it should not be wantonly insulted – which is what we have done. An evil day's work, and the evil this Government has done will live after them. The Turk

may forget; he is cynical, and used to knock-abouts; moreover, he is on his way to get all he wants.[45] But his sensitive co-religionists in India were looking for a sign, and they will conclude that it has been given them.[46]

The Khilafat movement met with an unexpected end in Turkey with the deposition of the Khalif, Mohammed VI, and with the abolition of the sultanate under the powerful secular leadership of Mustapha Kemal. But in India it had important consequences. Indian Muslims were roused by it to a strong sense of unity and communal feeling against the British which henceforth alienated their loyalty to the Empire. Political extremists, moderates and loyalists all combined in the spirit of Islamic unity, and shared one common outlook. As a historian observes of the situation:

> There was nothing in common between, say, the Aga Khan and Maulana Muhammad Ali or between Sayyid Ameer Ali and Dr. M. A. Ansari. But the 'loyalists' and the 'agitators' worked to the same end . . . The Khilafat movement . . . destroyed the myth of Muslim loyalty. The spectacle of the agitating Muslim was such a break with their traditional conduct that at first the British rubbed their eyes and refused to believe what they saw. The friends of yesterday had become the enemies of today.[47]

Forster's portrayal of the political outlook of the Muslims in *A Passage to India* is to be viewed against this particular background. By the time *A Passage to India* was published the Khilafat movement had of course ended, but the revolutionary consequences of the movement remained permanently, and they have crystallised into some significant themes and conflicts in Forster's story. The account of the transformation in the character of Dr Aziz who 'took no interest in politics'[48] but changed to the angry nationalist hating the English and, in fact, wishing in their place 'the Afghans . . . My own ancestors'[49] reflects the way the Khilafat movement had actually affected Muslim attitudes in India. Aziz is shown as inwardly moved by the Pan-Islamic sentiment and by a deep feeling for the past glory of Islamic culture —

> the feeling that India was one; Moslem; always had been . . . whatever Ghalib had felt, he had anyhow lived in India, and this consolidated it for them . . . the sister kingdoms of the north — Arabia, Persia, Farghana, Turkestan — stretched out their hands as he sang . . . and greeted ridiculous Chandrapore, where every street and house was divided against itself, and told her that she was a continent and a unity.[50]

His pride of Islam flows deeply within his own private life without erupting to the surface as a political passion, and he finds fulfilment in writing poems about 'the decay of Islam and the brevity of love'. But when the English disgrace Aziz, and he is made their enemy, his racial pride asserts itself in the form of a bitter political grudge against the Englishman. He assumes the uncompromising spirit of an anti-British Khilafat revolutionary: 'I have become anti-British and ought to have done so sooner, it would have saved the numerous misfortunes', he declares to Fielding. 'Down with the English anyhow. That's certain. Clear out, you fellows, double quick, I say. We may hate one another, but we hate you most.'⁵¹ Hamidullah, Mohamoud Ali, and even the loyalist Nawab Bahadur (he 'had financed the defence, and would ruin himself sooner than let an "innocent Moslem perish" '),⁵² all share the violent feelings of Aziz against the English. Their unity reflects, precisely, the kind of unity that had occurred among the Muslims at the time of the Khilafat movement.

The Hindu–Muslim entente brought about by the Khilafat movement is also presented with all its peculiar ramifications in *A Passage to India*. Dr Aziz's trouble unites the Hindus and Moslems in Forster's story. 'Another local consequence of the trial', we are told, 'was a Hindu–Moslem entente. Loud protestations of amity were exchanged by prominent citizens, and there went with them a genuine desire for a good understanding.'⁵³ In the trial Aziz is defended by both a Moslem pleader and a Hindu barrister who is 'anti-British . . . loathed at the club . . . [and] regarded as a political challenge.'⁵⁴ (It will be remembered that during the Khilafat agitation in 1921 when the Ali brothers were arrested for their provocative anti-Government speeches, Gandhi defended them publicly, and himself repeated the speeches as a way of protest against the Government's action.) Aziz is acquitted by a Hindu magistrate, and finally leaves British India to take employment in the Hindu state of Mau. 'His genuine hatred of the English' prompts him to forget the differences between Hindus and Muslims, and he thinks 'I am an Indian at last.'⁵⁵ The story ends with that note of Hindu–Muslim unity and the political slogans: 'India shall be a nation! No foreigners of any sort! Hindu and Moslem and Sikh and all shall be one! Hurrah! Hurrah! for India!'⁵⁶

In actual history, the 'entente' was however a temporary affair. The general pattern of Hindu–Muslim relations in British India had been dubious in the past, and the Khilafat agitation provided a purely temporary bridge between the two communities, for both found it politically expedient to combine together against the British. However strong their unity may have been at the time of the Khilafat agitation, it did not last long. There was no constructive force behind it to sustain it for longer. Their real binding force was their political opposition to the British, but after their initial thrust against the Government they expressed their opposition in their own separate ways. While the Muslims claimed more and more separate privileges for their own community, the Indian National Congress demanded a fully democratic and a free India based on the abolition of communal privileges. The religious differences between the two parties sharpened their political conflicts, the effects of which were several violent communal riots and, ultimately, the partition of India. Forster was aware of these separatist tendencies in Hindu–Muslim relations, which the temporary entente on the cause of the Khilafat did not abolish. In *A Passage to India* he throws light on this situation in subtle ways. Aziz, and Das, the Hindu magistrate, are shown one day after the trial shaking hands 'in a half-embrace that typified the entente'. 'You are our hero', says Das, complimenting Aziz, 'the whole city is behind you, irrespective of creed . . .' Aziz remarks: 'I know, but will it last?' 'I fear not' says Das, who, we are told, 'had much mental clearness'.[57] 'Between people of distant climes there is always the possibility of romance', says Forster, commenting on the situation generally, 'but the various branches of Indians know too much about each other to surmount the unknowable easily. The approach is prosaic. 'Excellent', said Aziz, patting [Das's] stout shoulder and thinking, 'I wish they did not remind me of cow-dung'; Das thought, 'Some Moslems are very violent'. They smiled wistfully, each spying the thought in the other's heart . . .[58] Commenting on the purely political purpose of the entente Forster says more particularly: 'As long as someone abused the English, all went well, but nothing constructive had been achieved, and if the English were to leave India, the committee would vanish also.'[59]

The discernment which comes across in Forsters's view of the Khilafat movement is also seen in his observations on the Non-cooperation movement in general. Unbiased by political propaganda – either for it from the Indian side or against it from the British side – he looked at the Non-cooperation movement as it actually worked and as it reflected and influenced the core of the struggle within British India. His portrayal of it shows his sympathy with the Indian cause as well as his scepticism about some particular aspects of the movement. At the time of his second visit to India the Non-cooperation movement was in its most vigorous and successful phase. It is necessary briefly to look at the actual progress of the movement and its implications in the context of the Indian national movement in general in order to assess fully the value of Forster's account.

The resolution on the movement which had been adopted at the special session of the Indian National Congress at Calcutta in September 1920 was reaffirmed by the annual Congress session at Nagpur at the end of that year. Protesting against the Khilafat and the Punjab wrongs the first resolution had declared that 'there is no course left open for the people of India but to approve of and adopt the policy of progressive non-violent Non-co-operation inaugurated by Mahatma Gandhi, until the said wrongs are righted and swarajya is established'.[60] Non-cooperation was urged against the authorities of the British Government in all fields: Indians who had received British titles and honours were to surrender them, Indian members in the Legislative Councils were to resign, elections to the new Councils, attendance at Government courts of law, durbars and all official functions were to be avoided, Indians were to refuse recruitment to military and clerical service and British controlled labour, all foreign goods were to be boycotted, hand spinning was to be revived, Indian children were to be withdrawn gradually from Government-controlled schools and colleges, national schools and colleges were to be established for them, and above all every Indian – 'man, woman, and child' – was to practise 'discipline and self-sacrifice'. The ideas of the movement were addressed to leading public men as well as the masses, and they were being put into effect widely. The surrender of British titles and honours had been started by Tagore,[61] and some members of the Supreme Legislative Council had resigned their seats even before the formal call for it was made by the Congress. In all other respects, such as the boycott of elections, law courts, Government schools and colleges, etc. and the opening of national schools and colleges, there was immediate success.

The widely shared feeling of national protest was manifested also in numerous public meetings and demonstrations by national volunteers; in the boycott of the visits by the Duke of Connaught and the Prince of Wales; and in the massive offers of resistance to Government authority by individuals and masses of people who were willingly courting arrest and going to prison. Throughout the period from September 1920, the date of the Calcutta resolution, to March 1922, when Gandhi was arrested and imprisoned, the Non-cooperation movement reigned over Indian political life, and under its impact the Indian national movement acquired a shape and a strength of position which were not to be diminished under any circumstances. By March 1922 the initial strength of the movement had been weakened by occurrences of violence in some parts of the country, and Gandhi, before his arrest, had called off the campaign of mass civil disobedience. Yet the cause of nationalism had been so strengthened by Gandhi's movement that nothing could weaken it. On the other hand it was advanced rigorously by all the successive political strategies that were adopted, until the final achievement of independence. The Swarjists[62] were keen on following a policy of positive 'obstruction' within the Legislative Councils and political committees by which they thought of forcing the British authorities to give up power. Working for the same end as the non-cooperationists they offered opposition to the Government by remaining within the machinery of the Government. The Congress resolution of 1929 carried the resolution on non-cooperation a step further by defining India's goal as the attainment of complete independence, and thereafter the nationalist agitation hardened more and more. In 1930–1 the campaign of civil disobedience was revived in a more vigorous way than before, and in 1942 the 'Quit India' agitation came as a climactic challenge, demanding that the British must give independence and leave India to solve her own problems. The reasons for which the British ultimately gave India independence are various. But one major factor behind their decision was that their position in India had become unacceptable to the socially and politically awakened Indians. The conflicts in British India at the end of the First World War had shown proofs of that awakening, and the Non-cooperation movement gave that awakening the character of a strong national agitation which worked with indomitable force till the end, successfully playing its part towards the dissolution of imperial India. It will now be seen how Forster's account of the Non-cooperation movement, based on his own analysis and remarkable political foresight, sums up this total achievement.

A reader unacquainted with all of Forster's relevant writings would find even in the apparently fictional story of *A Passage to India* a number of intriguing allusions to the Non-cooperation movement and evidence of Forster's personal reactions to it. The incident of the arrest of Dr Aziz, for example, which (though only apparently unrelated to any political cause) is the main event behind the upheaval in Forster's story, may be seen as a reminder of the numerous actual arrests of Indians during the period of the Non-cooperation movement. In 1921–2 political arrests and imprisonments were the order of the day: about 30,000 Indians, including the Ali brothers, Gandhi and Jawaharlal Nehru were in prison. The outlook of the 'moderate' leaders like Gandhi and Nehru had been revolutionised. On the occasions of their trials both leaders made statements actually declaring the sentiment Aziz voices after his trial, that they had lost their loyalty to the British:[63] Nehru stated that ten years earlier he was virtually an Englishman who had imbibed all the prejudices of Harrow and Cambridge, but was transformed in the space of ten years into 'a rebel'; 'We wanted to know you ten years back', Aziz announces to Fielding,'–now it's too late'.[64] The organisation of the Indian side after Aziz's trial closely follows the ideas of the Non-cooperation movement: the Hindus and Muslims are united against the British; the Nawab Bahadur 'announces that he should give up his British-conferred title'; the students of the Government College 'are on strike . . . they won't learn their lessons'–they jeer in front of the City Magistrate's court calling out that 'the English were cowards'; and Mohammedan ladies swear 'to take no food' (recalling Gandhi's method of fasts for public causes) until Aziz is released. 'A new spirit seemed abroad, a rearrangement, which no one in the stern little band of whites could explain',[65] comments Forster, and his words reflect the actual situation of bewilderment of the Government at the time of the Non-cooperation movement. In addition to these details, *A Passage to India* draws attention to the Swarajists' policy of 'obstruction'–'to kick and scream on committees', as Aziz sees it[66]–and it anticipates too extremist tendencies within the Congress such as those which were to grow after the Non-cooperation movement, leading to the fiercer national agitations of 1930–1 and 1942. When Aziz says: 'Until England is in difficulties we keep silent, but in the next European war–aha, aha! Then is our time',[67] he in fact anticipates the extremist position the Indian National Congress was to take in withdrawing support from the side of Britain during the Second World War.

With all the strength of the Non-cooperation movement Indian nationalism had nevertheless two main pitfalls before it, namely, the deeper communal rifts between the Hindus and Muslims, and the general opposition to nationalist tendencies from native India ruled by the princes. *A Passage to India* throws light on the first element by drawing attention to the religious riots during Moharrum, and it introduces the second through the theme of Professor Godbole's non-cooperation with Aziz's cause. When the Hindus and Muslims of Chandrapore have all combined to avenge Aziz, Godbole remains aloof: the terms 'anti-British' and 'seditious' bored him, and he leaves Chandrapore for the native state of Mau, his birthplace, 'to start a High School there [which eventually becomes a granary] on sound English lines, that shall be as like Government College as possible'[68] and be named after either Fielding or King-Emperor George the Fifth. Godbole's aim is in contradiction to the spirit of the Non-cooperation movement which disapproved of Government schools and colleges and encouraged the establishment of national ones in their place. His loyal outlook and his aloofness from the agitation against the English precisely reflect the spirit of Princely India.

One other intriguing aspect of *A Passage to India* with a possible connection with the events of the Non-cooperation movement is Aziz's own departure from British India to become a doctor at Mau: 'his retreat to a remote jungle, where the sahib seldom comes'.[69] 'His impulse to escape from the English was sound', comments Forster, and perhaps he means to indicate by the theme of Aziz's retreat from British India the earnestness of the Non-cooperation ideal as a complete revulsion against the British influence on India. Gandhi had rejected Western materialism, Western science and medicine, and the Western way of life altogether, and his idealism was criticised by British observers as retrograde: Forster, for his own part, while sympathising with Gandhi's movement as an expression of earnest protest seems to have remained sceptical about some tenets of his spiritualism. 'Look at you, forgetting your medicine and going back to charms', says Fielding chiding Aziz[70] – an obvious allusion to Gandhi's denunciation of Western medicine. A fuller account of Forster's actual reaction to the non-cooperation movement will however be obtained by looking at some factual sources outside *A Passage to India*.

Evidence of Forster's first personal reactions to the movement is seen in the private letters he wrote from Dewas. In one of the earliest letters from there, dated April 1921, he writes longingly about the 'present movements in India' and remarks about the great power held by Gandhi: 'the Government [is] frightened of Bolshevism and Gandhi'.[71] Direct evidence of Gandhi's popular influence was seen by him even from over the border of Dewas's 'loyal' territory. 'Our other provincial centre, Alot . . . caused us some anxiety', he says, 'for it had a railway station in J. B. [Dewas Junior Branch] territory; and the disciples of Gandhi used to alight there and shout subversive slogans at us over the border.'[72] In September 1921 he toured in British India and was at Nagpur to attend a Maratha educational conference. He writes of the strong anti-British feeling and the influence of Gandhi he witnessed there:

> Nagpur is British India – Capital of the Central Provinces – We entered the City of Nagpur on elephants and there were camels also and riderless horses draped in costly stuff. It was a pathetic pageant, and under our feet were crowds of the Nagpur people, the most fanatical and anti-British in India, all contemptuous or indifferent, and many of them wearing the white Gandhi cap.[73]

Returning from the tour he found Dewas intolerable by contrast to the liveliness of British India, and he hoped that the state's backwardness and separatism would disappear under the influence of the powerful currents of nationalism in British India: 'Poor little Dewas', says an extract from his journal between 25 September and 1 October 1921, 'thou art wretched scenically. Yet this is not a place to settle in. It is unlikely I shall ever see it again, and Gandhi would wipe it far more thoroughly than any P.A.'[74]

At the end of October 1921 Forster left Dewas, and came to Hyderabad for a short stay with his friend Masood. Hyderabad was also outside British India. It was the Nizam's 'Dominion', and like Dewas had remained predominantly loyal. But it was certainly more enlightened and progressive than Dewas, for which Forster was generally pleased. 'I have come . . . into a world whose troubles and problems are intelligible to me', he writes in a letter dated 12 November 1921, 'Dewas made much ado about nothing and no ado where a little would have been seemly.'[75] Forster's writings based on this period, however, give little account of the general situation in Hyderabad; his interest and attention were centred on the operations of the Non-cooperation movement in general, and especially on two important developments in that movement. At that time the non-cooperationists were preparing for their boycott of the Prince of Wales's visit,[76] and also for the launching of the campaign of mass civil disobedience. Both these objectives gave their movement tremendous force and interest, and Forster's own personal interest in these developments is seen in his letter of 12 November 1921. 'About the Prince of Wales's visit', he writes in his letter,

> I might also write much. It is disliked and dreaded by nearly everyone. The chief exponents are the motor-firms and caterers, who will make fortunes, and the non-co-operators and extremists, who will have an opportunity for protest which they would otherwise have lacked . . . The National Congress meets in December at Ahmedabad, and it will certainly carry through its resolution in favour of Civil Disobedience,

and if there is general response, this expensive royal expedition will look rather foolish.[77]

The boycott of the visit of the Prince of Wales, which was completed during Forster's stay in India, was entirely successful. The Congress resolution on the campaign of mass civil disobedience was also duly carried At Ahmedabad. By the beginning of 1922, when Forster left India, the Non-cooperation movement had thus made its full impact. Forster published his own personal account of the Indian situation in *The Nation and the Athenaeum*[78] and it will be seen that his reports presented the circumstances impartially – which other British newspaper reports and official accounts did not do.

The main points in Forster's account were three, namely:
(i) the Indian Non-cooperation movement had to be recognised as a real and unanswerable national protest against the British; (ii) the visit of the Prince of Wales was a failure; and (iii) the dissolution of British India was inevitable. On the first point, one has to look at the general background of British public opinion on the Non-cooperation movement in order to appreciate the real value of Forster's own account. The Imperial Government of India and the British Government – as well as important newspapers in Britain – all viewed the Non-cooperation movement as retrograde and anarchical. Lord Chelmsford, the Viceroy, thought of Gandhi's denunciation of the 'satanic' Government as a joke.[79] After him, Lord Reading, who liked and respected Gandhi personally, also held the view that 'the vast majority of the population in India are loyal to the crown', and that Non-cooperation was against India's interest.[80] The India Office annual statement of Indian events for 1921 presented to the House of Commons a brief history of the Non-cooperation movement, and described it as a 'campaign of misdirected energy' and 'utter sterility'.[81] *The Times* in its special supplement on India of 17 November 1921 denounced 'the fanatical pessimism of Mr. Gandhi', and in order to show that his cause was weak, observed that 'Non-cooperation and the Khilafat movement are kept alive by incessant public meetings', Even *The Nation and the Athenaeum*, which usually presented accounts of India with understanding and sympathy, was muddled in its approach to the Non-cooperation movement. Its account of the movement reported on 6 August 1921 (pp. 670–1) described the movement as 'the revolt of passivity', 'unconstructive and negative', 'a retrogression' and 'a lapse into the instinctive Buddhism of the East'. Against this background of muddled and hostile public opinion on the subject Forster's writings appeared, with some factual information and some irresistible judgements.

To illustrate the wide effect of the Non-cooperation movement at the popular level Forster cited concrete instances from his own experience in India. 'When the Collector of B—— fined a pleader two hundred rupees', he wrote, citing one instance, for appearing before him in a Gandhi cap, he thought no doubt, that the matter would stop where it was. He told the pleader to come back in two hours' time; who did, still wearing the cap, and was fined two hundred more rupees. The pleader appealed; the case was tried locally, by an English judge, and decided against the Collector; and the population of B——, which had hitherto worn any old thing on its head, at once trotted into Gandhi caps and escorted the Collector with shouts of 'Mahatma Gandhi ki jai' whenever he went out for a ride on his not very good motor-bicycle. The population ought to have weighed the illegality and the insolence of the Collector against the fairness of the judge and to have given the British Raj the benefit of the doubt. But the mind of a mob doesn't work thus. The attack on an educated Indian reacted in thousands of uneducated veins, and swelled the cause of Nationalism.[82]

Forster described how not only the extremist politicians, but also the 'moderates', important officials and common men and women – all classes of Indians – were involved in the movement, and showed self-sacrifice in the cause of swaraj.

The spirit of self-sacrifice in Indians is often spasmodic and temporary [he wrote], but while it lasts it is supreme, nothing can stand against it, and at the moment of writing most of the educated population is ready to go to jail. The Moderates are deserting the Government because their protests against the arrests have been ignored. Important Indian officials resign their posts, often under pressure from the zenana. The wife and daughters of a member of the U.P. Government go on hunger-strike and his withdrawal from public life can only be a matter of hours. A man whose brother has been arrested condoles with the sister-in-law; she, and his own sisters, repulse him indignantly; there is nothing to mourn here, they say, it is those who have not gone to jail who should feel sorrow and shame. Another lady, whose husband expects arrest, tries to learn how to carry on his *Swaraj* work in his absence, although unsympathetic to *Swaraj*, and prefers to remain unguarded, when he leaves her, rather than return to the comfort of her family. These three instances (all with names attached) happened to come to my notice; there must be thousands more, proving that the women as well as the men are desperate.[83]

The most concrete evidence of the Indians' feeling of disaffection and their ability to demonstrate that feeling in an organised manner was shown by the result of the Prince of Wales's visit. Exaggerated and inaccurate reports of success were being published in Britain on the subject of this visit. Forster's account of it, the second main theme in his reports, gave an accurate and discerning picture. The Prince's visit had apparently been

arranged by the British Government and the Government of India to keep
the prestige of the British Government by superimposing an image of
loyalty on India, and to wean the non-cooperators to the path of co-
operation. It was neither wanted by the Indians nor thought helpful by
those local authorities who considered the general situation seriously. The
non-cooperators had decided to demonstrate their protest before the
Prince by boycotting his visit, and provincial governors like Willingdon
had expressed their disagreement with the proposed visit because of the
widespread anti-British agitation. But these considerations were ignored,
and the visit was arranged on the initiative of Lord Reading, the Viceroy,
who assumed that India's loyalty to the Crown was an unquestionable
fact.[84] On the occasion of the visit the Prince was described in *The Times* as
'the ambassador of Peace', and his visit was hailed in these words:

> The visit of the Prince of Wales to India comes at an appropriate
> moment, when another great stage in the evolution of a system of self-
> government for the Indian peoples has been successfully inaugurated
> and is now being closely tested . . . We believe that in one respect at
> least the spirit of India remains unaltered. Her peoples, as the Prince will
> find, have not lost that instinctive devotion to the principle of kingship
> and to a personal ruler which has been developed among them from the
> beginnings of recorded history . . . In every part of the Indian Empire a
> sincere allegiance to the Crown continues to be manifest.[85]

Forster observed that this description of the background to the Prince's
visit was untrue, and in his account of the real circumstances he
emphasised first that the assumptions about India's continued loyalty to
the Empire were wrong:

> With the exception of the contractors and the extremists, scarcely
> anyone in India wished the Prince of Wales to come. The Army did not
> want him, nor did the Civil Service outside Simla, nor did the Native
> Rulers, whose finances are scarcely recovering from the visit of his great
> uncle, nor did the educated Indians, whether friends or hostile to the
> Government, nor did the people . . .
> Imperial pride and the will of a Viceroy are the agents through which
> Fate has worked. It was unseemly to our weavers of Empire that a royal
> progress should be twice postponed; it would look as if they doubted
> Indians' enthusiasm; it would look what it was, in fact. Prestige can only
> be maintained by pretending that it has not been questioned. And this
> high logic was confirmed by the considered conclusion of Lord Reading.
> Whom the Viceroy consulted it is difficult to say; I am told, on good
> authority, that in inviting the Prince he acted against the advice of his
> Provincial Governors, who reported public opinion as everywhere

hostile . . . The Viceroy has pointed out . . . that we must expect nothing from this visit but the honour of it.[86]

When the Prince was on his tour in India detailed news of the wide boycott of his visit was not published in Britain. On the contrary, the tour was publicised as a success. 'The visit of the Prince of Wales', wrote *The Times*, 'has served to demonstrate that changing India, for all its conflict and seeking and suffering, is still at heart loyal to the Crown . . . It was a bold experiment, which, so far, has been abundantly justified by its results.'[87] *The Times* also reported that 'the non-co-operators have put forth all their energies in order to render impossible a great popular reception of the Prince'; that the demonstrations and boycott were, however, 'not voluntary, but due to intimidation by Gandhi's agents and Khilafat volunteers'; that 'in Poona the Prince was joyfully received', and that in Calcutta 'the hartal was partially successful, but it soon broke down, and during the following days the population to an increasing extent gave expression to its pleasure in the presence of the son of the King-Emperor'.[88] To realise how grossly exaggerated and inaccurate such reports about the Prince's visit were one has to look at Forster's observations, and also at the accounts by the Prince of Wales himself.

In Forster's view the Prince's visit had been a 'waste of money'[89] and a complete failure. Large numbers of Indians had forsaken their loyalty, and were not interested in his mission of goodwill. Their expressions of protest against him were very real, and the protest was indeed against the Imperial British as a class. Their boycott and demonstrations, notwithstanding Government repression and small breaches at one or two places, were eminently successful, and this was in Forster's judgement a most positive sign that India was growing firmly independent of British control, and that British presence there was becoming irrelevant. Emphasising these important considerations Forster reported thus on the event of the 'Prince's progress':

The reception at Bombay was not bad, and after it the Prince disappeared into the deserts of Rajputana, dining with the Maharajah of Rutlam, staying with the Maharajah of Udaipur, who is descended from the sun, etc., all of which is easy and safe. But when he appeared in British India, at Allahabad, a changed atmosphere awaited him, because, during his tour in the Native States, the Government had taken to repression. The day of his landing (November 17th) had, in Calcutta, been observed as a *Hartal* and as a full-dress rehearsal of the reception intended for him. Eye-witnesses – awed Englishmen – bring amazing accounts. They say that the volunteer organization was perfect, with police and permits complete, and displayed a calm enthusiasm that was very impressive, and an efficiency that could only come from careful preparation. The discovery that Indians can run a great city without

European assistance filled the Calcutta merchants with dismay, and they appealed to Lord Ronaldshay. The volunteer organizations were declared illegal, and extensive arrests followed, both in Bengal and elsewhere in British India.

As a result of this firm policy the Prince, when he reached Allahabad, was greeted by five miles of deserted streets, and by scarcely any bunting. He is said to have resented the insult, and if so, it shows how completely he has been secluded from reality, for he ought to have known that such an insult was possible at any moment of the tour.[90]

Forster's report is confirmed by the Prince's own matter-of-fact account of his experiences. The Prince also thought that his Indian visit was a waste of large sums of money, and had failed to achieve its purpose. The reports of his success published in British newspapers were inaccurate. India was far from loyal to the Crown, the Prince thought, and no longer interested in the 'white men' living there. The Prince's observations on his tour were contained in two private letters he wrote in India at the end of his visit to the Viceroy and to the British Secretary of State for India. Both letters, as will be seen from the relevant extracts cited below, give a poignant account of the failure of his visit, and are an acute comment on the situation of British India during the period of the Non-cooperation movement. In the first of the two letters, written from Calcutta on 28 December 1921 to Lord Reading, the Prince said:

. . . I must tell you at once that I am not at all happy about the results of the tour as far as it has gone. £25,000 of English money and goodness knows how many lakhs of rupees are being spent over it, and I must honestly say that I have not as yet been able to justify that vast expenditure.

The ostensible reason for my coming to India was to see as many of the natives as possible and to get as near to them as I could. At least I presume it was the main reason, and I looked upon that as my duty. Well, I am afraid that I have not had many opportunities of doing this, either in British India or in the Native States.

Of course you know only too well how much my visits to British Indian cities have been boycotted by Gandhi and his disciples, and it has been obvious to me that the non-co-operators have prevented thousands of natives from turning out to see me. You will no doubt have had reports from Bombay, Poona, Ajmer, Lucknow, Allahabad, Benares and Patna. The cases of each have been the same – hartals and more or less emptied streets.

I do not so much worry about the native populations ignoring my visits to their cities, because only very few of them understand, and given the smallest lead, they follow like sheep; but I must say I was very angry and felt very insulted when at the University of Lucknow, Allahabad and Benares practically all students (in the case of Allahabad *all* the students) refused to meet me or to attend the University functions. At Benares it was quite a big ceremony, conferring of honorary degrees etc. and it would have been humorous if it had not been so sad this way they tried to 'kid' me by filling up the empty students seats with High School boys, boy scouts and Europeans. I suppose they hoped I would never get to hear of what had been done, or realise what a b.f. they had made of me!!!

I do realise that it is a responsibility for you and your Government to have a Prince of Wales touring India at such a critical and disturbed time, and I sympathise with you and do understand people having the wind up a bit. But surely it is better to take a few risks and so give this tour a chance of even only a little use than to carry on as I am now doing . . .

I feel sure that you will agree with me when I say that it is a great pleasure to work hard on a tour like this provided one can always feel that one is always doing some good to the Empire, but it makes it desperately hard and a real worry and anxiety if one has a constant feeling that the money and the time are being absolutely wasted. I am not at all sure that a tour of this kind that does not carry success is not worse for the Empire in the long run than no tour at all.[91]

The second letter, written from Bombay on 1 January 1922 to Montagu, was in the same vein as the first, but in it the Prince firmly rejected the news published in Britain of his success and of Indians' manifestations of loyalty. The Prince wrote:

. . . I am nearly half-way through now, and feel that it is only right that you should have my impressions of present-day India, and my views as to the utility and results of this tour.

Let me tell you at once that the newspaper accounts at home of the various visits, ceremonies and receptions have almost invariably been hopelessly exaggerated, and reading those accounts from this end I feel that comouflage is almost invariably the dominant feature.

Naturally I deplore this, as I cannot bear to think that people at home are being given a wrong impression, which they most certainly are. They think my tour is a success, and I must reluctantly tell you that it is no such thing.

I can assure you that my impressions of India are not merely based on the absence of crowds in the streets or the non-attendance of students at futile University ceremonies.

I make it my business to talk to as many of our people out here as I can – soldiers, civil servants, and more frequently the police, who, from the nature of their work can usually give a more accurate picture of the whole situation out here than anyone else; and as regards the present condition of life in India they one and all say the same thing – that they won't let their sons come out here to earn their living in the Indian Army, Indian Civil Service etc. etc. and that not now would they even recommend these services to any good fellow. The reason for this is, that India is no longer a place for a white man to live in.

I am sorry to have to paint you such a gloomy picture but I cannot refrain from doing so, as I know that, as Secretary of State you want to, and should know the truth . . .[92]

Forster's account read alongside those of the Prince of Wales accurately reflects the awakening of revolutionary feeling in India in the 1920s against the British and the Empire. The Non-cooperation movement was a most forceful manifestation of that awakening. Forster looked at the movement as such, without entering into the question of its ideological merits and demerits. Not that he thought that question unimportant, but he thought that it was irrelevant to the main tune of his subject. He knew that the whole movement involved many complex and controversial considerations – that it had its spiritual as well as its social and political aspects, and there were also the questions of its ideology and its practical application. He looked at all these different aspects objectively and rationally. While the social and political success of the movement impressed him, he remained sceptical about its spiritual effects. Gandhi had interpreted the policy of non-violent non-cooperation as 'a religious movement . . . a movement of self-reliance'.[93] Forster did not doubt the complete integrity of Gandhi's personal leadership. He looked at 'the doctrine of non-violence' and 'the doctrine of simplicity, symbolized by the spinning wheel' as 'pratical teachings', and he also believed that Gandhi's 'inprisonments, the fastings, the willingness to suffer' showed 'spiritual proofs of moral firmness'.[94] But he doubted whether the Non-cooperation movement actually fulfilled Gandhi's spiritual aspirations: whether the many Indians who joined in the movement 'could share, with Mr. Gandhi, a martyrdom deliberate, long-drawn, and obscure'.[95] As for the practical application of non-violence, Gandhi's basic principle in non-cooperation, Forster observed quite realistically that 'the methods of Non-co-operation pass inevitably into violence; the line between persuasion and compulsion is difficult to draw'.[96] These examples of his reflections show Forster's scepticism about particular aspects of the movement, but notwithstanding that scepticism he recognised clearly that the movement had achieved a remarkable social and political effect in India, and that it had also a value and significance of universal importance: 'Non-co-operation is only one aspect of a wider tendency that envelops not India in particular but all the globe – the tendency to question and to protest . . . A new spirit has entered India. Would that I could conclude with a eulogy of it! But that must be left to writers who can see into the future and who know in what human happiness consists.'[97]

Forster returned from his second visit to India seeing signs of the dissolution of the Empire. His personal diary of the last days of his visit in Hyderabad records that he was 'touched by the spectacle of the relics of British life there: deserted bungalows and bandstands, etc'.[98] A deeply felt personal realisation of the end of imperial India, and an inquisitive look at the face of the new and the traditional India, are the keynote of his writings about India from this period. The themes of *A Passage to India* and his subsequent writings about India are intimately related to these two main interests.

5 Through 'The Ruins of Empire': *A Passage to India* and some Later Writings about India

In a review, written after *A Passage to India*, of a book about the caves at Ajanta and Bagh, Forster wrote: 'The reader of any book about India should remember as he closes it that he has visited only one of the Indias'.[1] *A Passage to India*, however, seen purely as a book about India,[2] gives an inclusive and dynamic picture. As a portrayal of India, in which aspect the novel is looked at in this chapter, it gives an honest, realistic and imaginative account, and it is a complete view recorded at a particular stage in Forster's interpretation of India. Apparently its subject is the dissolution of the British Empire of India – the novel shows the weakening of the British Raj and the firm desire of politically minded Indians to be independent of Britain's control – but that is only one side of Forster's total view. The other side of it, which is more important from Forster's point of view, is concerned with looking at India and Indians, as such, independently of the political context.

Like Forster's earlier special reports on the social and political scene in British India, surveyed in the last chapter, *A Passage to India* portrays the political conflict and links it mainly with the lapses in the imperial policies of the Government in the past; but the novel's outlook is on the future. It presents India not as a sad concluding spectacle in British imperial history,[3] but as a subject of vital and permanent interest. Its purpose is to show that while imperialism, officialism and an impersonal governmental approach in Britain's connection with India had led to the estrangement between India and the Empire, there was ground for a more meaningful and an essentially human approach to the question. India and Indians were to be understood and interpreted at a more meaningful level, and with imagination and goodwill, so that a more valuable bond, based on fellowship rather than a mere political relationship, between Indians and the British might grow. 'The nations *must* understand one another, and quickly; and without the interposition of their governments', Forster wrote in his 'Notes on the English Character', remarking that towards such an understanding his 'notes' might make a contribution;[4] the same idea of creating understanding among nations is the embracing spirit also in all his writings about India, and especially in *A Passage to India*.

The peculiar distinction of Foster's outlook in *A Passage to India* can be adequately judged by looking at the novel against some other important novels of the time dealing with India. It will be seen that while the other books are concerned with the declining situation of the Empire as the single and exhaustive source of interest, *A Passage to India* considers that interest only as a starting-point. It looks at India as a subject with a permanent interest, which the other books do not do. To illustrate the point, the approaches of some other novels may briefly be looked at first.

Two novels which are deeply absorbed in the contemporary political question of Britain's losing control over India are Edmund Candler's *Abdication* (1922),[5] and Hilton Brown's *Dismiss* (1923).[6] They both deal with the effects of the constitutional reforms of 1919, under which Indians had been promised a responsible government and were called upon to share power with the British in governing India. Both novels present the situation as blind, sad and lost – the result of short-sighted liberal policies on the part of the British Government.

Riley, the principal character in *Abdication*, was drawn to India by his sympathy with the Indian tradition of mysticism and spiritual faith. But at Thompsonpur, where he is employed as the editor of an Anglo-Indian gazette, he finds himself in the hybrid atmosphere of Anglo-India and in a situation of intense political anarchy, caused by the Non-cooperation and the Khilafat movements. He is in sympathy with the enlightened spirit behind the Indian agitation, and is even disliked by the Anglo-Indians, who think him to be anti-British, but he is not convinced that India is in a fit position to be given self-government. Therefore, when Indians have the promise of 'swaraj' under the new constitution and the political situation of the country deteriorates, Riley feels inwardly distressed:

> Either we must clear out of India and take our army with us, or we must drop all talk of Swaraj, and hold the country by armed force. Then what of the pledge? Even if the Home Government consented to turning the country into an armed camp it would only be for a year or two. The masses are already being taught to hate us. The nationalist leaders will get at the army next. After that the deluge.[7]

Riley is asked to resign his editorship for being sympathetic towards the Indians, and he leaves in desperation. Travelling through Tibet, operating on cataracts, he is thinking of going back to England through Turkistan; he has forgotten Thompsonpur and the gazette, and thinks only in passing of Britain's short-sighted policy of 'abidcation' of power in India; at the same time he also thinks of Gandhi:

> If we are sincere . . . we ought to welcome him [Gandhi]. He has

opened a door; whether his countrymen pass through or not we shall see; the Englishman who would bang the door to, or deny that it exists, is either a knave or a fool. Give them Swaraj. What does it matter if they knock one another on the head, or neglect their drains, or leave their dead animals in the middle of the road? Race-hatred, which is the one thing that ultimately matters, would disappear . . . we have done everything for the Indians in a very superior and disagreeable way . . .[8]

The theme of 'abdication' of power by the British is dealt with in a equally limited context in Hilton Brown's *Dismiss*. This novel is concerned with the way the constitutional reforms had affected the world of the British civil servant in India. The principal figure, Drew Allan, is the son of a Scots family. He has grown up in an atmosphere where the name India meant nothing at all, but as his sister marries an official in India, he has his mind fixed on the Indian Civil Service. Coming to India as a member of the service he finds the people of his own race, civil servants like himself, uninteresting, caught and bound to the machinery of government. He does not understand the Indian at all:

If the people of my own race presented me with problems I found the Indian an enigma altogether. I find him so in many ways still. So far as generalizations can be applied I should call him by nature essentially domestic, loving his own little possessions, his own small interests, his own petty family affairs. These form his workaday world; outside these – in politics, for instance – he is a creature of dreams. He has the Oriental's love of the spacious word and the high-sounding phrase; he can live upon words to a quite incomprehensible extent; but behind and beneath all this he embodies, I believe, a real gift for devotion to an ideal. As such, it should be possible to make of him almost anything – to lead him on long progresses and to distinguished heights. How he has developed instead – how he has been allowed to develop – all this vile momentum of hate and bitterness, God alone knows. You may search the histories but they do not answer.[9]

Drew's isolation is intensified by his own emotional frustrations, and by political changes in India which bring disillusionment in his career in the Civil Serivce. The Reforms have 'Indianised' the Service. Drew has to work under an Indian secretary (a Christian), Devadoss, whom he finds competent and most delightful, but he sees that such Indians are only too rare. He is 'deeply disappointed in the mental calibre of most of them', and thinks that the idea of handing over power to Indians was utterly premature: 'If the Progressive party were made up of Devadosses, we could hand over India – with reservations – tomorrow'.[10] As revolutionary agitation spreads and becomes violent, Drew is posted to Yelrud, which is a difficult division. The Nationalists of Yelrud persist in their demonstrations, and Drew, feeling that the storm could burst at any time, asks for a counter-demonstration of British troops. But the authorities do not send any, for it is against their policy. In a helpless situation, as the outpost of Chinnavale and the few policemen there are burnt by a violent mob, Drew decides to leave the Service immediately. He resigns, and spends the rest of his life withdrawn from the political situation, on the Mahamalai hills overlooking the plains of Mysore.

Two other novels which together give a more powerful and more absorbing account of India than either *Abdication* or *Dismiss*, and yet are overwhelmingly nostalgic on the theme of the breaking-up of Brtish India, are Edward Thompson's[11] *An Indian Day* (1927), and *A Farewell to India* (1931), both published after *A Passage to India*. Both novels portray the lives of some individual Englishmen, chiefly educational missionaries, who have settled in India and are deeply in love with the country. Vincent Hamar, in *An Indian Day*, is a judge in the Civil Service, who is fair-minded and believes in justice. The Anglo-Indians think that he is sympathetic to India because he has not sentenced some Swarajists. In disgrace with his countrymen, he is transferred to a small place called Vishnugram. Hamar is not sorry about it. He is, indeed, quite pleased with the idea of going to Vishnugram, as it has a historical past and beautiful jungles. There he meets Rob Alden and John Findley, two dedicated missionaries, who are passionately in love with their work for Indians and are also interested in Indian thought and philosophy. The earnest evangelist who was bent on reforming the heathen mind did not understand Alden's and Findley's outlook and the average Anglo-Indian thought of them as knaves.

Both novels, forming a sort of sequel, narrate the story of Findley's and Alden's unremitting hardships. Findley's daughter dies when, gravely ill, she is being sent to England, and his wife jumps into the sea. Alden is in constant difficulty owing to persistent political unrest among the students of the local college of which he is in charge, and he is also attacked by the Anglo-Indian press for his sympathy with his students. But love of work, and a deep sentimental attachment for Vishnugram bind them both to India. Their spirit is not deterred by Indian political propaganda against the Englishmen (the revolutionary Indian thought of every individual Englishman living in India as belonging to 'the United English Nation' and was hostile to them). Asked by Alden what is wrong with all Englishmen, Jayananda Sadhu, an Indian ascetic (formerly of the Indian Civil Service, from which he resigned to agitate against the partition of Bengal), says:

> Your nobly moral airs. The way you have persuaded yourselves that the Empire is just a magnificent philanthropic institution, disinterestedly run for the sake of an ungrateful world. That's where *your* brag comes in. You don't brag about your poetry – or your men of science – or your martyrs – or any of those things that really exist.[12]

Indian nationalism turns increasingly revolutionary in *A Farewell to India*, where Jayananda Sadhu explains that he had left the Civil Service and become a revolutionary because of the humiliation he felt the Indians were subjected to at Curzon's Delhi Durbar. Alden, too, agrees that the humiliation India had suffered was unforgivable, but what he did not like was the dishonesty of it all – Indians screaming about the injustice of the English growing tea and jute, where none grew before, and also the British boasting of their great gifts to the country.

Political tension builds up not only between British and Indians, but also between the Hindus and Muslims. Hamar, taking the official view, thinks that big businessmen are going to join Gandhi's movement and see that it does not fail. Alden's love of India prompts him to wish that she should have peaceful partnership with the rest of the Empire; but the Indians' faces show dislike, resentment, wrath and hatred. The Indian national flag is flown everywhere. Although Alden loves India deeply, the changing India is something which he does not understand entirely. As he says to Hilda Hamar, his sister-in-law: 'There's something elemental in this land, that's in revolt against us . . . The age from time to time, in one land or another, gets sick of a certain people, and gets rid of them. It isn't reason, it isn't even the sword, that kicks them out . . . the age is tired of us, and wants a change. I guess it's going to have one'.[13]

Alden has to leave India on receiving medical advice that he should go home and never come back, as he has strained his heart. The college gives him a big farewell; and there are sentimental poems also by students who were troubling him a few days before. He leaves for England, but with a great longing to come back. His last wish in India is that if he does not come back but dies in England, his sister-in-law shall build a shrine for him in his beloved jungles, since he loves the land so much.

The one outlook which is common to all these four novels is that they look at India as a lost world – a world that the British have found challenging in many ways, engaging, and also lovable, but one that they are going to lose for ever. The political situation is looked at as overpowering – stupid, meaningless, yet fatal; a deep feeling of loss resulting from the political event of estrangement between India and the Empire dominates their outlook. In this respect these novels reflected the typically imperialistic outlook on India, in the context of a most important issue of the time. The political upheaval in India and the question of Britain giving her self-government, which meant the eventual end of Britain's connection with India, were not only matters that touched personally some individual Englishmen living in India but also matters of public importance, which were looked at with serious public interest. Apart from the four novels, two important general studies about India which also appeared in the same period were concerned with the theme of 'the lost empire' in a far more serious way and in an essentially disinterested spirit. They are: Al Carthill's *The Lost Dominion*,[14] published in the same year as *A Passage to India*, and Michael O'Dwyer's *India As I Knew It: 1885–1925*,[15] published in the following year, 1925. In these books, the question of Britain granting responsible government to India is approached from different angles, yet with an equal and totally serious concern. Al Carthill sees that Indian nationalism is spurious – 'there was, and is, no Indian nation',[16] and that there cannot be a national government where there is no nation; nevertheless, he thinks, Britain ought to abandon power on moral grounds. He says that although Whiggery has perished from England, and Liberalism, 'its favourite bastard',[17] is fast perishing, their effects on the English moral outlook is deep; and morally Britain must recognise India's claim: 'Many are the lost possessions of England. From some she has been driven in battle: others she has abandoned through negligence: others she has surrendered as useless and noxious: some have been bartered. The case of India is up to the present the first and only example of the abandonment of a valuable possession on moral grounds'.[18]

Michael O'Dwyer, on the other hand, maintains that the British Raj has been valuable for India in many ways and is still important to India's interest. The reforms were a thoughtless concession given to the small group of political extremists. But still, he says, answering Al Carthill, 'the Dominion is *not* lost'.[19] In his view, the British must remain firmly in their position of 'trust and their mission in India', and care for the 'real India' of the poor and the illiterate masses, and not for the politicians:

> Those responsible for the Reforms . . . went astray because they did not understand the *real India*, and what it wants – authority, justice, and the power necessary to enforce them. They legislated only for English-educated India, a minority of less than 1 per cent, which was vocal and which they thought they understood. But events have proved that even here they were wrong. Meantime *the real India* is steadily drifting away from the justice and authority to which it was so securely moored . . .[20]

Seen against this background of the prevalent imperialistic attitudes in writings about India of the 1920s, Forster's approach in *A Passage to India* has the remarkable distinction of being essentially non-imperialistic. The theme of the 'dissolution' of the Empire is looked at by him without a sense of loss: over this question *A Passage to India* does not express either the bitterness that is present in *Abdication*, or the tone of disgust and withdrawal that is present in *Dismiss*. It is free from the sentimentality and nostalgia for India that permeate *An Indian Day* and *A Farewell to India*; it has neither the assumption of moral righteousness conveyed in *The Lost Dominion*, nor the tone of blind conservatism expressed in *India As I Knew It*. Although all these books look at India s a subject limited within a past context, *A Passage to India* looks beyond that context and approaches India in order to create possibilities independently of the terms of the Empire.[21]

To understand India is the keynote of Forster's approach in the novel. The complexities of India's past traditions, the great variety presented by the range of her physical nature, the more intriguing variety of her people, and the intricacies of the contemporary political situation too – all these subjects are approached in order to be understood, and they are presented in the novel in an artistic form that is fully comprehensive and distinctive. In dealing with its immense theme and purpose, *A Passage to India* attains to a status of creative writing which is more lively than actual history and more meaningful than normal fiction. It presents historical facts with imagination, and tempers imagination with factual observation. Its creative approach is essential for comprehending the complexity and vastness of the subject: any approach to India other than for understanding, other than the deep and the creative, would be inadequate.

The story of the novel is itself significantly concerned with illustrating the limitations in a conventional approach to India. Adela Quested, 'the queer, cautious girl' from England, has come on a visit to India in the company of Mrs Moore, an elderly lady, to meet Mrs Moore's son, Ronny Heaslop, the city magistrate at Chandrapore, whom there is a possibility of her marrying: she is also anxious to 'see the real India'. Her approach to India has the excitement of a conventional visit, although she assumes herself to be unconventional. The India of her imagination is composed of the usual items of publicised romantic glamour: 'an elephant ride', and 'catching the moon in the Ganges'; and she insists that Mrs Moore too must not miss seeing that India – 'I will fetch you from Simla when it's cool enough. I will unbottle you in fact . . . We then see some of the Mogul stuff – how appalling if we let you miss the Taj! – and then I will see you off at Bombay'.[22] Mrs Moore, on her part, is in India because she has been 'commissioned' by her son to bring Adela from England; she has a duty to perform in seeing her son married; and, incidentally, she is interested in seeing 'the right places' too.

At the English club at Chandrapore where no Indians are admitted, it is suggested by Fielding, the principal of the local Government College, that in order to see the real India one has to 'try seeing Indians'. Fielding is sympathetic to Indians and has friends among them, but at the club he is disliked, and his idea of trying to see Indians is mocked: 'As if one could avoid seeing them', sighs Mrs Lesley. Fielding's idea, however, appeals to Adela, for it has the appearance of unconventionality. 'I am tired of seeing picturesque figures pass before me as a frieze . . . It was wonderful when we landed, but that superficial glamour soon goes',[23] she says, and she wants to meet Indians.

A 'bridge party' is arranged under 'British auspices' at the Collector's bungalow, for Adela and Mrs Moore to meet Indians. It is not a success, for the Indian guests were awkward: they arrived early and 'were only gazing sadly over the lawn'. Adela and Mrs Moore are later introduced by Fielding to Aziz, a doctor at Chandrapore hospital, who invites them all to a picnic on the Marabar hills, where there are the 'famous' caves. The expedition to Marabar fills Adela with excitement: she likes to hear from Dr Aziz about the Moguls, about Akbar's universal religion, and she thinks, inspired temporarily by Akbar's 'fine' idea, that the barriers are to be broken down in India, and that there will be 'universal brotherhood'. The picnic, however, ends in disaster: Adela, while being shown the caves by Dr Aziz, has a hallucination that she is molested by him. In a fit she is brought back to the 'civil station'; Dr Aziz is arrested and has to appear on trial.

The English and the Indian communities of Chandrapore are roused to bitter hostility against each other. Indians, long embittered because they are hated and also deprived of jobs by the English, look at the case of Aziz as an insult to the whole of India – to Hindus as well as Muslims – and are all united against the English. The English meet at the club to discuss the situation. They think that the law must be enforced, justice must be done; it is also suggested that the situation should have been left in the control of troops. The Collector, however, decides that there should be the least possible provocation of the natives lest there be a riot. The women and children are sent off to the hills for safety.

The case against Aziz is tried by an Indian magistrate, a subordinate of Ronny. (The English community is angered by the idea that an Indian should be judge over an English girl). There is a well-formulated charge against Aziz, prepared by the English Superintendent of Police; and to defend him Indians have brought a strongly anti-British Hindu barrister from Calcutta. The elaborate preparations on both sides, however, prove of little use, as the trial ends in a simple and unexpected way when Adela confesses during the trial that Dr Aziz did not follow her into the cave.

Aziz is released, and the Indians celebrate their 'victory' over the English. In bitterness against the English, Aziz leaves Chandrapore to work and live in the Hindu native state of Mau, outside the limits of British India. Adela returns to England, getting 'the worst of both worlds': she has antagonised the Indians, and has also 'renounced her own people' in India by asserting Aziz's innocence. Ronny cannot marry her, 'it would mean the end of his career'. 'Disaster had shown her limitations'; she understands that she has suffered because her whole approach to India has been senseless, and she assents when Fielding reminds her: 'You have no real affection for Aziz, or Indians generally . . . The first time I saw you, you were wanting to see India, not Indians, and it occurred to me: Ah, that won't take us far. Indians know whether they are liked or not – they cannot be fooled here. Justice never satisfies them, and that is why the British Empire rests on sand'.[24]

Mrs Moore's approach to India, like Adela's, is conventional, though in another way. She does not look at India with Adela's eye for anything superficially curious, she applies her own simple and benevolent Christian outlook instead: ' "India is part of the earth. And God has put us on the earth in order to be pleasant to one another. God . . . is . . . love." She hesitated . . . but something made her go on. "God has put us on earth to love our neighbours and to show it, and He is omnipresent, even in India, to see how we are succeeding" '.[25] With her intuitive sympathy and pious tenderness Mrs Moore has endeared herself to both Aziz and Professor Godbole, though only in a vague way; and similarly (though only by the curious fact of her being absent from India at the time of the trial of Dr Aziz, which she did not wish to see) her memory among the Indians at Chandrapore has turned into a charming and inexplicable popular legend. There is no real dimension of life in her contact with India: her simple, pious outlook is too soon confounded, and, wearied and pushed into 'the twilight of the double vision in which so many elderly people are involved',[26] she wishes for relief by departing from India:

> So Mrs. Moore had all she wished; she escaped the trial, the marriage, and the hot weather; she would return to England in comfort and distinction, and see her other children. At her son's suggestion, and by her own desire, she departed. But she accepted her good luck without enthusiasm . . .Mrs. Moore had always inclined to resignation. As soon as she landed in India it seemed to her good, and when she saw the water flowing through the mosque tank, or the Ganges, or the moon, caught in the shawl of night with all the other stars, it seemed a beautiful goal and an easy one. To be one with the universe! So dignified and simple. But there was always some little duty to be performed first, some new card to be turned up from the diminishing pack and placed, and while she was pottering about, the Marabar struck its gong.[27]

Mrs Moore's departure from India is described in the novel with expressions of pity, pathos and irony. Her naive idea of India in the days of her arrival in the country is seen also in her thoughts at the time of her departure:

> The swift and comfortable mail-train slid with her through the night, and all the next day she was rushing through Central India, through landscapes that were baked and bleached, but had not the hopeless melancholy of the plain. She watched the indestructible life of man and his changing faces, and the houses he has built for himself and God, and they appeared to her not in terms of her own trouble, but as things to see. There was, for instance, a place called Asirgarh which she passed at sunset and identified on a map — an enormous fortress among wooded hills. No one had ever mentioned Asirgarh to her . . .[28]

While the train descends through the Vindhyas Mrs. Moore sees only a half-view of Asirgarh. She arrives at the end of her journey in Bombay, and is filled with regret that her visit to India has been incomplete. Her old longing for India is revived when she is to sail back:

'I have not seen the right places', she thought, as she saw embayed in the platforms of the Victoria Terminus the end of the rails that had carried her over a continent, and could never carry her back. She would never visit Asirgarh or the other untouched places; neither Delhi nor Agra nor the Rajputana cities nor Kashmir, nor the obscurer marvels that had sometimes shone through men's speech: the bilingual rock of Girnar, the statue of Shri Belgola, the ruins of Mandu and Hampi, temples of Khajraha, gardens of Shalimar. As she drove through the huge city which the West has built and abandoned with a gesture of despair, she longed to stop, though it was only Bombay, and disentangle the hundred Indias that passed each other in its streets. The feet of the horses moved her on, and presently the boat sailed and thousands of coco-nut palms appeared all round the anchorage and climbed the hills to wave her farewell. 'So you thought an echo was India; you took the Marabar caves as final?' they laughed. 'What have we in common with them, or they with Asirgarh? Good-bye!'[29]

Mrs Moore's, and Adela's, general outlook on India at least acquires an edge of sensitivity as a result of their experiences during their visit, but the British living in India, with the exception of Fielding, all remain insensitive. The principal figures among them are all officials—the collector, the superintendent of police, the civil surgeon, and the city magistrate—whose only interest in India is in governing her: 'to do justice and keep the peace'.[30] They are not interested in knowing Indians socially, nor are they interested in Indian art, literature, or culture: 'Their ignorance of the Arts was notable, and they lost no opportunity of proclaiming it to one another; it was the Public School attitude, flourishing more vigorously than it can yet hope to do in England. If Indians were shop, the Arts were bad form.'[31] The officials' wives are portrayed as more indifferent to India than their husbands. They are dull, they express racial hatred openly, and they are also inhuman: Mrs Callendar, the civil surgeon's wife, thinks that 'the kindest thing one can do to a native is to let him die'.[32]

There is, on the whole, an element of dramatic exaggeration in Forster's portrayal of the Anglo-Indian official,[33] but the exaggeration is deliberate, and is intended to show the futility of an outlook to India that is based chiefly on officialdom. Forster was, in fact, not ignorant that it could be possible for an Anglo-Indian official to be true to his 'duty', and perform it within the context of a larger and more meaningful outlook on India. (His high appreciation for men like Alfred Lyall and Malcolm Darling has already been referred to in the third chapter.) He illustrates that outlook in the character of Fielding. Fielding is not portrayed as an ideal character, or as a perfect spokesman for the author's views: his past life 'had included going to the bad and repenting thereafter'; in middle age, when he entered India, he 'bribed a European ticket inspector' to take his luggage into his compartment in the train at Victoria terminus; and it may be remembered also that his nomination to the principalship of the 'little college' at Chandrapore was obtained 'through the influence of friends'. But however incomplete in his private life, Fielding has an essentially personal approach to society in general, which he also applies to the society of Anglo-India. He believes in the value of fellowship between individuals, and in human culture, and he cannot sympathise with the communal barrier between the British and Indians: 'Neither a missionary nor a student, he was happiest in the give-and-take of a private conversation. The world, he believed, is a globe of men who are trying to reach one another and can best do so by the help of goodwill plus culture and intelligence—a creed ill suited to Chandrapore, but he had come out too late to lose it'.[34] If he has no racial feeling against Indians, he does not sympathise with the Indians' communal feeling against the British either. He is disliked by his fellow Anglo-Indians and is considered a renegade when he openly sympathises with Aziz during his trial, but he stands by his own personal loyalty to the individual, and not by his community. His role in the novel illustrates that it was possible for an Englishman to live in British India in terms of a social and personal relationship with Indians, and provides a basis for the kind of outlook towards India which *A Passage to India* encourages.

Yet the total outlook of the novel (which may for present purposes be regarded as Forster's own outlook) is larger than Fielding's. Fielding is unable to grasp that his desire for friendship with Indians must recognise and absorb the condition of the Indians' political aspirations as well. He cannot imagine that the British Empire will be abolished or that India can become a nation; when Aziz emotionally portrays the future of India as a nation with 'no foreigners of any sort', Fielding mocks the idea: 'India a nation! What an apotheosis! Last comer to the drab nineteenth-century sisterhood! Waddling in at this hour of the world to take her seat! She, whose only peer was the Holy Roman Empire, she shall rank with Guatemala and Belgium perhaps!'[35] It was sad that in contemporary India the possibility of friendship between an Englishman and an Indian was dependent on whether India was going to be politically free of Britain's domination, but it was the reality, and the situation had to be looked at realistically. Fielding had illusions about a relationship with India and Indians within the continuity of Britain's imperial presence in India, which Forster himself had not. Forster had understood that the Empire was no longer a reality, and that a link with India and Indians must be sought independently of Britain's imperial interests, within the terms of the real situation.

For this reason *A Passage to India* puts the contemporary political situation into persepctive. In its picture of the British administration at

Chandrapore it shows the imperialist policies in their worst form, and also
draws attention to the Indians' political demand for complete freedom
from British domination. In a criticism[36] of the political theme in *A Passage
to India* it has been pointed out that the novel does not take into account the
fact that the imperial administration was also sensitive to Indian feelings;
although the administration had been actually involved, since the Reforms
of 1919, in the work of preparing Indians for self-government by giving
them an increasing share of power and authority, there is, the critic
maintains, no trace of this side of the picture in Forster's account. It is true
of course that the emphasis in the novel's political picture is on showing the
lapses in the imperial policies; but it is false to say that the novel does not
take notice of the new progressive elements in the imperial machinery – the
effects of the recent constitutional provisions of dyarchy, 'Indianisation' of
the Civil Service, and other democratic reforms. The effects of 'Indianisation' are seen in the novel's general picture of British and Indian
officials working together, holding important posts in the administration at
Chandrapore. It is also shown in the story of Aziz's trial, where Das, a
'subordinate' Indian magistrate, presides over the trial (it may be
remembered that the case is a criminal case involving an English girl, and
that a subordinate Indian magistrate did not have the authority before the
reforms of the Indian Criminal Procedure in 1923, to try such a case); by
making Das preside the novel throws light on an entirely new development
in the imperial system.[37] There are, besides, other instances in the novel
where direct reference is made to the new sympathetic imperial policies:
for example, it is pointed out that the Collector of Chandrapore is reluctant
to call troops to control the situation in the city, because he knows not only
that important Indians like the Nawab Bahadur would be annoyed, but
that the Government of India and the British Parliament are also
watchful.[38] Thus the political theme in the novel is not blind to the new
policies which were in operation in the 1920s; but, by focusing attention on
the main political issue of the time, which was the irreconcilable Indian
national challenge to the Empire, it shows that the effects of the reforms
had been minimal. Politically awakened Indians, like Aziz, thought that
reforms and attempts at conciliation were useless as long as the Indian
people were not treated as equals by the British.

Apart from drawing attention to the fact that the Indians' political
aspirations were a part of their enlightenment, and that these aspirations
could not be ignored,[39] the political theme of *A Passage to India* does not
have any other relevance within the context of the novel's total outlook on
India. Forster's interests in looking beyond the confines of Anglo-India at
the face of Indian society and civilisation are stimulated, first of all, by
distinctive qualities of the Indian way of life and of individual Indians. He
is struck deeply by the peace and restfulness, and the traditional warmth
and generosity of Indian social life, which he sees as the marks of a
civilisation unknown to the West:

Civilization strays about like a ghost here, revisiting the ruins of empire, and is to be found not in great works of art or mighty deeds, but in the gestures well-bred Indians make when they sit or lie down. Fielding, who had dressed up in native costume, learnt from his excessive awkwardness in it that all his motions were makeshifts, whereas when the Nawab Bahadur stretched out his hand for food or Nureddin applauded a song, something beautiful had been accomplished which needed no development. This restfulness of gesture – it is the Peace that passeth Understanding, after all, it is the social equivalent of Yoga. When the whirring of action ceases, it becomes visible, and reveals a civilization which the West can disturb but will never acquire. The hand stretches out for ever, the lifted knee has the eternity though not the sadness of the grave. Aziz was full of civilization this evening, complete, dignified, rather hard . . .[40]

The three Indians who are offered for study in their distinct individuality as comprehending the vast range of attraction and complexity in the Indian character are Aziz, Godbole and the man who pulled the punkah in the Court at Chandrapore. Aziz is a well-bred, enlightened, anglicised, modern Indian, whose personality includes an attractive blend of intensely individual and traditional features, with elements of influence from English education. He is spontaneous, imaginative, fond of poetry, sentimental, deeply generous, hospitable, proud of his own Muslim community and of his motherland as a whole, prejudiced against the Hindus temperamentally, but deeply prejudiced against the Anglo-Indians as a class. He is happy in his private life with his children, sentimental about his dead wife and content in his profession – despite the irritant of the relationship with his superior, Major Callendar, the civil surgeon. His curiosity about 'Post-Impressionism' in the West, which was ignored by Fielding, his independence, which was looked down upon by Ronny Heaslop as making 'the spoilt Westernized' type, his personal generosity, which was abused in a racially divided society, his conception of the value of pathos in personal life and in art, his inborn religious prejudices and his emotional feeling for his nation – all these qualities in Aziz show him as a modern and enlightened Indian, not simply a product of British India, but truly and deeply 'Indian', his complex character the result of contacts with many civilisations.[41]

Against the enlightened and sophisticated Aziz is set the character of Professor Godbole, presented in the novel as an essentially conservative, conventionally religious, uncertain, yet mysteriously attractive figure. He is not studied purely as a type (against Aziz, say, who happens to be a Muslim) to represent the traditional Hindu character in general; yet his portraiture is composed from certain elements which Forster had gathered chiefly from his contacts with society in the Hindu states of Dewas and Chhatarpur. Godbole appears on the whole rather enigmatic

—corresponding, evidently, to some elements in Forster's own experience in the Native States; in a significant way, however, he is seen as a more intriguingly Indian character than Aziz. (This point will be illustrated in the next chapter, where Godbole's character is scrutinised in the context of Forster's view of Hinduism in general.)

All the other Indians in the novel including Aziz's poor relative, Mohammed Latif, belong, like Aziz and Godbole, to a particular social level which however complex has evolved, in one way or another, in contact with intelligible trends of civilisation. But the Indian who is seen as distinct from everyone else—from Indians belonging to society as well as from the British—is the man 'of low birth',[42] the outcaste Indian, who is employed to pull the punkah in the city magistrate's Court. He is humble, 'splendidly formed', beautiful, and strong. He is shown sitting almost naked, on the floor of a raised platform, in the back of the Court. The proceedings of the trial are not understood by him, the social and political conflicts between the British and Indians do not touch his mind. Forster's portrayal of this unique figure in the Indian world is drawn with deep feeling, and it has a central relevance to the total outlook of the novel. He is drawn realistically, and also as a symbolic presence. By portraying him as he is—deprived and condemned by society—Forster draws attention to one most enigmatic feature of the Indian social tradition, and also comments on the actual scene of social inequality, poverty and deprivation in India: 'This man would have been notable anywhere; among the thin-hammed, flat-chested mediocrities of Chandrapore he stood out as divine, yet he was of the city, its garbage had nourished him, he would end on its rubbish heaps'.[43]

Symbolically, the punkahwallah's presence in the court room reflects on the meaninglessness of the communal and class conflicts in Anglo-India. Physically naked, he is presented in the novel as a man in his natural form, as the human individual, who is equal with all other indivduals[44] and higher than communities and religions. His presence points out, in the novel's local context, that the British in the days of their imperial power might have looked at Indians as equals; and in the wider context it points out the way that any individual human being might look at any other.

The portrayal of Indian life in the novel is seen alongside an intelligent portrayal of Indian nature. Forster has said that the three sections into which *A Passage to India* is divided 'also represent the three seasons of the Cold Weather, the Hot Weather, and the Rains, which divide the Indian year'.[45] Evocations of the great variety of Indian nature, linked in a correspondence with Indian life in various ways, can be seen in some of the most poetic passages in the novel. In the opening chapter, for example, the description of the city of Chandrapore, viewed from the slope of the 'little civil station', is characteristic:

It is a tropical pleasaunce washed by a noble river. The toddy palms and neem-trees and mangoes and peepul that were hidden behind the bazaars now become visible and in their turn hide the bazaars. They rise from the gardens where ancient tanks nourish them, they burst out of stifling purlieus and unconsidered temples. Seeking light and air, and endowed with more strength than man or his works, they soar above the lower deposit to greet one another with branches and beckoning leaves, and to build a city for the birds. Especially after the rains do they screen what passes below, but at all times, even when scorched or leafless, they glorify the city to the English people who inhabit the rise, so that new-comers cannot believe it to be as meagre as it is described, and have to be driven down to acquire disillusionment.[46]

In contrast to such a picture where nature is shown in close association with Indian life, there is the short prosaic description of the 'civil station' where the British officials live in a society, aloof and small, of their own:

As for the civil station itself, it provokes no emotion. It charms not, neither does it repel. It is sensibly planned, with a red-brick club on its brow, and farther back a grocer's and a cemetery and the bungalows are disposed along roads that intersect at right angles. It has nothing hideous in it, and only the view is beautiful; it shares nothing with the city except the overarching sky.[47]

The correspondence between the Indians' life and nature is shown always in the form of a pageant which is deeply imaginative, and at the same time real. When the hot weather comes to Chandrapore and stifles human activity, its horror is evoked with the same touches of imagination and realism with which the atmosphere at Mau at the coming of the monsoon rains is described. Here are two excerpts to illustrate the point:

The heat leapt forward in the last hour, the street was deserted as if a catastrophe had cleaned off humanity during the inconclusive talk . . .
  All over the city and over much of India the same retreat on the part of humanity was beginning, into cellars, up hills, under trees. April, herald of horrors, was at hand. The sun was returning to his kingdom with power, but without beauty – that was the sinister feature. If only there had been beauty! His cruelty would have been tolerable then.[48]

The sky grey and black, bellyfuls of rain all over it, the earth pocked with pools of water and slimy with mud. A magnificent monsoon – the best for three years, the tanks already full, bumper crops possible. Out towards the river (the route by which the Fieldings had escaped from Deora) the downpour had been enormous; the mails had to be pulled across by ropes. They could just see the break in the forest trees where the gorge came through, and the rocks above that marked the site of the diamond mine, glistening with wet. Close beneath was the suburban residence of the Junior Rani, isolated by floods, and Her Highness, lax about purdah, to be seen paddling with her handmaidens in the garden and waving her sari at the monkeys on the roof . . .[49]

The rain settled in steadily to its job of wetting everybody and everything through, and soon spoiled the cloth of gold on the palanquin and the costly disk-shaped banners. Some of the torches went out, fireworks didn't catch, there began to be less singing, and the tray returned to Professor Godbole, who picked up a fragment of the mud adhering and smeared it on his forehead without much ceremony . . .[50]

Viewing contemporary social and political events in the wider perspective of the traditional and more permanent aspects of Indian life and nature *A Passage to India* thus portrays an India of perennially attractive interest; it portrays an India whose people, their stream of life, their civilisation, religions and culture, all have peculiar attractions. Its account is not an exhaustive account, but it has the distinction of being comprehensive and fully evocative. While meaning to present a book about India Forster was deeply aware of the magnitude of his task; he knew that the immensity of his subject could always be approached, each approach being rewarded with a greater understanding; only a complete and final interpretation of India would always elude the grasp:

How can the mind take hold of such a country? Generations of invaders have tried, but they remain in exile. The important towns they build are only retreats, their quarrels the malaise of men who cannot find their way home. India knows of their trouble. She knows of the whole world's trouble . . . She calls 'Come' through her hundred mouths, through objects ridiculous and august. But come to what? She has not defined. She is not a promise, only an appeal.[51]

Forster's interests in India were sustained, after the publication of *A Passage to India*, through his many connections with the country. He continued to contribute a number of articles to periodicals, all written in a direct and interpretative style, on various aspects of Indian society, of the traditions of Indian religions, of Indian art and architecture, and of contemporary Indian thought. He was engaged in broadcasting to India on subjects of literary interest for a period during and after the Second World War,[52] and invited by the All-India centre of the P.E.N. club he also visited in India, for the third time, in 1945. Through all these ways his contacts with India became deeper, and his writings, which took the form of detailed observations on individual items of interest concerning India, were to provide valuable supplementation to his interpretation in *A Passage to India*.

There are two main directions in his later writings about India. In some of these articles he looks at the changing Indian society, emerging from British domination to acquire an independent status, while in certain other articles he searches for permanent meanings in some of India's long-established traditions. Reflecting on the social and political scene he says, in an article written after his third visit, that Indian society in the period immediately preceding Independence showed more signs of Westernisation and at the same time a stronger desire for political emancipation. He observed that there was an intenser political awareness, industrialisation had increased, the 'purdah' was breaking down, and people looked socially happier and freer than before. The Indians' excitement over politics, he observed, prevailed in all other spheres of Indian life, even in the sphere of their literary and artistic activities: there was great poverty still, but the economic solution was not pursued with the attention it deserved – the attainment of the political solution had taken precedence over the attainment of the economic. 'I do not know what political solution is correct' – Forster remarked, 'but I do know that people ought not to be so poor and look so ill, and that rats ought not to run about as I saw them doing in a labour camp in Bombay'.[53] Commenting on a more disturbing feature of the economic situation he drew attention to the great inequality that existed (and still exists) between the well-to-do Indians and the poor: 'For the well-to-do, life is much easier in India than in England. The shops are full of tinned delicacies for those who can afford them – butter, cheese, even plum puddings. For the poor, life is much harder there than here'.[54]

Alongside the social and political scene he has looked with deep interest also at certain aspects of the literary and the cultural scene of modern India. The importance of writers like Tagore and Iqbal[55] had already drawn the attention of the world, and Forster's acquaintance with them is not so important as his acquaintance with, and his appreciation of, some contemporary Indian writers of a lesser stature than Tagore's or Iqbal's, whom he has, in fact, made known outside India. Modern Indian writers like Mulk Raj Anand, Raja Rao and Ahmed Ali (now of Pakistan), who have made a mark by their writings in English, all confess that their recognition by the English speaking world is due to Forster's sympathy and initiative in introducing them;[56] and Forster, while writing about the merit of these writers, has shown that they possess a highly distinctive courage and depth of vision. He praises the great evocative power of Ahmed Ali's *Twilight in Delhi*,[57] and of Mulk Raj Anand's *Untouchable* he writes:

This remarkable novel describes a day in the life of a sweeper in an Indian city with every realistic circumstance. Is it a clean book or a dirty one? Some readers, especially those who consider themselves all-white, will go purple in the face with rage before they have finished a dozen pages, and will exclaim that they cannot trust themselves to speak. I cannot trust myself either, though for a different reason: the book seems to me indescribably clean and I hesitate for words in which this can be

conveyed. Avoiding rhetoric and circumlocution, it has gone straight to
the heart of its subject and purified it. None of us are pure – we shouldn't
be alive if we were. But to the straightforward all things can become
pure, and it is to the directness of his attack that Mr. Anand's success is
probably due.[58]

Forster's praise for these Indian artists is not uncritical: where he has
found a deficiency he has pointed that out also. For example, commenting
on the state of contemporary Indian poetry, drama and criticism he wrote,
in the account of his third visit: 'Poetry often echoes T. S. Eliot or Auden.
Drama is not prominent. Criticism weak. Indians have a marked capacity
for worship or for denunciation, but not much critical sense, as criticism is
understood in the west'.[59] Similarly it may be seen that although he is
delighted with the achievements of Indian folk art, and with the work of
some modern painters of Calcutta like Jamini Roy,[60] in modern Indian
cinema before the 1950s he finds nothing to commend.[61]

Since the account of his third visit to India, Forster has written nothing
in detail about contemporary India: his attention has chiefly been
concerned with certain more permanent aspects of the Hindu
tradition – which will be looked at in the next chapter. In independent
India, there have been some social and political changes which remain
outside his surveillance. Yet he has taken notice of the fact, and in writing a
note on *A Passage to India* in 1957, has said so: 'The India described in *A
Passage to India* no longer exists either politically or socially. Change had
begun even at the time the book was published [1924] and during the
following quarter of a century it accelerated enormously'.[62] He observes
that the end of the British Raj, the abolition of the Native States, the rapid
industrialisation, the breaking of social barriers of caste and purdah, and
the impact on contemporary India of the United States and the Soviet
Union – all these factors have changed the face of the India of his
book – 'Assuredly, the novel dates'.[63] This remark may be true of the novel
outwardly, only so far as its account of the limited social and political
picture of Anglo-India is concerned. Yet in the fact of Forster's recognition
of the changes that have taken place in a later period, outside his survey,
one sees not his limitations but the mark of his essentially dynamic outlook
on India. Forster had himself looked at the society of Anglo-India as a
passing and temporary phenomenon. In *A Passage to India* and his later
writings about India he was searching outside that coterie for more
substantial elements of the traditional India.

6 Some Aspects of Hinduism and Islam

A Passage to India portrays some aspects of Hinduism and Islam with sensitiveness and intense curiosity. The novel is not to be read as a systematic exposition of the Hindu and the Muslim ways of life, or as an account of the author's own formulated opinions on these two religions;[1] its approach to the religions is, in fact, fundamentally realistic: detached, self-conscious, and also ironical. Yet it will be seen that in significant ways the novel reflects on some main questions concerning the two religions, and also throws light on an interesting stage in the author's intellectual confrontations with these two religious beliefs of India. It shows him seriously questioning some aspects of Hinduism and Islam, and emerging finally more in sympathy with Hinduism than Islam. Scrutinising the possibilities of a value in the spiritualism of India, which might be tenable for him personally, he seems to have seen in Hinduism, rather than in Islam, such a possibility. *A Passage to India* shows his personal outlook on Hinduism only in a tentative form; but there is evidence that the novel registers the process of his recognition of a higher value in Hinduism – which he was to affirm directly and more specifically in some of his subsequent writings about India.

The themes connected with the religions of India in *A Passage to India* are based on material obtained from Forster's actual experiences during his two Indian visits prior to the appearance of the novel. As he had little actual contact with Buddhism or any other religion of India apart from Hinduism and Islam (his personal records of his visits refer almost exclusively to these two religions), *A Passage to India*, although it introduces the reader peripherally to many more religious sects and beliefs of India, directs attention mainly to the Hindus and the Muslims, and to certain aspects of their religions.[2] The Muslims appear to dominate in the novel: Dr Aziz is the central character, and the story is more concerned with him than with the Hindu protagonist, Professor Godbole. Aziz and his Muslim associates also are presented in a more intelligible way than Professor Godbole, and the mass of Hindus living in the Native State of Mau: 'Hindus, Hindus only, mild-featured men, mostly villagers, for whom anything outside their villages passed in a dream'.[3]

One reason for this apparent partiality for the Muslims *vis-à-vis* the Hindus in the novel may be found in the peculiarity of the author's actual experiences in India. During his two visits, before the publication of the novel, Forster seems to have felt easier in the society of Muslims than in that of Hindus. The personalities and religion of his Muslim friends were evidently more intelligible to him than the personality of the individual Hindus he had known, and their religion. One may find some positive evidence of this in his private accounts during the period of the two visits. For example, there is a striking contrast between his portrayal of the character of Syed Ross Masood, Forster's Muslim friend, and that of the character of the Hindu Maharajah of Dewas. While Forster shows absolute understanding of Masood's mental qualities and outlook, and is always in complete sympathy with him, he presents the Maharajah of Dewas with a mixture of affection, suspicion, sympathy and praise, but never shows that he comprehends him fully. 'Masood (afterwards Sir Syed Ross Masood) was my greatest Indian friend . . .' he says; 'he came of an eminent Moslem family . . . his ancestors had been nobles at the Moghul Court, and his descent from the Prophet was better documented than that of the Maharajah from the sun.'[4] It is true that in *The Hill of Devi* the Maharajah is also portrayed as a 'beloved' figure: 'enlightened', 'versatile and resourceful', and 'one of the sweetest and saintliest men I have ever known'; and that his deep religious instincts are praised, and the tragedy of his last days is painted with the utmost sympathy; but Forster confesses his sincere doubts about him too: 'Quite often I did not understand him – he was too incalculable'; 'I never feel certain what he likes, or even whether he likes me'; 'one can never be certain of saints', and so on.

As for the other Hindu Maharajah, of the State of Chhatarpur, who was also known to Forster personally and who may have contributed partly to the portrayal of the Hindu element in *A Passage to India*, Forster's private accounts show him as a highly comical and bewildering person: he is described as 'a most unusual character', 'fantastic and poetical', 'nonsensical and elusive', 'mystical, and sensual, silly and shrewd'. Forster's association with these two Maharajahs resulted chiefly in a great degree of light-hearted entertainment, and an increasing curiosity about Hinduism. When he says that they both threw light on Indian religion for him,[5] one must realise how limited the enlightenment was: through a process of comedy and enjoyable bewilderment, without seriously taking into account its theology or philosophy, he seems to have looked at Hindu religion as it was practised by the two Maharajahs and their states.

Against such lighter connections with the figures behind his approach to Hinduism, Forster's connections with Masood are strong, far more significant, and many-sided. 'There was never anyone like him, and there never will be anyone like him . . .' he says of Masood. 'My own debt to him is incalculable. He woke me up out of my suburban and academic life, showed me new horizons and a new civilization and helped me towards the understanding of a continent . . . *A Passage to India* . . . would never have been written without him.'[6] Alongside Masood's enlightened outlook and interests Forster also remembers 'his services to Islam', and that his 'real work . . . lay with his own community'.[7] It is likely that Forster's high degree of appreciation of Masood's character influenced his general outlook on the Muslims and on Islam.

One may also see in Forster's personal account some direct evidence of his general feeling of uneasiness with Hinduism, as against a feeling of ease and comfort with Islam. In a letter he wrote from the Hindu State of Chhatarpur he contrasts his different feelings about the two religions. The letter was written when, after several months' stay in Dewas, Forster had been on tour: he had been in touch with the Muslim atmosphere at Agra, revisiting the Taj, and listening to a prayer from a distant mosque, and had come to stay temporarily at Chhatarpur as the Maharajah's guest. He says:

> After nine years, I revisited the Taj . . . I have never seen the vision lovelier . . . a muezzin with a most glorious voice gave the evening call to prayer from a Mosque. 'There is no God but God'. I do like Islam, though I have had to come through Hinduism to discover it. After all the mess and profusion and confusion of Gokul Ashtami, where nothing ever stopped or need ever have begun, it was like standing on a mountain.[8]

The same note of contrast is struck also in another letter, written at a later date, when Forster had left Dewas for good and was staying with Masood in the Muslim State of Hyderabad. 'I am having a lovely time here', the letter says,

> and enjoying every moment of it. Masood in such good form, the weather perfect and exhilarating, beautiful things to look at, interesting people to talk to, delicious food, romantic walks, pretty birds in the garden, no Baldeo and no religion. Not but what Mr. Hydari, when least expected to do so, unlaces his boots and prostrates himself in a tight tweed suit during a picnic, but when it is over it is over, and he does not require red powder or drums to see him through. I have passed abruptly from Hinduism to Islam and the change is a relief.[9]

Apart from these instances where Forster draws a direct contrast between his feelings for Hinduism and for Islam, one comes across several other instances, in his private accounts, where Hinduism is alluded to, directly and indirectly, in a rather disparaging, and essentially non-serious and whimsical vein. In a letter written during his early days in Dewas to Lowes Dickinson, he refers to the Hindu character as 'unaesthetic', and writes: 'One is starved by the absence of beauty. The one beautiful object I can see is something no Indian has made or can touch – the constellation of the Scorpion which now hangs at night down the sky.'[10] There are detailed references in various parts of his journal to Hindu mythology, and to gods and goddesses, in the forms they are actually worshipped by Hindus, but such references are nearly everywhere made in a flippant and hilarious vein, as may be seen in the following selection.

Vishnu is the subject of the first: 'It gave me a shock to meet a tortoise in the Krishna Waterworks. It sat on the central slab – Vishnu himself no doubt . . .'[11]

In the following passage the subject is the goddess Chamunda, worshipped in Dewas, enshrined on the hill of Devi: 'There was a great popular festivity . . . The Temple on the summit thronged with worshippers . . . We went up on an elephant . . . made an offering to the Goddess (youngest and most amiable of seven sisters, but I should not like to meet her on a dark night) . . .'[12]

Krishna's birth ceremony is the subject in the following three excerpts; the idol Krishna is addressed as 'Dolly':

This month is to be devoted, not to say abandoned, to Religion, and we move down to the Old Palace in the heart of the town to be stung by mosquitoes and bitten by bugs. I have already helped to choose the 'Lord of the Universe' some new clothes. He is fortunately only six inches high, but he had to have eight suits, and he has several companions who must also be dressed, and the bill for this alone will not be far short of £30 . . .[13]

The shrine . . . looked like a Flower Show on the last day, just before the people come to take away their exhibits. Dolly was there, smothered in the rubbish, lost in the scuffle in fact . . . I wonder what it is all about. It is certainly the most important thing in these people's lives. His Highness will also sing. Electric light (£100 this) will be specially installed, and Dolly must also have a new bed and a new mosquito net.[14]

There was a palanquin, large and gorgeous, and shaped like a gondola with silver dragons at each end. Dolly got in with his rose leaves and tea services and a chrome picture of Tukaram, the Maratha Saint, and banana leaves and fans and the Village of Gokul and I don't know what else. Still I could not see him. But H.H. brought me quite close. I saw the thing at last – face like an ill-tempered pea: curious little lump for so much to centre round.[15]

The next passage is concerned with a festival sacred to Ganpati, and with some other forms of Hindu worship: 'Festivals are endless. Today Ganpati (the Elephant God) has a little show, the day before yesterday the bullocks were worshipped, tomorrow ladies may eat practically nothing but vegetable marrows . . .'[16]

Rama, an avatar of Vishnu, and Hanuman, Rama's loyal companion and messenger, are together dealt with in the following two quotations:

'Chhatarpur was wilder, smaller . . . Beyond the city were hills. Monkeys scampered up and down the slope – black-faced because they had not helped Rama in the wars . . .'[17] 'Yesterday, after my usual early visit from royalty, I walked to the Temple of Ram-whose-hands-reach-to-his-knees, not to be confused with the Temple of the Monkey God (Hanuman-who-knocks-down-Europeans) which is close to the Guest House.'[18]

These citations, showing a deliberately irreverential posture before the various Hindu divinities, proceed from an essentially light-hearted approach to the religion in general. 'Religion approaches, to me in a very tangible form', Forster writes in a letter describing the Gokul Ashtami celebrations at Dewas, 'as I have been hit on the head by an iron bar belonging to a sacred swing . . . I was not the least hurt – a miracle why. My skull must be pretty thick . . . Collision with this holy article seems to have made me active . . .'[19] The celebrations are described in elaborate detail and with deep curiosity, but Forster does not hide his actual incomprehension at many aspects of the ceremony. His elaborate descriptions indeed show a mixture of reactions: his innocence, his irreverence, his curiosity, his doubts, his joy and his confusion – all his different feelings about this particular Hindu ceremony are honestly conveyed. In the beginning of an elaborate letter on the subject a feeling of discomfiture is expressed, along with curiosity:

This ought to be an interesting letter. It is the fourth day of the Festival and I am getting along all right though I collapsed at first. The noise is so appalling. Hymns are sung to the altar downstairs without ceasing. The singers, in groups of eight, accompany themselves on cymbals and a harmonium. At the end of two hours a new group pushes in from the back. The altar has also a ritual which is independent of the singing. A great many gods are on a visit and they all get up at 4.30 a.m. – they are not supposed to be asleep during the Festival, which is reasonable considering the din, but to be enjoying themselves. They have a bath and are anointed and take a meal, which is over about 9.0 a.m. At 12.0 is another service, during which three bands play simultaneously in the little courtyard, two native bands and one European, affecting a merry polka, while these united strains are pierced by an enormous curved horn, rather fine, which is blown whenever incense is offered. And still I am only at the beginning of the noise.[20]

'Well, what's it all about?' the letter proceeds to explain in a matter-of-fact way, offering a direct personal comment:

It's called Gokul Ashtami – i.e. the *8 days* feast in honour of Krishna who was born at *Gokul* near Muttra, and I cannot yet discover how much of it is traditional and how much due to H.H. What troubles me is that every detail, almost without exception, is fatuous and in bad taste. The altar is a mess of little objects, stifled with rose leaves, the walls are hung with deplorable oleographs, the chandeliers, draperies – everything bad.[21]

From the beginning to the end the 'queerness' of the main ceremony and other rituals of worship is emphasised: 'I shall never be at the end of the queerness . . . It is the noise, the noise, the noise which sucks one into a whirlpool, from which there is no re-emerging';[22] 'I must get on to the final day – the most queer and also the most enjoyable day of the series';[23] 'By 10.0 we reached the Tank and the queer impressive ceremony of drowning the Town of Gokul was performed . . .'[24]

The one beautiful feature of the celebrations, Forster says, was 'the expression of the faces of the people as they bow to the shrine'.[25] He is inclined to look at this feature as a sign of 'religious ecstasy', but feeling doubtful, he writes about it sceptically. His account scrutinises the Maharajah's ecstatic dances before Krishna's altar, and conveys his own feeling of inability to grapple with the phenomenon fully:

> I have never seen religious ecstasy before and don't take to it more than I expected I should, but he manages not to be absurd. Whereas the other groups of singers stand quiet, *he* is dancing all the time, like David before his ark, jigging up and down with a happy expression on his face, and twanging a stringed instrument that hangs by a scarf around his neck. At the end of his two hours he gets wound up and begins composing poetry which is copied down by a clerk, and yesterday he flung himself flat on his face on the carpet. Ten minutes afterwards I saw him as usual, in ordinary life. He complained of indigestion but seemed normal and discussed arrangements connected with the motor cars. I cannot see the point of this, or rather in what it differs from ordinary mundane intoxication. I suppose that if you believe your drunkenness proceeds from God it becomes more enjoyable. Yet I am very muddled in my own mind about it all, for H.H. has what one understands by the religious sense and it comes out through all his life.[26]

In Forster's view the devotional singing and the various outward gestures of the worshippers appeared meaningless, silly and fanatical. He observes:

> Some praised God without attributes, others with attributes: the same mixture of fatuity and philosophy that ran through the whole festival. A lady fanatic was in the Dewan's group. She was gaudily yet neatly dressed in purple and yellow, a circle of jasmine flowers was round her chignon and in her hands were a pair of tongs with which she accompanied herself. We could not discover whether she was praising God with or without attributes.[27]

Forster did not look at Hindu idolatry as entirely devoid of significance, and in fact he was delighted with some aspects of Gokul Ashtami celebrations, but his accounts give no evidence that Hindu religion, in its external appearance through ceremony and rituals, exercised any deep attraction on his mind. Looking at it sensitively, yet remaining almost wholly outside its field of impact, Forster thus sums up his personal outlook on Hinduism in the midst of his actual experiences in Dewas:

> It is difficult to make vivid what seems so fatuous. There is no dignity, no taste, no form, and though I am dressed as a Hindu I shall never become one. I don't think one ought to be irritated with Idolatry because one can see from the faces of the people that it touches something very deep in their hearts. But it is natural that Missionaries, who think these ceremonies wrong as well as inartistic, should lose their tempers.[28]

His outlook is based on his observation of the curious and bewildering ceremonies at Dewas; and, in contrast, the situation of Islam – far less complicated, centred on the worship of the one God, and generally devoid of idolatrous ceremonies – appealed to him vaguely as reassuring; being more intelligible, it appeared also more congenial. In a rather spontaneous and uncritical way he seems to have felt predisposed towards Islam, and he has made no attempt to examine his special feeling for it. His liking for it is just stated in a summary way, and nowhere in the accounts of his personal experiences in India does he attempt to approach the subject of Islam as deeply, or in the same proportion, as he has dealt with Hinduism.

This was the peculiar state of Forster's attitudes to the two religions when he returned from his second visit in India: his mental outlook had been exposed to a wider field of observations, connected this time with Hinduism rather than with Islam, and he had found more interesting things to write about in Hinduism than in Islam; but evidently the complexity of Hinduism had still eluded him while he had entirely comprehended the essential meaning of Islam, and that is why he was able to look at Islam in greater sympathy. This situation is the key to the general outlook on the two religions reflected in *A Passage to India*.

The novel faithfully presents the full range of Forster's actual experiences concerning Hinduism and Islam. Hinduism is portrayed on a wide and bewildering canvas, Islam on a more handy and presentable one: also, broadly speaking, the Hindu character is presented as queer, and the Muslim as perfectly intelligible. This broad pattern of differentiation may be illustrated by reference to some relevant instances. The two religions are introduced in the novel in two distinctive tones. In the first part, Islam is presented through the eyes of Aziz as more valuable than a faith; the mosque is described as an abode of rest and graciousness, and its atmosphere is made familiar by the reference to the English parish church

and by the quotation of a perfectly understandable inscription for a tomb.
Hinduism and Christianity are portrayed as uncongenial:

> At the edge of the civil station he [Aziz] turned into a mosque to rest. He
> had always liked this mosque. It was gracious, and the arrangement
> pleased him. The court-yard – entered through a ruined gate – con-
> tained an ablution tank of fresh, clear water, which was always in
> motion, being indeed part of a conduit that supplied the city.
>
> The courtyard was paved with broken slabs. The covered part of the
> mosque was deeper than is usual; its effect was that of an English parish
> church whose side has been taken out. Where he sat, he looked into three
> arcades whose darkness was illuminated by a small hanging lamp and
> by the moon . . . A mosque by winning his approval let loose his
> imagination. The temple of another creed, Hindu, Christian, or Greek,
> would have bored him and failed to awaken his sense of beauty. Here
> was Islam, his own country, more than a Faith, more than a battle-cry,
> more, much more . . . Islam, an attitude towards life both exquisite and
> durable, where his body and his thoughts found their home . . .
>
> On the right, over in the club, the English community contributed an
> amateur orchestra. Elsewhere some Hindus were drumming – he knew
> they were Hindus, because the rhythm was uncongenial to him . . . the
> mosque – that alone signified, and he returned to it from the complex
> appeal of the night, and decked it with meanings the builder had never
> intended. Some day he too would build a mosque, smaller than this but
> in perfect taste, so that all who passed by should experience the
> happiness he felt now. And near it, under a low dome, should be his
> tomb, with a Persian inscription:
> > Alas, without me for thousands of years
> > The Rose will blossom and the Spring will bloom,
> > But those who have secretly understood my heart –
> > They will approach and visit the grave where I lie.[29]

In contrast to this direct and straightforward narration there is, in the
last part of the novel, the rhetorical and ironical passage on the Hindu
theme. The celebrations of Krishna's birth, the decorations surrounding
the idol, the idol itself, the devotional chanting of the choir, and the
question of the significance of the whole ceremony, are all presented in
their muddled and incomprehensible form:

> Some hundreds of miles westward of the Marabar Hills, and two years
> later in time, Professor Narayan Godbole stands in the presence of God.
> God is not born yet – that will occur at midnight – but He has also been
> born centuries ago, nor can He ever be born, because He is the Lord of
> the Universe, who transcends human processes. He is, was not, is not,

was. He and Professor Godbole stood at opposite ends of the same strip of carpet.

> 'Tukaram, Tukaram,
> Thou art my father and mother and everybody.
> Tukaram, Tukaram,
> Thou art my father and mother and everybody.
> Tukaram, Tukaram,
> Thou art my father and mother and everybody.
> Tukaram, Tukaram,
> Thou art my father and mother and everybody.
> Tukaram . . .'

This corridor in the palace at Mau opened through other corridors into a courtyard. It was of beautiful and hard white stucco, but its pillars and vaulting could scarcely be seen behind coloured rags, iridescent balls, chandeliers of opaque pink glass, and murky photographs framed crookedly. At the end was the small but famous shrine of the dynastic cult, and the God to be born was largely a silver image the size of a teaspoon. Hindus sat on either side of the carpet where they could find room, or overflowed into the adjoining corridors and the courtyard . . .

They sang not even to the God who confronted them, but to a saint; they did not one thing which the non-Hindu would feel dramatically correct; this approaching triumph of India was a muddle (as we call it), a frustration of reason and form. Where was the God Himself, in whose honour the congregation had gathered? Indistinguishable in the jumble of his own altar, huddled out of sight amid images of inferior descent, smothered under rose-leaves, overhung by oleographs, outblazed by golden tablets representing the Rajah's ancestors, and entirely obscured, when the wind blew, by the tattered foliage of a banana. Hundreds of electric lights had been lit in His honour (worked by an engine whose thumps destroyed the rhythm of the hymn). Yet his face could not be seen. Hundreds of His silver dishes were piled around Him with the minimum of effect. The inscriptions which the poets of the State had composed were hung where they could not be read, or had twitched their drawing-pins out of the stucco, and one of them (composed in English to indicate His universality) consisted, by an unfortunate slip of the draughtsman, of the words, 'God si Love'.

God si Love. Is this the final message of India?[30]

Against these two contrasting back-drops more aspects of the two religions are viewed. Islam is not presented without reflections on some of its lapses in its contemporary form: superstitions and some forms of idolatry found among the Muslim community make Aziz unhappy. 'You know, my dear fellow', he says to Nureddin, 'we Moslems simply must get rid of these superstitions, or India will never advance. How long must I hear of the savage upon the Marabar Road'.[31] Or again, when Aziz has moved from

Chandrapore to the Hindu Native State of Mau, it is observed that he
'found that even Islam was idolatrous, he grew scornful, and longed to
purify the place'.[32] But on the whole, these observations do not alter the
general impression of Islam presented in the novel as perfectly intelligible
and claiming the author's sympathy.[33]

The details about Hinduism, on the other hand, are presented in an
ambivalent way. Aspects of Hindu gods, Hindu mythology, Hindu forms
of worship, Hindu scripture and Hindu philosophy are touched upon with
irony; the Hindu character is also portrayed as comical and incomprehensible. However, it will be seen that there is evidence underneath this
apparent picture that the author is being strongly drawn by some deeper
source of attraction in Hinduism, and that, in the process, he emerges
towards a position of strong personal sympathy with it.

As with the references in Forster's personal letters irony, frivolity and
realism are the keynote too of the various references to Hindu mythology
and polytheistic worship in *A Passage to India*. Here is a characteristic
example: 'The Ganges, though flowing from the foot of Vishnu and
through Siva's hair', it is remarked, 'is not an ancient stream. Geology,
looking further than religion, knows of a time when neither the river nor
the Himalayas that nourished it existed, and an ocean flowed over the holy
places of Hindustan'.[34] Similarly, the various gods that are supposed to be
worshipped in the Hindu State of Mau are referred to as follows:

> Beyond the Guest House rose another grey-green gloom of hills, covered
> with temples like little white flames. There were over two hundred gods
> in that direction alone, who visited each other constantly, and owned
> numerous cows, and all the betel-leaf industry, besides having shares in
> the Asirgarh motor omnibus. Many of them were in the palace at this
> moment, having the time of their lives; others, too large or proud to
> travel, had sent symbols to represent them. The air was thick with
> religion and rain.[35]

There is an amusing allusion in one passage to Lakshmi, the Hindu goddess
of wealth: 'Just as the Hindu clerks asked Lakshmi for an increase in pay, so
did she [Adela] implore Jehovah for a favourable verdict'.[36] In an equally
amusing context the *Bhagavad Gita* too is mentioned: Mr McBryde, the
District Superintendent of Police at Chandrapore, asks Fielding to 'read
any of the Mutiny records; which, rather than the *Bhagavad Gita*, should be
your Bible in this country'.[37] As a final example, the Vedantic concept of
'Brahm' as the Highest Being is alluded to in nonsensical juxtaposition
with the demons of dead Europeans in India:

> A hundred years ago, when Europeans still made their home in the
> countryside and appealed to its imagination, they occasionally became
> local demons after death – not a whole god, perhaps, but part of one,

adding an epithet or gesture to what already existed, just as the gods contribute to the great gods, and they to the philosophical Brahm.[38]

The Hindu character, so far as it is presented through the portraiture of Professor Godbole, is seen as mainly curious, elusive and amusing. Some critics have looked at Godbole far more seriously, as Forster's study of an ideal Hindu character embodying the Hindu way of love,[39] though such an interpretation may be valid so far as only one aspect of Godbole's character is concerned, that is his faculty for religious ecstasy. When Godbole is shown singing hymns and dancing before the altar of Krishna, during the god's birth ceremony, he is presumably meant to portray the devotional Hindu's mental faculty for direct and heightened apprehension of the presence of God through love. (As has already been pointed out, Forster had actually been intrigued by this particular phenomenon encountered, during the Gokul Ashtami celebrations at Dewas, in the similar behaviour of the Maharajah.) But apart from illustrating this particular point, Godbole's character for most of the novel hardly remains true to the Hindu ideal of love.[40] He does not embody an ideal fully; so far as his Hindu aspects are concerned, they are in fact based on Forster's limited observations in Dewas of the Hindu character, and the rest of his qualities are Forster's own creation.

Forster has said about Godbole: 'I never met anyone like him. Godbole was mainly constructed by me. He was to a large extent a created character.'[41] Some elements in Godbole, however, resemble the familiar image of the Chitpavan Brahman (the 'Godboles' belong to this particular sect of Hindu Brahmans); and some other interesting details in him may be traced to sources in the personality of the two Hindu Maharajahs of Dewas and Chhatarpur. It is necessary to look at this point closely in order to approach the question of Godbole's real significance in the novel.

With the general figure of the Chitpavan (the name means 'purified by fire') Brahman of the Deccan Forster seems to have been very well acquainted. These Brahmans held a formidable place in British India. Their traditional pride of being the purest among the Brahmans and of their past imperial power, their ambition and shrewd ability, their loyalty as well as their opposition to the British position in India – all these were well known. To an observer of the Indian situation at the beginning of the present century, the Chitpavan Brahman was a familiar figure: Tilak and Gokhale, central figures in the Indian national movement, both came from this community. (In accordance with the traditionally complex outlook of their community, Tilak was fiercely anti-British, while Gokhale never gave up his loyalty to the Crown.) Forster's acquaintance with the Chitpavan Brahman may have been acquired from common knowledge;[42] it evidently came to him through two other closer sources, however – through his association with Dewas, and through his familiarity with Valentine Chirol's reports on the subject of the political unrest in India.[43] In the

Dewas Court the Deccani Brahman was looked upon as an enemy, and Forster was acquainted (through a confidential report by Malcolm Darling) with the Maharajah's past feud with this community. Valentine Chirol's reports on the contemporary situation in India contained detailed accounts of the Chitpavan Brahman as the most controversial figure; Forster's acquaintance with these accounts must have been deep, for his own portrayal of Godbole shows a strong resemblance with Valentine Chirol's sketch of the general image of the Chitpavan Brahman. The points of similarity between the two accounts are cited below.

Describing the Chitpavan Brahmans and the part played by them in the context of the political unrest in British India Valentine Chirol writes:[44]

Fundamental as is the antagonism between the civilization represented by the British *Raj* and the essential spirit of Brahmanism, it is not, of course, always or everywhere equally acute, for there is no more uniformity about Brahmanism than about any other Indian growth. But in the Deccan Brahmanism has remained more fiercely militant than in any other part of India, chiefly perhaps because nowhere had it wielded such absolute power within times which may be still called recent. Far into the 18th century Poona had been the capital of a theocratic State in which behind the throne of the Peshwas both spiritual and secular authority were concentrated in the hands of the Brahmins. Such memories are slow to die and least of all in an ancient and conservative country like India, and there was one sept of Brahmans, at any rate, who were determined not to let them die.

The Chitpavan Brahmans are undoubtedly the most powerful and the most able of all the Brahmans of the Deccan. A curious legend ascribes their origin to the miraculous intervention of Parashurama, the sixth Avatar of the god Vishnu, who finding no Brahmans to release him by the accustomed ritual from the defilement of his earthly labours, dragged on to the shore the bodies of fourteen barbarians that he had found washed up from the ocean, burnt them on the funeral pyre and then breathed life and Brahmanhood into their ashes. On these new made Brahmans he conferred the name Chitpavan, which means 'purified by fire' . . .

About two centuries ago . . . the Chitpavan Brahmans began to play a conspicuous part in Indian history . . . The Mahratta Empire became essentially a Chitpavan Empire. The British arms ultimately defeated the dreams of universal dominion which, in the then condition of India, the Chitpavans might well have hoped to establish on the ruins of the great Moghul Empire. But the British rule did not destroy their power. They were quick to adapt themselves to new conditions and above all to avail themselves of the advantages of Western education. Their great administrative abilities compelled recognition, and Chitpavans swarm to-day in every Government office of the Deccan . . . They sit on the

Bench, they dominate the Bar, they teach in schools, they control the vernacular Press, they have furnished almost all the most conspicuous names in the modern literature and drama of Western India as well as in politics . . . From the Deccan, moreover, their influence has spread practically all over India, and, especially, in the native States, which have recruited amongst the Chitpavans some of their ablest public servants. Amongst Chitpavans are to be found many of the most enlightened and progressive Indians of our times and many have served the British Raj with unquestioned loyalty and integrity. But amongst many others – perhaps indeed amongst the great majority – there has undoubtedly been preserved for the last hundred years from the time of the downfall of the Peshwa dominion to the present day, an unbroken tradition of hatred towards British rule, an undying hope that it might some day be subverted and their own ascendancy restored . . .

Chirol goes on to describe the anti-British activities of Tilak and his associates, their seditious propaganda through the press, 'through religious songs in which legends of Hindu mythology were skilfully exploited to stir up hatred of the foreigner', and their equal hatred of the Europeans and the Muslims. In *A Passage to India*, Forster's portrayal of Godbole draws attention to all the essential details depicted by Chirol. The pride, ambition, social importance and subtle ability of Godbole's community, and its jealous attitude to the British power in India, are talked about in a conversation between Fielding and Aziz:

[Fielding] 'Besides the ladies I am expecting one of my assistants – Narayan Godbole.'
[Aziz] 'Oho, the Deccani Brahman!'
[Fielding] 'He wants the past back too, but not precisely Alamgir.'
[Aziz] 'I should think not. Do you know what Deccani Brahmans say? That England conquered India from them – from them, mind, and not from the Moguls. Is not that like their cheek? They have even bribed it to appear in text-books, for they are so subtle and immensely rich. Professor Godbole must be quite unlike any other Deccani Brahmans from all I can hear say. A most sincere chap.'[45]

Godbole shows a sense of his community's assumption of purity: 'He took his tea at a little distance from the outcastes'; for him Europeans, Muslims, and all other non-Hindus were untouchable – 'the touch of a non-Hindu would necessitate another bath'. He apparently illustrates also his community's claims to superior learning and the knowledge of Hindu philosophy. And in line with his community's general importance in Indian society, he is also shown, in the first part of the novel, as receiving the regard due to someone in his position at Chandrapore. 'All his friends trusted him without knowing why – ', and later as taking up the important official position of minister of education in the Hindu Native State of Mau. As for his political outlook, Forster presents Godbole as leaning towards the loyal side of his community rather than the anarchist (as minister of education Godbole wants to name his proposed High School either after Fielding or the King-Emperor).

Besides these details, the main items in Forster's portrayal of Godbole's looks and general deportment also correspond to the image of the Chitpavan Brahman portrayed by Valentine Chirol. Here is a quotation from Forster's description of Godbole on his first appearance in the novel:

> He was elderly and wizen with a grey moustache and grey-blue eyes, and his complexion was as fair as a European's. He wore a turban that looked like pale purple macaroni, coat, waistcoat, dhoti, socks with clocks. The clocks matched the turban, and his whole appearance suggested harmony – as if he had reconciled the products of East and West, mental as well as physical, and could never be discomposed.[46]

The same complex combination of features, derived from the East and the West, is seen in the outlines presented by Valentine Chirol:

> Every Chitpavan to-day claims descent from one or other of the fourteen divinely Brahmanized barbarians, whom some believe to have been hardy Norsemen driven in their longships on to the sandy shores of what is now the Bombay Presidency. At any rate, as has been well said of them, Western daring and Eastern craft look out alike from the alert features and clear parchment skin and through the strange stone-grey eyes of the Chitpavan.[47]

Apart from the type figure of the Chitpavan community, some interesting qualities Forster had seen in the Maharajahs of Dewas and Chhatarpur also seem to have contributed to his creation of Godbole. The essentially comical aspects of Godbole may be compared with the similar qualities of the Maharajah of Chhatarpur: Godbole's missing the train for the journey to Marabar, for 'he had miscalculated the length of a prayer', reminds the reader that the Maharajah of Chhatarpur meditated 'when I can for two hours, and when I am busy for forty-five minutes'. Similarly, Godbole's adoration of Krishna ('I say to Shri Krishna, "Come! come to me only . . . O Lord of the Universe, come to me"')[48] is a reminder of the Maharajah's own peculiar faith in God as described by Forster on one particular occasion: 'He now says I am a "wizard" and implores me to open my heart so that God may fill it and him . . .'[49] Forster remarks about the Maharajah of Chhatarpur that 'he concentrated on his health, on philosophy and religion and on his troupe of Krishna dancers, when he had one . . . He was exasperating, undignified, unreliable, but endearing'.[50] All these qualities are found to be present in Godbole. The Maharajah's 'concentration' on health is reflected in Godbole's attention to food: 'he only ate – ate and ate, smiling, never letting his eyes catch sight of his hand' (*Passage*, VII, p. 76). In the Chhatarpur Court too Forster had observed that the Brahmins ate 'endlessly meals off banana leaves' (*The Hill of Devi*, p. 133). The Maharajah's interests in philosophy were fatuous, as are Godbole's: Forster writes of Godbole's talk about good and evil actions (*Passage*, XIX, p. 185) in the same curious vein as he does about the Maharajah's talk about 'Love and Beauty and Wisdom' (*The Hill of Devi*, p. 31). The Maharajah's 'exasperating, undignified and unreliable' nature is shown in Godbole's action when he refuses to be concerned in any way about Aziz's situation after the Marabar incident: Godbole's behaviour makes Fielding think 'really, Indians were sometimes unbearable' (*Passage*, XIX, p. 184). As for the Maharajah's 'endearing' quality, the presence of this quality in Godbole is especially remembered by Fielding too, when he says at the end of the novel: 'I never really understood or liked them [the Hindus], except an occasional scrap of Godbole. Does the old fellow still say "come, come"?' (*Passage*, XXXVII, p. 333).

From the Maharajah of Dewas Godbole seems to have derived his strange principles in the matter of food,[51] his inspired moments of religious feeling – seen in the novel when he performs his dance during Krishna's birth ceremony – as well as his sense of universal love. It may be remembered that the Maharajah of Dewas had told Forster that he believed 'men, birds, everything – are part of God'; that belief is apparently enacted by Godbole when, during the celebrations of Krishna's birth, he thinks lovingly of Mrs Moore and also of the little wasp:

> Thus Godbole, though she was not important to him, remembered an old woman he had met in Chandrapore days. Chance brought her into his mind while it was in this heated state, he did not select her, she happened to occur among the throng of soliciting images, a tiny splinter, and he impelled her by this spiritual force to that place where completeness can be found. Completeness, not reconstruction. His senses grew thinner, he remembered a wasp seen he forgot where, perhaps on a stone. He loved the wasp equally, he impelled it likewise, he was imitating God . . . Up and down, a third of the way to the altar and back again, clashing his cymbals, his little legs twinkling, his companions dancing with him and each other.[52]

Without looking at Godbole's religious ecstasy as a pure and supreme Hindu spiritual faculty, Forster presents it sceptically, as he had, in fact, looked at the presence of that faculty in the Maharajah of Dewas. It is remarked ironically that Godbole's loving recollection of Mrs Moore might be 'a trick of his memory or a telepathic appeal', and that his universal love could not have extended to the stone 'where the wasp clung – could he . . . no, he could not, he had been wrong to attempt the stone, logic and conscious effort had seduced, he came back to the strip of red carpet and discovered that he was dancing upon it'.[53]

The above account of the possible background to Forster's creation of Godbole shows that his character is based on certain precise elements in Forster's contacts with Hindu India and not on an abstract and idealistic approach to it. Neither in the detailed references to Hindu gods and mythology, nor in the character of Godbole does he attempt to present in the novel a convincing picture of the Hindu religion;[54] and the main reason for this may be that Forster had found his actual contacts with Hinduism limited, though intensely curious and endearing.

A comparative study of the treatment of Hinduism and Islam in the novel shows however a deeper aspect of Forster's total view of the two religions. It is true that he views Islam as a more congenial subject to interpret, and Hinduism as much less so – 'Study it for years with the best teacher, and when you raise your head, nothing they have told you quite fits'[55] – yet, evidently, the novel derives its main interest so far as the interpretations of the two religions are concerned more from its deeper curiosity about Hinduism than from its general assumption of familiarity with Islam. The picture of the Hindu world, apparently inadequate, unsympathetic and incomprehensible, never lacks in curiosity and realism. 'What I want to discover is its spiritual side, if it has one', says Fielding, and when Aziz remarks: 'It is useless discussing Hindus with me . . . Why so curious about them?' – Fielding replies, 'It's difficult to explain . . . I can't explain, because it isn't in words at all, but why do my wife and her brother like Hinduism, though they take no interest in its forms? They won't talk to me about this. They know I think a certain side of their lives is a mistake, and are shy.'[56]

Fielding's reflections on 'the spiritual side' of Hinduism could be read as the concluding note of Forster's interpretation of Indian religions in the novel. Looking through the appearance of largely unintelligible mythology, ceremony and aspects of individual religious behaviour, as Fielding searches for an essential meaning in Hinduism he discovers that he has gained a compelling insight into one part of it. He can see that there is in Hinduism the possibility of a spiritual meaning which, it seems to him, Christianity as well as Islam lacked. He sees, himself an unbeliever in God or Providence,[57] that unlike Christianity or Islam Hinduism presents religion as 'a living force'[58] by conceiving of God as an immediate reality apprehensible by man, and he is deeply drawn by this idea. Both he and Aziz remain outside the world of experience connected with the celebration of Krishna's birth, and the Hindu 'way' of a living contact with God remains alien to them both; yet Fielding has an inner sense that by emphasising the idea of man's nearness to God Hinduism gives religion a significance which Christianity or Islam does not: 'There is something in religion that may not be true, but has not yet been sung', Fielding says to Aziz; 'something that the Hindus have perhaps found'.[59] He thinks that

It belonged to the Universe that he had missed or rejected. And the mosque missed it too. Like himself, those shallow arcades provided but a limited asylum. 'There is no God but God' doesn't carry us far through the complexities of matter and spirit; it is only a game with words, really, a religious pun, not a religious truth.[60]

Fielding's new insight is Forster's own; and it is developed, as may be seen from some of Forster's writings about India after *A Passage to India*, into a fuller appreciation of two main elements in the Hindu tradition: the Hindu conception of Krishna, and the meaning of Hindu temple architecture. Forster's closest acquaintance with Krishna's story is seen in *The Hill of Devi* in a detailed account of the god's birth legend. The description of the legend, based on information derived from the *Bhagavad Purana*, Book X, and the *Vishnu Purana*, Book V,[61] shows that Forster is personally attracted by the qualities of liveliness and humanity in the Hindu conception of Krishna. He narrates the story about the birth with interest. The god, being 'the Supreme God, the incarnation of Vishnu', escaped the plans of Kamsa, the wicked king of Mathura, to kill him at birth – this part of the legend is shown as cognate with the story about the birth of Jesus and Herod's murder of the innocents[62] – but when it comes to Krishna's childhood and later life, Forster is fascinated by the numerous intriguing qualities which Hindu legends have attributed to the god. In Krishna's childhood he sees a picture of familiar human activity, warmth and fun, and remembering the celebrations of Gokul Ashtami at Dewas he find meaning in his own bewildered observations of the past:

'Various and wonderful instruments are played when he is born' and the sportive cowboys 'smear one another with butter' as we did. In infancy he and his brother 'drag their feet with the tinkling sounds of ornaments on them through the moist places and looked beautiful with their limbs besmeared with mire'. He steals trifles, he 'commits nuisance in the premise of the house', then 'stands like a very quiet boy'. He even eats earth and dirt; 'look in my mouth, then' he says, and 'the whole Universe of mobile and immobile creatures is seen inside it'. As he grows up he goes with his friends to the fields and woods, breakfasts by a stream while the cows stray, eats while they sit around him, 'his flute between his belly and his garment, the soft morsel in the left hand and fruits between his fingers walled in by his comrades, and laughing and making them laugh'. 'He, the one deity of all sacrifices, exhibiting the gaiety of lads, while the celestial world looked on'. 'Thy glory purifies all the world' sing the bees. They dance, sing, fight, imitate birds and animals, and when he is tired he 'goes beneath a tree and rests on beds of tender leaves, with his head cushioned on a herdsboy's thigh'. The frivolity, triviality goes on, and every now and then it cracks, as at our festival, and discloses depths.[63]

Some of Forster's later accounts[64] show that the complex legends
associated with Krishna have a deeper appeal for his imagination. He sees
that there are discrepancies in the many legends: 'How is it that the warrior
who drives Arjuna into battle and lectures him *en route* on the nature of the
universe is also a dark-skinned cowboy who seduces hundreds of cow-
girls?'[65] – but the discrepancies are the result of an interesting mixture of
two popular traditions of Krishna worship. There is an old tradition which
conceived of the god of the *Mahabharata*, the warrior, as the incarnation of
Vishnu; there is also a later tradition which grew around 'a godling of a
group of cattle-keepers in the Jumna valley'.[66] The god of the *Mahabharata*
is profound, while the godling in the legend of the cattle-keepers is
essentially mundane –

> cheerful, disrespectful to the priesthood and to his elders, scandalously
> amorous . . . [he] was tidied up in two directions – one social, the other
> mystic. Socially he became a king, who was legally married to hundreds
> of queens and was consequently respectable. Mystically, his amours – or
> rather the longings that were felt for him – symbolized the longings of
> the soul for God.[67]

The way the two traditions have coalesced to make Krishna a complex and
intriguing figure appeals to Forster, and he looks at Krishna not only as the
most versatile god in the Hindu pantheon, but also as the form of godhood
most congenial to his imagination:

> Warrior, counsellor, randy villager, divine principle, flautist, great king:
> these are some of Krishna's aspects, and to them must be added the
> destroyer of dragons, the Hercules–Siegfried hero who makes the earth
> habitable for men. It is no wonder that in India so varied a deity
> exercises a wide appeal. Hindu religion has the high distinction of being
> non-propagandist. But if it abandoned that distinction, as Buddhism in
> Ceylon appears to be doing, and competed with Christianity and Islam
> as the unique representative of Truth, it might well push Krishna
> forward as its champion. There is no one in its contemporary pantheon,
> neither Siva nor Durga, who would function nearly as well.[68]

Krishna's attractions may not have inspired in him an actual belief in
the Hindu god,[69] in the place of his disbelief in Christ, but it has evidently
made Hinduism more endearing for Forster than Christianity. He sees that
the Hindu conception of Krishna includes, apart from ideas about the
immortal life, some familiar truths of day to day life like pleasure, fun and
personal love, and that is why the idea of Krishna is nearer to him than the
idea of Christ. 'It may seem absurd to turn from Christ to Krishna', he says
in an account of his own personal outlook on religion, 'that vulgar blue-
faced boy with his romps and butter-pats: Krishna is usually a trivial

figure. But he does admit pleasure and fun and jokes and their connection with love. And in one of his aspects, that of charioteer to Arjuna, he manages to produce the most famous of the Indian's utterances.'[70]

Forster's inclination to Hinduism is also based on his appreciation of an essential significance in the tradition of Hindu temple art and architecture. His early accounts of Indian art and architecture showed his deep curiosity about some traditional monuments, and they also expressed his inability to understand the full significance of the elaborate and complicated architecture of the Hindu temple (although he had been impressed by the traditional style in a profound.way).[71] A more perceptive account is seen in his later studies on the subject.[72] As with his approaches to Hinduism in general, so with his approach to the tradition of Hindu art also: his understanding is achieved through a process of sustained personal interest and keen study.[73] His later writings on the subject emphasise that the essential significance of Hindu art lies in its portrayal of the experiences of life in their fullness—in its depiction of elements from the individual's mundane as well as spiritual experiences. He sees that the temple presents the idea of a synthesis. Its large and elaborately designed exterior, containing intriguing sculptures of all forms of life—gods, men and animals—and sculptures portraying spiritual as well as erotic themes, represents the complex panorama of creation that surrounds the individual. And in contrast to the complex exterior, the small, plain, dark interior of the temple signifies the individual's own inner life. In the inner cell, the individual has contact with nothing else but his god, of whom he, in his inner life, realises himself to be a part. This symbolical representation of the conceptions of the extensive and complex variety of life, and the sanctity of the individual's inner life, gives Forster an insight into the quality of completeness in Hindu spiritualism. He considers Hindu temple architecture as the manifestation of a valuable attitude to life, which looks at the immensity of creation and also emphasises that the individual and his inner life are at the centre of it.

Forster's point will be illustrated by a brief look at some main aspects of the Kandariya Mahadeva temple at Khajuraho which he visited in 1912 and 1921, and wrote about after the latter visit as 'one of the glories of India'. The architecture of this temple, one of the surviving twenty temples (originally a group of eighty-five, 1000 A.D.) at Khajuraho shows the culmination of the Indo-Aryan style, and it symbolises the traditional Hindu philosophical view of life. The temple is a compact structure, built on an elevated platform, and its exterior is composed of several smaller domical temple-like structures merging into each other in an ascending order, like the successive peaks of a mountain, to form one complete edifice. (To the outside view, there are elaborate sculptural decorations of all forms, including various representations in the friezes of erotic acts between men and women.)[74] The summit of the temple is above the innermost part of the shrine, which is the place of the deity, to be approached by the individual worshipper. Behind this arrangement is the Hindu philosophical idea that the temple represents Meru, the world-mountain, which connects earth with heaven. Its summit reaches towards the Highest Being, and worshipping in the shrine below the individual man, who is a part of the Highest Being, realises his own connection with Him. He sees the particular deity whom he worships as one of the forms of the Highest Being, directly present before him.

Reflecting on the Hindu thought of the individual man's direct participation in godhood, as the concept was revealed to him in the architecture of the temples at Khajuraho,[75] Forster writes:

> I became easier with the Indian temple as soon as I realised, or rather as soon as I was taught, that there often exists inside its complexity a tiny cavity, a central cell, where the individual may be alone with his god. There is a temple-group in the middle of India (the Khajuraho temples), once well known to me, which adopts this arrangement. The exterior of each temple respresents the world mountain, the Himalayas. Its topmost summit, the Everest of later days, is crowned by the sun, and round its flanks run all the complexity of life – people dying, dancing, fighting, loving – and creatures who are not human at all, or even earthly. That is the exterior. The interior is small, simple. It is only a cell where the worshipper can for a moment face what he believes. He worships at the heart of the world-mountain, inside the exterior complexity. And he is alone. Hinduism, unlike Christianity and Buddhism and Islam, does not invite him to meet his god congregationally; and this commends it to me.[76]

Forster affirms the value of Hindu spiritualism, looking at it as non-propagandist in outlook, and as centred upon the conception of the importance of the individual. He finds it meaningful not only in the context of his own personal belief in the individual but also in the context of the general situation of modern society. As society gets more and more regimented and totalitarian it tends to become oblivious of the individual man's existence as an individual. Religious and political propaganda drive the individual to seek his identity in the abstract conception of the community or state, and to lose his sense of his own real being and the truth of his inner life. Forster looks at this tendency as non-human. If having discarded Christianity he shows a deep personal inclination towards Hinduism, it is because he sees that Hinduism more than Christianity comprehends the individual man as a human as well as divine reality.[77]

Conclusion

Introducing a programme of talks called 'My Debt to India', broadcast by the B.B.C. during the Second World War, Forster remarked: 'I am not so foolish as to say that I understand your country. But I have good grounds to say that I love it'. He spoke of his own debt to India, recalling in particular his friendships with Syed Ross Masood, the Maharajah of Dewas Senior, and Sir Akbar[1] and Lady Hydari of Hyderabad: 'round these friendships there gathered opportunities for insight and for vision and for work'. India predominated in his creative life; his Indian friendships, his love of the vivacious Oriental way of life, his interest in India's ancient and flowing civilisation and in her modern social, political and economic developments – all provided meaning and inspiration to his work for over half a century.

His interpretations of India do not constitute an exclusive compartment in his total work as a writer but form an integral part of the whole body of his writings, reflecting a total vision of life which is also embodied in his non-Indian writings. His interest in Indian civilisation is related to his deep and sensitive feeling for the distinctive qualities and characteristics of various forms of human civilisations: it is the kind of interest which also inspired his earlier writings about Greece and Italy, and his book about Alexandria. He saw in the civilisation of India, as in these other great civilisations of the world, a concrete picture of a part of human society with many years of complex history and distinctive traditions of its own.

His continuing attentiveness to the social and political developments in modern India reflected his own fundamental concern for the growth and importance of a democratic society and his belief that through democracy individual men all over the world might find a fuller scope for development as individuals and thus come to understand one another better, and make human society happier. He greeted India as she became independent and, though the partition of the country made him sad, saw in the emergence of the new India as an independent democracy and a partner of the Commonwealth a realisation of his own conception of a human society based on racial and social equality. In modern India Indians, British and other non-Indians now live in a condition of racial equality (which could not be possible within the multi-racial society of imperial India, because it was undemocratic in character), just as do British, Indians, Pakistanis and other non-British people in present-day British society. The clouds of racial prejudice and authoritarianism may not have disappeared altogether from

either country, yet Forster saw in the free relationship between India and
Britain the possibility of a growing understanding between the two peoples
which had not been achieved in the past, and he saw in Indian democracy
and in the freedom of the Indian people the essential terms for the
realisation of that possibility. In his view all democratic peoples of the
world, if they were allowed to remain democratic and free from the
tyranny of totalitarianism and repression, might progress towards the
achievement of a better relationship between one another.[2]

Apart from showing his human interests Forster's India also reflects, on
the imaginative plane, his larger sense of life in its universal form. His work
does not necessarily include a full account of the complexities of
metropolitan India, since his concern is not for a 'total' picture in that
sense. But with its immensity, variety, contradictions and complexities of
human and non-human life, his vision of India reflects the deep mystery of
the creation as a whole: 'Perhaps life is a mystery . . . Perhaps the hundred
Indias . . . are one, and the universe they mirror is one'.

Appendix A

Forster's Tribute to Mahatma Gandhi

The organizers of this meeting [of Cambridge Majlis] have asked me, before I call on the principal speakers, to pay a short tribute myself. In doing so I do not desire to emphasize the note of grief. Grief is for those who knew Mahatma Gandhi personally, or who are close to his teaching. I have neither of these claims. Nor would it be seemly to speak with compassion and pity of him, as though it were on him rather than on India and the world that the blow has fallen. If I have understood him rightly, he was always indifferent to death. His work and the welfare of others was what mattered to him, and if the work could have been furthered by dying rather than living, he would have been content. He was accustomed to regard an interruption as an instrument, and he remarks in his *Autobiography* that God seldom intended for him what he had planned. And he would have regarded death, the supreme interruption, as an instrument and perhaps the supreme one – preferable to the full 125 years of life for which in his innocence he had hoped. The murder seems so hideous and senseless to us – as an English friend of mine put it, one would have liked that old saint to fade away magically. But we must remember that we are looking at it all from outside; it was not a defeat to him.

But although neither grief nor pity are in place this evening, we may well entertain a feeling of awe and a sense of our own smallness. When the news came to me last week, I realized intensely how small I was, how small those around me, how impotent and circumscribed are the lives of most of us spiritually, and how in comparison with that mature goodness the so-called great men of our age are no more than blustering school boys. Read the newspapers tomorrow, see what they advertise and whom, observe the values they imply and the actions they emphasize. Then think anew of the career and character of Mahatma Gandhi, and the feeling of awe will return with a salutary shock. We, to-day – we are inventive and adaptable, we are stoical and learning to bear things, our young men have acquired what may be termed the 'returned warrior' attitude, and that is all very well. But we are losing the sense of wonder. We are forgetting what human nature can do, and upon what a vast stage it is set. The death of this very great man may remind us, he has indicated by his existence the possibilities still to be explored.

His character was intricate, and this is not the place to analyse it. But all who met him, even the critical, have testified to the goodness in it, a goodness irradiated by no ordinary light. His practical teachings – the doctrine of non-violence and the doctrine of simplicity, symbolised by the spinning wheel – proceeded from that goodness, and it also inspired his willingness to suffer. He was not only good. He made good and ordinary men all over the world now look up to him in consequence. He has placed India on their spiritual map. It was always on that map for the student and scholar, but the ordinary man demands tangible evidence, spiritual proofs of moral firmness, and he has found them in the imprisonments, the fastings, the willingness to suffer, and in this death. The other day I passed a taxi-rank, and heard the drivers talking to one another about 'Old Gandhi' and praising him in their own way. He would have valued it more than any tribute the scholar or the student can bring. For it sprang from simplicity.

'A very great man' I have called him. He is likely to be the greatest of our century. Lenin is sometimes bracketed with him, but Lenin's kingdom was of this world, and we do not know yet what the world will do with it. Gandhi's was not. Though he impinged upon events and influenced politics, he had his roots outside time, and drew strength thence. He is with the founders of religion, whether he founds a religion or not. He is with the great artists, though art was not his medium. He is with all the men and women who have sought something in life that is neither chaos nor mechanism, who have not confused happiness with possessiveness, or victory with success, and who have believed in love.

(Reproduced from *Mahatma Gandhi: Essays and Reflections on His Life and Work, Together with a new Memorial Section*, ed. S. Radhakrishnan (London, 1949, pp. 386–8.)

Appendix B

Call Me A Non-Believer: Interview With E. M. Forster

Once again I had dropped in as before, but on this occasion it was midday; Mr. Forster looked immaculate in his morning suit and did not have to suffer another session of our dialogue in his pyjamas.

I began by asking about the late W. S. Blunt. I said I had been reading Blunt's Diaries [reviewed by Forster in 1920] and was greatly struck by his strong pro-Indian feelings in the early days of the Indian movement for self-government. Mr. Forster remembered his personal meeting with Wilfrid Blunt and described him as a 'very witty and entertaining man'. On my telling him how Blunt had once advised the late Mr. Gokhale to carry a couple of bombs in his pocket when he went to the India Office Mr. Forster laughed and remarked 'O yes, he was the sort of man who would say that . . . though he wouldn't have done it himself!'

Talking about the Indian political events of 1907–8 – the days when Gokhale was in London pleading for reforms – I expressed my doubts that Mr. Forster should at such a time have remained untouched by the events. I said: 'Mr. Forster, you say in your memorial essay on Syed Ross Masood that until you met him, i.e. until 1907 India was to you a vague jumble of rajahs, sahibs, babus and elephants, and that you were not interested in such a jumble. I find it difficult to take you seriously there. I find it difficult to believe that you were not interested in the political events that were then going on in India.'

Upon this Mr. Forster remarked: 'I don't think really I turned my attention to India in any important way in those days', and he confessed in reply to my subsequent questions that he never met Gokhale, Tilak or Edwin Montagu, and had no connexion with the Liberal Club of Cambridge: 'Never been very much interested in politics . . . incidentally, of course, I have.'

We then talked of the reception of *A Passage to India* when it was first published, and answering my curiosity to hear something more about Lord Reading's reactions Mr. Forster said: 'Lord Reading did not approve of me as far as he knew anything about me, I never met him myself.'

Continuing the topic of the British official reaction to the book I said in a lighter vein: 'Mr. Forster, I have heard it said somewhere that some British civil servants on their voyage to India took to reading your book with great interest, but once they had read it, it seems they all threw their copies into the sea!'

'Did they indeed! How good for the sea!' Mr. Forster interjected with laughter and added after a pause that 'it may only be gossip.'

'My book', Mr. Forster said, 'when it came out, attracted very little notice. I think in the *Nation* it was well reviewed. I read some conservative papers who just dismissed it as trivial. It was not condemned, not noticed, not given that attention. *The Morning Post* was non-favourable – didn't think it important enough to be denounced.'

What *The Times* thought – if it said anything at all about the book – Mr. Forster could not remember. (I discovered later that the review in *The Times Literary Supplement* was favourable though brief.) Mr. Forster agreed that he never wrote anything for *The Times* apart from a couple of letters and the personal tribute to the Maharajah of Dewas in which he wanted to correct some errors in the Maharajah's official obituary published in that paper. '*The Times* is not very important now as you know', Mr. Forster commented, and on my asking which papers he read he said, '*The Times*, generally, and *The Guardian*, a little.' While I was taking it down briskly, perhaps I gave Mr. Forster the impression that approaching him through politics I was entirely at the wrong end and, possibly to revert me to his central position, he remarked: 'But, as you know, my own trend is not political. I am looking for other things.'

We turned to talk briefly about Godbole and Fielding. When I suggested that Godbole might have the peculiar shrewdness and power of a Chitpavan Brahmin Mr. Forster appreciated the point, but to the question whether he had actually met Godbole's original at Dewas or elsewhere, Mr. Forster answered: 'I never met anyone like him. Godbole was mainly constructed by me. He was to a large extent a created character.'

Concerning Fielding I remarked that his sympathies with the Indians came particularly close to Sir Malcolm Darling's social sympathies, and I quoted Sir Malcolm's own comments about this idea ('That is going into rather deep waters', Sir Malcolm had told me in the course of a recent interview with him). Mr. Forster pondered for a moment and said: 'I don't think I thought of Darling when I was writing about Fielding.'

In the end our conversation turned on the question of Mr. Forster's unbelief. On my asking in what particular way Hugh Meredith had influenced his unbelief Mr. Forster remarked: 'Talking with him certainly influenced me. He became a professor at Belfast, as you know; he did a great deal of teaching and influencing people.'

The last question I picked on was a plain and straight one: 'Mr. Forster, you will be ninety in the New Year ("Yes, good heavens!" he interjected), do you still regard yourself as an unbeliever?'

'Yes,' replied Mr. Forster, 'I think I should call myself one.'

'Unbeliever?' I repeated.

'Yes, perhaps', answered Mr. Forster and halting for a moment corrected himself: 'Non-believer perhaps – a better description.'

'I thought you were inclined to believe in Krishna, Mr. Forster?'

'Not any more than any one else', Mr. Forster remarked and (somewhat hopefully for me) added: 'I like things about Krishna worship.'

(This account of my interview with Forster in July 1968 was first published as 'Call Me An Unbeliever: Interview With E. M. Forster', *The Statesman*, Calcutta, 23 September 1968.)

Notes

1 'The Indian Boom', *Daily News and Leader*, 2 February 1915, p. 7.
2 See 'Hymn Before Action', *Abinger Harvest*, pp. 380–1. Dated 1912, 'Hymn Before Action' is Forster's first complete piece of writing on an Indian subject. Brief references to Hindu, Buddhist and Islamic mythologies are seen however in a short story, written earlier – see 'Mr. Andrews' (1911), *Collected Short Stories of E. M. Forster* (London, 1948) pp. 184–5.

In 'Hymn Before Action' Forster points out that Krishna's ideas that death is negligible, being a passage to rebirth, and that man must renounce thought of the fruits of action but not action itself, are unknown to Christianity and the Westerner. It is interesting to contrast Forster's 'Hymn Before Action' with Kipling's poem of the same name (1896). The latter shows an essentially Christian consciousness, while Forster's piece shows his characteristically non-Christian outlook.

3 Forster has observed that the meaning of traditional Hindu art and architecture was not understood by him in the first instance. Of the architecture of Ellora caves and the temples of Khajuraho he says in an earlier article:

> The Indian artist . . . has covered vast surfaces with seething blobs of figures which indifferently beckon to each other, to the architecture, and to the visitor, until all the universe reels and coalesces. Isolate these figures in museums, photograph or frame them, and you will get a result that is often interesting and sometimes beautiful, but you will be telling Vishnu that he is Vishnu and nothing else, and Siva that he cannot both create and destroy . . . (*The Athenaeum*, 21 May 1920, pp. 667–8)

Forster's appreciation of Indian temple architecture developed with his increasing acquaintance with the spiritual element in Indian tradition.

4 The name 'Vikramaditya', meaning 'the sun of power', was adopted by several Hindu kings in ancient India. Among them Chandragupta II (Chandragupta Vikramaditya), who ascended the throne of the Guptas about 375 A.D., is the most celebrated name. Forster writes elsewhere about the great achievements of the Gupta period. (See 'The Art and Architecture of India', *Listener*, 10 September 1953, pp. 419–21.)

Kalidas, the author of *Sakuntala*, *Vikramorvasi* (plays), *Malavikagnimitra, Raghuvamsa, Kumarasambhava* (epics), and *Meghaduta* (lyrical poem), is among the most celebrated poets of ancient Sanskrit literature. The first English translation of *Sakuntala* by Sir William Jones, which appeared in 1789, made Kalidas familiar to British scholars. Forster describes *Sakuntala* (a special version prepared for the English stage) as 'august . . . humorous, enchanted, gracious'. (See 'The Golden Peak', *The Athenaeum*, 14 May 1920, pp. 631–2; see also, 28 November 1919, p.

1267, where Forster remarks that the action of the play *Sakuntala* is 'human and amusing, and the atmosphere not so much religious as fanciful'.)

5 *Abinger Harvest*, pp. 338–41. The city of Ujjain, the river Sipra and the religious fairs are all introduced into Forster's picture of India in *A Passage to India* (see ch. ix, p. 109).

6 The one Indian city which Forster describes with complete delight is Jodhpur, the city of the Rajputs. 'The civilization of Jodhpur, though limited', he writes,

> has never ceased to grow. It has not spread far or excelled in the arts, but it is as surely alive as the civilization of Agra is dead. Not as a poignant memory does it touch the heart of the son or the stranger. And when it does die, may it find a death complete and unbroken; may it never survive archaeologically, or hear, like Delhi, the trumpets of an official resurrection. (*Abinger Harvest*, p. 348)

7 See 'Advance India!', *Abinger Harvest*, p. 342.

8 Ibid., p. 343.

9 The Indian National Congress resolution of 1906 protested against the partition of Bengal, and called for the launching of the Swadeshi and boycott movement. (See 'Resolutions of the Congress of 1906', in C. H. Philips *et al.* (eds), *The Evolution of India and Pakistan – 1885 to 1945: Select Documents*, London, 1962, pp. 159–60.)

10 *Abinger Harvest*, p. 344.

11 See Indian Diary: Aurangabad, 27 March 1913, in the E. M. Forster archive of King's College, Cambridge.

12 'The Mission of Hinduism', *Daily News and Leader*, 30 April 1915, p. 7.

Chapter 2

1 (i) 'Reflections in India, I: Too Late?' 21 January 1922, pp. 614–15; unsigned. (ii) 'Reflections in India, II: The Prince's Progress', 28 January 1922, pp. 644–6; unsigned. (iii) 'The Mind of the Indian Native State', 29 April, 13 May 1922, pp. 146–7, 216–17; unsigned. (Reprinted in *Abinger Harvest*, 1936, pp. 368–79.) (iv) 'India and the Turk', 30 September 1922, pp. 844–5; signed F.

These anonymous contributions to *The Nation and the Athenaeum* have been identified as Forster's by B. J. Kirkpatrick in *A Bibliography of E. M. Forster* (London, 1968).

2 *The Hill of Devi*, p. 56.

3 Inaugurated after the special session of the Indian National Congress held in Calcutta in September 1920.

4 See the MSS. of *A Passage to India*, B95.

5 *The Hill of Devi*, p. 76.

6 Ibid., pp. 91–2.

7 Ibid., p. 155.

8 Ibid., pp. 137, 67, 136.

9 See *Census of India, 1921*, vol. xiii, 'Central India Agency: Report and Tables', by Lt Col. C. E. Luard, C.I.E., Superintendent of Census Operations (Calcutta, 1923) pp. 5–7.

10 Cf. *The Hill of Devi*, pp. 143–4.

11 *Imperial Gazetteer of India* (published under the authority of His Majesty's Secretary of State for India in Council, Oxford, 1908) vol. XI, pp. 279–80.

12 Sir Malcolm Darling, *Apprentice to Power: India, 1904–1908* (London, 1966) pp. 172–3.

13 Ibid., p. 145.

14 Cf. *The Hill of Devi*, pp. 21–4, 27–8.

15 Ibid., p. 67.

16 Ibid., p. 91.

17 Ibid., pp. 86–7.

18 Ibid., p. 100.

19 Ibid., pp. 135–6.

20 Ibid., p. 137.

21 Ibid., p. 168.

22 Ibid., p. 174.

23 S. Gopal, *The Viceroyalty of Lord Irwin 1926–1931* (Oxford, 1957) pp. 123–4.

24 *Abinger Harvest*, p. 371. Forster refers to the exaggerated 'Dessera budget'. 'Dessera', 'Dassera' or 'Dussera' is one of the annual Hindu festivals, and is celebrated in varied manner and with varied significance throughout India. Forster writes about its origin and celebrations in Dewas:

The Festival is – in its origin – a military review held at the end of the Rains, when war under old conditions again became possible, and since everything in India takes a religious tinge, it has turned into a general worship of implements, and of the collective power of the State. I should enjoy it were the State not in debt, but with a heavy load round one's neck it seems so inappropriate.' (*The Hill of Devi*, p. 138)

25 *Abinger Harvest*, pp. 371–2.

26 Ibid., p. 372.

27 *The Hill of Devi*, p. 87.

28 *Abinger Harvest*, p. 370.

29 Ibid., pp. 369–70.

30 *The Hill of Devi*, p. 39.

31 Ibid., p. 124.

32 Percival Spear, *India, Pakistan and the West* (London, 1961) pp. 138–9.

33 *Abinger Harvest*, pp. 368–9.

34 *Report on Indian Constitutional Reforms* (London, 1918) p. 129.

35 Reported in *The Times*, 12 November 1919, p. 13.

36 *Abinger Harvest*, p. 374. In 1922 the princes wanted stronger measures of protection than they had enjoyed before, and Lord Reading, the Viceroy, going against the wishes of the Legislative Assembly, certified a special Bill to give them additional protection. 'The action of the Viceroy clearly disturbed the Assembly today . . .', it was reported in London, 'the Press Bill was passed as a certified measure by the Council of State today without a division'. (See *The Times*, 26, 27 September 1922, p. 9.)

37 See *The British Crown and the Indian States: An outline sketch drawn up on behalf of the Standing Committee of the Chamber of Princes*, by the Directorate of the Chamber's special organization (London, 1929) pp. xxiii–xxiv.

The Treaty of 1818, Article 3, under which Dewas received protection from the British Government (mentioned by Forster, *The Hill of Devi*, p. 38), includes the following interesting passages:

The British Government will protect the Rajahs of Dewas in their present possessions . . . The British Government will further protect the Rajahs of Dewas against the attacks of enemies, and will aid them in the settlement of any of their rebellious subjects, and will mediate in a just and amicable manner any dispute that may arise between them and other States and petty Chiefs. (Cited in *The British Crown and the Indian States*, pp. 217–18.)

By the treaty, the senior and the junior branches of the state were together required to provide 'a contingent of 50 horse and 50 foot to be at the disposal of the British Government, in return for the guarantee of protection. In 1827 the contingent was raised to 75 horse and 200 foot. This obligation was afterwards commuted to an annual contribution of Rs. 28474-9-2' (*The British Crown and the Indian States*, p. 231).

38 *Abinger Harvest*, pp. 373–4.
39 Ibid., p. 370.
40 Ibid., p. 375.
41 *The Hill of Devi*, pp. 25–6.
42 Ibid., p. 55.
43 Sir Valentine Chirol's complimentary account of the Maharajah of Dewas appeared in his articles in *The Times* on the subject of Indian unrest and was later reprinted in his book, *Indian Unrest* (London, 1910). As cited in this book (pp. 192–3), the Maharajah, 'one of the most enlightened of the younger Hindu Chiefs', had thus written to the Viceroy in answer to a communication on the problem of unrest:

It is a well known fact that the endeavours of the seditious party are directed not only against the Paramount Power, but against all constructed forms of government in India, through an absolutely misunderstood sense of 'patriotism', and through an attachment to the popular idea of 'government by the people', when every level-headed Indian must admit that India generally has not in any way shown its fitness for a popular government.

Sir Valentine Chirol remarked that the Maharajah 'goes so far as to state his personal conviction that history and all "sound-minded" people agree that India cannot really attain to the standard of popular government as understood by the West'.

44 *The Hill of Devi*, p. 76.
45 Ibid., p. 124.
46 Ibid., p. 159.
47 *Abinger Harvest*, p. 376.
48 Ibid., p. 377.
49 Jawaharlal Nehru, *The Discovery of India* (London, 1956) pp. 306, 312.
50 *Abinger Harvest*, p. 369. Frederick Lugard was known for his ideas of 'indirect rule' and had also put them into effect in Nigeria, where he was the Governor-General (1912–19). Cf. *The Concept of Empire: Burke to Attlee 1774–1947*, ed. George

Bennett (London, 1953) p. 394.
　51 *Abinger Harvest*, p. 378.
　52 Ibid.
　53 Ibid., p. 379.

Chapter 3

　1　21, 28 January and 30 September 1922.
　2　Among the critics who have attempted to look at aspects of Forster as an interpreter of India, the tendency is to read *A Passage to India* as Forster's only document on India, and they regard it as an unsatisfactory and distorted account. For example, Nirad C. Chaudhuri ('Passage to and from India', *Encounter*, II June 1954, pp. 20–1) says:

> Mr. Forster chose the sector of which he had personal knowledge. As an Englishman paying a short visit to India, he naturally saw far less of India in general than of his own countrymen and of the Indians with whom the latter had official business or perfunctory social relations . . . he could not observe the larger and the more important area without going considerably out of his way and making a special effort.
>
> He had not chosen his Indian types happily. In regard to the Hindu characters, he relied mostly on the types found in the Princely States. Certainly they were more traditional than those in British India, but they were so traditional that they did not represent modern India at all.

Similarly, Andrew Shonfield ('The Politics of Forster's India', *Encounter*, XXX January 1968, pp. 62–9) restricts his study to *A Passage to India* alone and writes:

> As an account of something which purports to be typical of Imperial India, the picture distorts . . .

One gets the impression that Forster had little understanding and no sympathy for the complicated and courageous politics of the Indian independence movement. He was aware of it all right, but insisted on treating it like noises off.
　3　Cf. 'Reflections in India', *The Nation and the Athenaeum*, 28 January 1922, pp. 645–6.
　4　*The Nation and the Athenaeum*, 21 January 1922, p. 614.
　5　On 13 April 1919, under General Reginald Dyer's command, armed soldiers fired on an enormous Indian crowd that had gathered at Jallianwala Bagh, Amritsar, to protest against repressive Government legislations. As many as 379 Indians were killed, and about 1200 were wounded. The impact of the event on the rise of the Indian national agitation, and Forster's reaction to it, are discussed in the next chapter.
　6　Dismemberment of the Turkish Empire was proposed under the Treaty of Sèvres (published in May 1920) to which Britain, as an Allied power, was a party, and this was taken by the Muslims in India as a violation of the Khalif's sovereignty and of Islam. They launched the 'Khilafat movement' protesting against the British Government's part in the Treaty.

7 The resolution on the Non-cooperation movement passed on 30 December 1920 at the Nagpur session of the Indian National Congress claimed the establishment of 'swaraj' within one year.

8 *The Hill of Devi*, p. 155.

9 See *Report on Indian Constitutional Reforms*, p. 276.

10 *The Nation and the Athenaeum*, 21 January 1922, p. 614.

11 Ibid.

12 Ibid.

13 Ibid.

14 See *Goldsworthy Lowes Dickinson*, p. 141. Lowes Dickinson had written to H. O. Meredith in January 1913: 'Why can't the races meet? Simply because the Indians *bore* the English. *That* is the simple adamantine fact.' Disagreeing with this, Forster says: 'I disagree with the last paragraph. Perhaps he was overtired, perhaps temperamentally averse, but he never found in Indian society either the happiness or the peacefulness which have made my own visits to the country so wonderful.'

15 *The Nation and the Athenaeum*, 21 January 1922, p. 615.

16 See 'Mem-Sahib's Point of View' (anonymous article), *Cornhill Magazine*, XLVIII (May 1920) 590–9.

17 *The Nation and the Athenaeum*, 21 January 1922, p. 615.

18 Ibid.

19 The Government of India Act of 1919 providing for constitutional reforms introduced 'a new policy' towards India. Its aim was the establishment of 'responsible government' in India by a gradual process of associating the Indians with ministerial responsibilities and by a progressive 'Indianisation' of the Civil Service. (Cf. 'A New Policy', *Report on Indian Constitutional Reforms*, p. 6.)

20 The Secretary of State for India visited and toured in India at the end of 1917, and drafted the *Report on Indian Constitutional Reforms*, which subsequently formed the Government of India Act of 1919. The Duke of Connaught, representing the King-Emperor, visited in the beginning of 1921 and inaugurated the newly constituted Indian Parliament. At the end of the same year the Prince of Wales, about whose visit Forster reported in detail, was also in India, pleading for goodwill and better Indo-British relations.

21 *The Nation and the Athenaeum*, 21 January 1922, p. 614.

22 Surendranath Banerjea (1848–1925) was member of the I.C.S. from which he was dismissed in 1874, teacher, journalist, liberal nationalist leader, President of the Indian National Congress in 1895 and 1902, minister for local self-government 1921–3, and author of *A Nation in Making* (London, 1925).

23 See *A Nation in Making* (Calcutta, 1963) pp. 311–21.

24 See Gandhi's letter, written about the time of Forster's article, published in *Amrit Bazar Patrika*, 2 February 1921, and cited in *The Collected Works of Mahatma Gandhi*, XIX (Delhi, 1966) pp. 310–12.

25 See *The Longest Journey*, Ch. XVII, p. 183.

26 See *Egypt*, published by the Labour Research Department (London, 1920).

27 *Abinger Harvest*, p. 315.

28 See Wilfrid S. Blunt, *My Diaries, Part II: 1900–1914* (London 1920) p. 408. During a conversation between Forster and the author at King's College, Cambridge, on 5 July 1968 (published in *The Stateman*, Calcutta, 23 September 1968, as 'Call Me an Unbeliever: Interview with E. M. Forster') Forster said about Wilfrid Blunt that he was 'a very witty and entertaining man', and, on the author's

talking about Blunt's pro-Indian sentiments and his advice to Gokhale about taking bombs to the India Office, added: 'O yes he was the sort of man who would say that . . . though he wouldn't have done it himself!'

29 Chapter XIII, p. 118.

30 *Daily News and Leader*, 2 February 1915, p. 7.

31 See *St. Antony's Papers, No. 8*, ed. Raghavan Iyer (London, 1960) pp. 9–71.

32 Ibid., pp. 70–1.

33 See Burke's speech on Fox's East India Bill cited in Bennett (ed.), *The Concept of Empire*, pp. 51–4.

34 Cf. ibid., pp. 63–4. The governor-generalship of Marquess Wellesley (1798–1805) was decisive in the extension of British power in India.

35 See ibid., pp. 354–7. Lord Curzon was Under-Secretary for India 1891–2, Viceroy 1899–1905, Lord President of the Council and member of the War Cabinet 1916–18, and Foreign Secretary 1919–24.

36 *Howards End*, ch. IV, p. 31.

37 Ibid., pp. 29–30.

38 Ibid., p. 29.

39 Ibid., p. 31.

40 Ibid., pp. 31–2.

41 Cf. 'The Gods of India', *New Weekly*, 30 May 1914, p. 338. Forster writes:

The Hindu is concerned not with conduct, but with vision. To realise what God is seems more important than to do what God wants. He has a constant sense of *the unseen* – of the powers around if he is a peasant, of the power behind if he is a philosopher, and he feels that this tangible world, with its chatter of right and wrong, subserves the intangible . . . (my italics)

42 *Two Cheers for Democracy*, p. 68.

43 *Original Letters from India (1779–1815): Mrs. Eliza Fay* (London, 1925) p. 20.

44 Cited in Eric Stokes, *The English Utilitarians and India* (Oxford, 1959) p. 13.

45 Apart from Bentham's direct influence on the governor-general and other men in high places in the East India Company's service, Eric Stokes observes that Benthamite ideas were being disseminated amongst the young Indian civilians at their training at Haileybury College (see ibid., pp. 51–2).

46 Ibid., p. 48.

47 Cited in ibid., pp. 53–4.

48 Ibid., p. 57.

49 Cf. ibid., pp. 48–9. John Stuart Mill joined as a clerk at the East India House in 1823 and rose to become chief of office in 1856. He opposed the Act in 1858 ending the Company's rule in India, and drew up the Company's petition against it to the Parliament. Declining to serve on the new Council for India under the Government, he retired on a pension.

50 Spear, *India, Pakistan and the West*, p. 159.

51 *Howards End*, ch. XII, p. 342.

52 The Earl of Cromer was member of Viceroy's Council in India 1880–3, and British Agent and Consul-General in Egypt 1883–1907.

After long service in Egypt and South Africa, Alfred, Viscount Milner was appointed member of Lloyd George's war cabinet 1916–18, Secretary of State for

War 1918, and Colonial Secretary 1918–21.

53 See Macaulay's Minute on Education cited in G. O. Trevelyan, *The Competitionwallah* (London, 1864) pp. 410–24.

54 *Listener*, 10 September 1953, p. 419.

55 *Egypt*, p. 4.

56 Ibid., p. 8.

57 Cf. Bennett (ed.), *The Concept of Empire*, pp. 352, 359.

58 *Howards End*, ch. xxiv, p. 215.

59 *The Nation and the Athenaeum*, 21 January 1922, p. 614.

60 See Forster's introduction to K. R. Srinivasa Iyengar, *Literature and Authorship in India* (London, 1943) p. 7. About the British Empire Exhibition at Wembley in 1924 Forster had written slightingly in 'The Birth of an Empire', *Abinger Harvest*, pp. 56–60.

61 *Report of the Church Missionary Society, III* (London, 1812), cited in Standish Meacham, *Henry Thornton of Clapham* (Cambridge, Mass., 1964) p. 128.

62 Cited in Stokes, *The English Utilitarians and India*, p. 31.

63 Cited in Bennett (ed.), *The Concept of Empire*, p. 101.

64 Cited in Iyer (ed.), *St. Antony's Papers, No. 8*, p. 44.

65 Unhappy over the continuing conflicts between Turkey and the Allied Powers after the First World War, Forster particularly criticised Britain's encouragement of the Greek aggressions in 1921–2, and wrote:

It is Great Britain, the protector of Islam, who appears as a solitary crusader, whose troops remain in Chanak, whose fleet holds the straits, and whose Ministers assert that the British Empire stands behind them.

That is how the present crisis will present itself to an Indian Mohammedan. What are we to say to him? What explanation shall we rig up next? . . . If it is not Christian fanaticism, then what is it? Our Government can make no reply. ('India and the Turk', *The Nation and the Athenaeum*, 30 September 1922, pp. 844–5).

66 'Missionaries', ibid., October 1920, p. 545.

67 Ibid., p. 546.

68 Ibid., p. 545.

69 Ibid., pp. 546–7.

70 Ibid.

71 Chapter iv, pp. 40–1.

72 *The Nation and the Athenaeum*, October 1920, p. 545.

73 *The Men Who Ruled India: II The Guardians* (London, 1965) p. 15.

74 Ibid., p. 76.

75 L. S. S. O'Malley, *The Indian Civil Service 1601–1930* (London, 1931) p. 207.

76 Lord Curzon said in his budget speech in 1904 that

the highest ranks of civil employment in India, those in the Imperial Civil Service, though open to such Indians as can proceed to England and pass the requisite tests, must, nevertheless, as a general rule, be held by Englishmen, for the reason that they possess, partly by heredity, partly by upbringing, and partly by education, the knowledge of the principles of government, the habits of mind, and the vigour of character, which are essential for the task, and that, the rule of

India being a British rule, and any other rule being in the circumstances of the case impossible, the tone and standard should be set by those who have created and are responsible for it. (Cited in O'Malley, ibid., p. 225)

The Reforms of 1919, under which an increasing number of Indians were to be admitted to the Service, made the I.C.S. unpopular among many British members and future aspirants from Britain. 'Forty officers from two services alone had already applied for leave to retire because of reforms', reported *The Times* on 13 February 1922. 'Eight officers appointed from England to the Civil Service had resigned their appointments before assuming them. Out of 86 candidates at the last examination only 26 were British, and of these three only were successful as against 13 Indians.' 'Premature retirement has become a normal incident of service', says O'Malley (*Indian Civil Service 1601–1930*, p. 148),

and up to the present one man out of every ten has exercised the right to retire on proportionate pension. The number of men who retired prematurely was relatively greater during the early years of the Reforms scheme, viz., one in six up to the end of 1923; and many others who had already completed twenty-five years of service also preferred to retire rather than continue under the new conditions.

77 Woodruff, *The Men Who Ruled India: The Guardians*, p. 17.

78 *A Passage to India*, ch. IX, p. 116.

79 *Goldsworthy Lowes Dickinson*, p. 34. Attention to this significant remark by Forster on Plato is drawn in J. B. Beer, *The Achievement of E. M. Forster* (London, 1962) pp. 35–6.

80 Woodruff, *The Men Who Ruled India: The Guardians*, p. 74.

81 *Daily News and Leader*, 2 February 1915, p. 7.

82 Forster's criticism of the public school background of the Englishman abroad is seen in detail in his the 'Notes on the English Character', *Abinger Harvest*, pp. 12–13. In *A Passage to India* (ch. V, p. 54) Ronny's 'public-school days' are remembered by Mrs Moore at the sight of his officialism and indifference.

83 Darling, *Apprentice to Power*, p. 45.

84 Ibid., p. 47.

85 Ibid., p. 38.

86 Ibid., p. 116.

87 About the Anglo-Indian officials who were in Egypt, Forster observes: 'Some of the officials have served previously in India; such may be useful for their administrative qualities, but they, and still more their women-folk, introduce a racial arrogance, from which the regular Anglo-Egyptian officials are free' (*Egypt*, p. 4).

88 Cf. *The Hill of Devi*, pp. 74–6.

89 Ibid., p. 131.

90 *Abinger Harvest*, p. 315.

91 Ibid., p. 23.

92 *The Nation and the Athenaeum*, 28 January 1922, p. 646.

93 Michael O'Dwyer, Lieutenant-Governor of the Punjab, had supported the Rowlatt Acts (1919), under which the Government was given wide repressive powers against the revolutionaries, and he had also supported the enforcement of

martial law and General Dyer's massacre operation at Amritsar.

94 *A Passage to India*, ch. v, p. 53.

95 O'Malley, *The Indian Civil Service: 1601–1930*, p. xi.

96 *Observer*, 21 February 1954, p. 9.

97 Fielding too thought that 'Away from us, Indians go to seed at once' (*A Passage to India*, ch. xxxvii, p. 334), but his feeling for India was inspired by his desire for personal relations with the Indians untainted by officialdom or the love of imperial power.

98 'Did he seem to tolerate us, the brutal conqueror, the sun-dried bureaucrat, that sort of thing?' Ronny asks Mrs Moore about Aziz (*A Passage to India*, ch. iii, p. 35). 'To speak of Indian Civil Servants as "sun-dried bureaucrats" is', observes O'Malley, 'a common *cliché* of the Indian politicians and journalists, who frequently also refer to the whole system of government in India as a bureaucracy.' (*Indian Civil Service: 1601–1930*, p. 157.)

99 *A Passage to India*, ch. v, p. 54.

100 Cited in S. D. Waley, *Edwin Montagu: A Memoir and an Account of His Visits to India* (London, 1964) p. 292.

101 Cf. *The Nation and the Athenaeum*, 21 January 1922, p. 614.

102 Cited in *Collected Works of Mahatma Gandhi*, vol. xix, p. 311.

103 Ibid., pp. 206–7.

104 Cf. *East India (Progress and Report)*, H.M. Stationery Office (London, 1922) p. 49 ('The Duke's Appeal') and p. 89 (the Prince of Wales's reply to the Address of the Bombay Corporation).

105 See the Prince of Wales's letter of 1 January 1922 to Montagu, cited in S. D. Waley, *Edwin Montagu: A Memoir*, p. 262.

106 *The Nation and the Athenaeum*, 21 January 1922, pp. 614–15.

107 Forster describes himself as 'an individualist and a liberal' in 'What I believe', *Two Cheers for Democracy*, p. 85.

108 R. J. Moore, *Liberalism and Indian Politics, 1872–1922* (London, 1966) p. 121.

109 Ibid., p. 2.

110 From Fowler's speech of February 1900, cited in ibid., p. 64.

111 That the Morley–Minto Reforms were introduced with the purpose of reinforcing the British Raj in India rather than advancing the cause of self-government is indicated in the following correspondence between the Secretary of State for India and the Viceroy:

Morley: Reforms may not save the Raj, but if they don't nothing else will.
Minto: I must utterly disagree. The *Raj* will not disappear in India as long as the British race remains what it is, because we shall fight for the *Raj* as hard as we have ever fought, if it comes to fighting, and we shall win as we have always won.

Cited in ibid., p. 126.

112 *Report on Indian Constitutional Reforms*, p. 5.

113 *The Nation and the Athenaeum*, 21 January 1922, p. 615.

114 *Abinger Harvest*, p. 346.

115 See the MSS. of *A Passage to India*, A61.

116 *A Passage to India*, ch. xi, p. 122.

117 Founded in 1923.

118 Cited in Sitaramayya, *The History of the Indian National Congress, I. 1885–1935* (Bombay, 1935) p. 180.

119 *Collected Works of Mahatma Gandhi*, vol. XIX, pp. 311–12.

120 *The Nation and the Athenaeum*, 28 January 1922, p. 645.

121 Gandhi did not support the extremist nationalist aspiration for an India outside the British Empire. When the Congress of 1929 under the leadership of Jawaharlal Nehru and Subash Bose resolved that its goal was to achieve complete independence, it did so against Gandhi's wishes. (See Sitaramayya, *History of the Indian National Congress*, pp. 330–1.) Even in 1931, at the Round Table Conference in London, Gandhi was pleading for 'partnership' with Britain: 'I want to become a partner with Great Britain. I want to become a partner with the English people . . . I do not want to break the bond between England and India, but I do want to transform that bond . . .' (*Mahatma Gandhi: Essays on his Life and Work*, ed. S. Radhakrishnan, 2nd ed., London, 1949, pp. 513–14.)

Chapter 4

1 See 'Congress Resolution on Non-co-operation', *Collected Works of Mahatma Gandhi*, vol. XIX, pp. 576–8.

2 For some time detailed news about the massacre was not known in Britain. Excited controversy started when the findings of the Committee of Enquiry presided over by the Scottish High Court Judge, Lord Hunter, were made public in 1920, and when General Dyer, censured by the committee, was relieved of his post in India.

3 See *The Nation*, 17 July 1920, pp. 488–9. In a series of articles published during 1919–21 *The Nation* pointed to the atrocities in the Punjab and the way the situation had affected the British position in India. See, for example, the following issues: 26 April 1919 ('India at the Cross Roads'), 30 August 1919 ('Whither India'), 29 May 1920 ('Mr. Montagu's Gesture'), 17 July 1920 ('The Choice in India), 8 January 1921 ('After Ireland, India'), 16 July 1921 ('The Gathering Storm in India'), 6 August 1921 ('The Choice of Passivity') and 1 October 1921 ('A New Turn in India'). During 1922 *The Nation and the Athenaeum* published Forster's reports on the Indian situation, 'Reflections in India', etc.

4 *Two Cheers for Democracy*, p. 80.

5 *A Passage to India*, ch. XIV, p. 142. When Mrs Moore and Adela were journeying with Dr Aziz on the 'branch' railway to the Marabar caves, the reader is told, the mail train rushed past them 'connecting up important towns such as Calcutta and Lahore, where interesting events occur, and personalities are developed'.

6 The alleged charge against Aziz is that he 'made insulting advances' to Miss Quested (*A Passage to India*, ch. XVIII, p. 174). An early version of the story in the manuscript shows Dr Aziz actually attempting to molest her.

7 Examples of threatening Indian posters were quoted in the Hunter Committee Report. One poster said:

. . . We the Indians will fight to the death after you. The flag of cruelty and oppression has been fixed in the ground. Alas, British, how you have cheated us . . . You have fired on the Indians and shot them to death . . . The treatments meted out to our girls at Amritsar are unbearable and we cannot expose them. It is very sad, that all our brethren are keeping silent at this moment.

What time are you waiting for now? There are many [English] ladies to dishonour. Go all round India, clear the country of the ladies and those sinful creatures and then will be the only time when we can all say together, 'Blessed be the Hindus, Mohammedans, and Sikhs'.

(Cited in Michael O'Dwyer, *India as I Knew It: 1885–1925*, London, 1925, pp. 292–3.) O'Dwyer, Lieutenant-Governor of the Punjab at the time of the troubles at Amritsar, writes, 'How critical the situation was for the small British colony, and especially the women and children, till the troops arrived, may be gathered [from the above poster]'.

8 'Amritsar, By An Englishwoman', *Blackwood's Magazine*, no. MCCLIV, vol. CCVII (April 1920) 441–6.

9 The Rowlatt Acts, named after the Honourable Justice Sydney Rowlatt, President of the Sedition Committee appointed to investigate revolutionary conspiracies in India, gave the Government drastic powers to deal with the revolutionaries and anarchists.

10 *Blackwood's Magazine* (April 1920) 442–6. (The case of Miss Sherwood, who had been the victim of a brutal assault during the Amritsar disturbances, is discussed later in the course of this chapter.)

11 *A Passage to India*, ch. XX, pp. 188–94.

12 Ibid., ch. XXIV, p. 225.

13 The list includes: (i) General Dyer's 'crawling' order; (ii) General Campbell's 'salaaming' order; (iii) Colonel Frank Johnson's orders directing that the students of four (out of ten) colleges at Lahore should attend roll-calls four times a day to keep them from spreading sedition; (iv) the order of the same officer arresting and interning in the Fort for twenty-four hours from fifty to one hundred students of a college where the martial law orders had been disobeyed; (v) public floggings (whippings with a cane) at Lahore; (vi) 'fancy' punishments by Captain Doveton at Kasur, e.g. making convicted men touch the ground with their forehead (a traditional method of expressing repentance in the Punjab) and skipping, in lieu of whipping, fine and imprisonment, etc.

14 *The Nation*, 17 July 1920, enumerated practically all these punishments, and made a forceful criticism of the military rule in the Punjab under which they had been imposed.

15 See *The Times*, 27 May 1920, p. 13, and *The Nation*, 17 July 1920, p. 488.

16 *A Passage to India*, ch. XX, p. 191.

17 Cited in Hunter Committee Report, pp. 83–4.

18 The Hunter Committee quotes General Dyer stating that the 'salaaming order' was necessary in order to correct the 'tendency' in India 'to abolish respectfulness'. The Committee's hearing on this order is interesting:

Committee questioned: Is it not enforcing humiliation on the Indian people, to make them alight from their carriages to salaam an European officer? Does it not savour of that?

General Dyer: You perhaps put the other way. It is rather this way. I go to the other extreme in insisting on the ordinary salutations being paid.

Q. It was necessary to go to the other extreme?

A. Perhaps so.

Q.   For what purpose? What was the necessity for going to the other extreme and making this order?

A.   The tendency of the present day is to abolish respectfulness. The Indian father will tell you that sons are not respectful even to their parents.

Q.   The Indian young men are not following the ways of respectfulness and you therefore thought that you would improve them by going to the other extreme and enforcing this order?

A.   I say I did not pass this order. I generally agreed.

Q.   This is the ground on which you defend it? I put it to you; if an order of this sort is in force would it not create considerable resentment and bitterness among the people, and would not they feel humiliated?

A.   I do not know. The feeling of bitterness already existed.

Q.   You thought that was bitterness sufficient and therefore any order of humiliation could not add to the bitterness.

A.   I do not think its effect would be much.

19 *A Passage to India*, ch. ii, pp. 18–19. See also ch. v, p. 44, where Mrs Turton, the Collector's wife, disapproves of Indians driving into the grounds of the English club on the occasion of the 'bridge party', and says: 'They ought never to have been allowed to drive in; it's so bad for them.'

20 Ibid., ch. iii, p. 36. The Indian word 'izzat' means prestige.

21 Ibid., ch. xxxv, p. 312.

22 Ibid., ch. xx, p. 195.

23 Ibid., p. 191.

24 Apart from the mass public acclaim which General Dyer received there were also individual opinions which appeared in the British press stating that the General's action had saved the situation in India. For example, a correspondent in *The Times*, 20 December 1919, wrote:

Sir . . . I quote from a letter received from an officer who was present on the occasion. Every Englishman in India knows General Dyer saved the situation by his promptness. If his small force had been rushed the whole of Northern India would have been in a blaze in a week and a second Mutiny would have eventuated.

'An Englishwoman' (*Blackwood's Magazine*, April 1920, p. 446) also wrote in the same vein: 'No European who was at Amritsar or Lahore doubts that for some days there was a very real danger of the entire European population being massacred, and that General Dyer's action alone saved them.'

25 See the MSS. of *A Passage to India*, A212.

26 See the India Office Annual Report, *East India (Progress and Condition)* (London, 1922) p. 50.

27 Ibid., p. 49.

28 *The Nation and the Athenaeum*, 28 January 1922, p. 645.

29 Lord Reading, the Viceroy, was blamed for not taking drastic measures against the non-cooperators and the Moplahs who were responsible for the

widespread disturbances. Michael O'Dwyer (*India as I Knew It*, pp. 392–4) writes:

> Mr. Gandhi . . . joined hands with the Ali brothers in the so-called Hindu – Muslim *entente* and used the Punjab 'atrocities' and the Khilafat 'grievances' to stir up a subversive movement which for over two years caused bloodshed and disorder in every province in India, led to the serious rebellion of 1920–21, which cost at least ten thousand lives, and was finally suppressed only when, in 1922, the Government of India summoned up courage to enforce the law and bring the chief apostles of sedition and anarchy to tardy justice . . . it is no longer a secret that, after three years of painful experience it was the threat of resignation by two Governors that compelled Lord Reading's Government to enforce the law in 1922 against the arch-criminal, Gandhi.

30 Lord Hardinge of Penshurst, *My Indian Years: 1910–1916* (London, 1948) pp. 86–7.

31 See 'Indian Entries', *Encounter*, XVIII, no. 1 (January 1962) 26.

32 Asked by an interviewer of the *Daily Herald* to comment on the Treaty of Sèvres Gandhi said on 16 March 1921, advocating the cause of Khilafat and the Indian Muslims' interest,

> Khilafat is essentially a religious movement, being idealistic and unconnected with Turkish pacification. It derives its sanction directly from the injunction of the Prophet. Until, therefore, Indian Mussalmans are placated, there can be no peace, and the *sine qua non* of Mussalman conciliation is that what is termed the Island of Arabia must remain under the exclusive Mussalman control and under the spiritual sovereignty of the Khalifa, whoever he may be for the time being. The prestige of Islam demands rendition of Smyrna and Thrace for Turkey, and evacuation by the Allied Powers of Constantinople, but the existence of Islam demands the total abrogation of mandates taken by Britain and France. No influence, direct or indirect, over the Holy Places of Islam will ever be tolerated by Indian Mussalmans. (Cited in *Collected Works of Mahatma Gandhi*, vol. XIX, p. 444.)

33 Aziz's outburst against the Englishmen at the end of *A Passage to India* – 'We shall drive every blasted Englishman into the sea' – echoes the angry claim of the Khilafat extremists, pronounced especially in the speeches of Mohammed Ali, which the British found particularly offensive. Michael O'Dwyer (*India as I Knew It*, p. 402) writes that in one speech Mohammed Ali 'announced that the object of non-co-operation was to drive out from India the British thieves by the same aperture they had entered as thieves'. The India Office Annual Report, *East India (Progress and Condition)*, p.63, remarks on 'the series of violent speeches' delivered by the Ali brothers in support of 'the liberation of India from the British yoke'. The report states that 'Mohammed Ali, in the course of a singularly offensive speech at Madras, announced that Englishmen would soon be compelled to leave India'.

34 Forster notes (*The Nation and the Athenaeum*, 30 September 1922, p. 844) that Lord Reading, the Viceroy, sympathised with the grievance of Indian Muslims while the British Government did not. Lord Reading and Montagu, Secretary of State for India, pressed the British Government to negotiate the Turkish question favourably in the interest of peace in India. The Government however did not give

up its pro-Greek policies. In a crisis caused by the Khilafat issue Montagu had to resign his post (see S. D. Waley, *Edwin Montagu*, pp. 271-4). He and Lord Reading both happened to be Jews, and, as such, the feeling in anti-Khilafat circles was that they were partial to the Muslim cause against the Christian. In *A Passage to India* (ch. XXXVI, pp. 320-1) Ronny Heaslop seems to imply this viewpoint when, writing to Fielding about the happenings in British India, he blames the Jews: 'You are lucky to be out of British India at the present moment. Incident after incident, all due to propaganda, but we can't lay our hands on the connecting thread. The longer one lives here the more certain one gets that everything hangs together. My personal opinion is, it's the Jews.'

35 *The Nation and the Athenaeum*, 30 September 1922, p. 844. Sir Syed Ahmed Khan was grandfather of Forster's friend, Sir Syed Ross Masood.

36 Ibid.

37 Ibid.

38 Ibid., p. 845.

39 Ibid.

40 See the *Daily News*, 4 October 1922: 'Another Little War', by A. A. Milne, former Assistant Editor of *Punch*, author of *Winnie-the-Pooh*, *Mr. Pim Passes By*, *Belinda*, and *The Dover Road*. Opposing the British Government's war support for the Greeks against the Turkish national army A. A. Milne wrote in his article:

They have almost brought it off, the War to End Peace, for which they have been striving for three years. What an incredible joke! A war 'to defend the freedom of the Straits and the sanctity of our graves in Gallipoli'; says 'Punch' magnificently. Of course you can't think of it like that, and it sounds quite dignified and natural. But you may also think, as I do, of those five or ten or twenty men, our chosen statesmen; sitting round a table; the same old statesmen; each with his war-memories thick upon him; each knowing his own utter incompetence to maintain a war or to end a war; sitting round a table now, in 1922, and solemnly discussing another little war. Is it not an incredible joke? Does none of them laugh?

What was this war to be about? I read the papers, and I am told that we are to fight: (i) for England's honour; (ii) for the freedom of the Straits; (iii) for the sanctity of our graves in Gallipoli. 'The sanctity of our graves' – isn't that funny? They died, and only if others die will their graves be sanctified; otherwise we should forget them; otherwise God should not receive them; otherwise they did not die. Graves are sacred only when England occupies the earth in which they are dug. There were airmen who fell within the German boundaries; their graves, alas! are not sacred. Foolishly we allowed the Germans to keep that land. We should be occupying it . . .

41 Reprinted in *Abinger Harvest*, pp. 43-6.

42 Ibid.

43 Ibid.

44 *The Nation and the Athenaeum*, 30 September 1922, p. 845.

45 Under the Treaty of Lausanne signed on 24 July 1923 (replacing the Treaty of Sevres) Turkey regained control over parts of eastern Thrace and Constantinople, and the Straits were demilitarised. Turkey was proclaimed a republic on 29 October 1923.

46 *The Nation and the Athenaeum*, 30 September 1922, p. 845.

47 K. K. Aziz, *The Making of Pakistan: A Study in Nationalism* (London, 1967) p. 113.

48 *A Passage to India*, ch. IX, p. 111.

49 Ibid., ch. XXXVII, p. 335.

50 Ibid., ch. IX, p. 110. Mirza Ghalib (1796–1869), one of the most celebrated Urdu poets, wrote of Muslim glory in India, and has inspired a whole generation of poets.

51 Ibid., ch. XXXVII, p. 335.

52 Ibid., ch. XXIV, p. 222.

53 Ibid., ch. XXX, p. 276.

54 Ibid., ch. XIX, pp. 181–2.

55 Ibid., ch. XXXIV, p. 305.

56 Ibid., ch. XXXVII, p. 335.

57 Ibid., ch. XXX, p. 277.

58 Ibid., pp. 277–8.

59 Ibid., ch. IX, p. 111.

60 See the Calcutta Congress Resolution on Non-cooperation (September 1920), cited in Sitaramayya, *History of the Indian National Congress*, vol. I, pp. 200–3.

61 Tagore did not favour the policy of non-cooperation, but he had surrendered his knighthood in protest against the massacre at Amritsar.

62 The Swaraj Party, formed as a splinter group within the Congress under C. R. Das and Motilal Nehru, advocated the policy of 'obstruction' from within the Legislatures and other committees, as opposed to Gandhi's policy of total non-cooperation. After the All India Congress Committee meeting at Patna, the Swarajist group rejoined the Congress under a common programme.

63 See statements made to the court by Gandhi and Jawaharlal Nehru, cited in Sitaramayya, *History of the Indian National Congress*, vol. I, pp. 238, 250.

64 *A Passage to India*, ch. XXXVII, p. 334.

65 Ibid., ch. XXIV, p. 223.

66 Ibid., ch. XXXIV, 305.

67 Ibid., ch. XXXVII, p. 334.

68 Ibid., ch. XIX, p. 184.

69 See ibid., ch. XXXIV, p. 304.

70 Ibid., ch. XXXVII, p. 334. See also ch. XXXIV, p. 305, where Aziz is said to have 'had to drop inoculation and such Western whims . . .'

71 See *The Hill of Devi*, p. 76.

72 Ibid., p. 104.

73 Ibid., pp. 124–5.

74 See ibid., p. 130.

75 Ibid., p. 154.

76 The Prince of Wales arrived in India on 17 November 1921 and left at the end of the year.

77 *The Hill of Devi*, pp. 154–5.

78 21,28 January 1922 ('Reflections in India, I & II').

79 See 'Viceroy's speech on Non-co-operation', cited in *Collected Works of Mahatma Gandhi*, vol. XIX, p. 580.

80 See Lord Reading's reply to the deputation on the proposed Round-table Conference, 21 December 1921, cited in Syed Sirdar Ali Khan, *The Earl of Reading*

(London, 1924) pp. 262–8.

81 Cf. *East India (Progress and Condition)*, pp. 31–2, 57.

82 *The Nation and the Athenaeum*, 21 January 1922, p. 615.

83 Ibid., 28 January 1922, p. 645.

84 Welcoming the Prince of Wales on his arrival at Aden, Lord Reading sent the following message of loyalty and goodwill on behalf of India:

> On arrival of your Royal Highness at the first outpost of the Indian Empire, permit me to tender you a loyal and enthusiastic welcome to Indian waters and to express India's warmest wish that your approaching visit may be a memorable and continuous success worthy of the traditional courtesy and hospitality of India. (Reported in *The Times*, 15 November 1921)

85 *The Times*, Indian Supplement, 17 November 1921.

86 *The Nation and the Athenaeum*, 28 January 1922, p. 645.

87 *The Times* (Review of the Year: India), 31 December 1921.

88 Ibid.

89 *The Nation and the Athenaeum*, 28 January 1922, p. 645.

90 Ibid.

91 Cited in S. D. Waley, *Edwin Montagu*, pp. 263–4.

92 Ibid., pp. 262–3.

93 Cf. *Collected Works of Mahatma Gandhi*, vol. XIX, p. 171.

94 See Forster's tribute to Mahatma Gandhi, cited in Radhakrishnan (ed.), *Mahatma Gandhi: Essays and Reflections on his Life and Work*, p. 387.

95 *The Nation and the Athenaeum*, 28 January 1922, p. 645.

96 Ibid., p. 646.

97 *Abinger Harvest*, p. 379.

98 Information (from unpublished records in Forster's diary, 11 December 1921) given in a letter to the author from Mr P. N. Furbank, 24 August 1969.

Chapter 5

1 *The Nation and the Athenaeum*, 11 July 1925, p. 462. (Review of *My Piligrimages to Ajanta and Bagh* by S. M. C. Day.) Forster looked at India as a land of many cultures and civilisations mixed together, and yet thought 'Perhaps the hundred Indias which fuss and squabble so tiresomely are one . . .' (*A Passage to India*, ch. XXIX, p. 274.)

2 That one of Forster's main intentions in writing the novel was to 'describe' India is seen in his own note:

> I began this novel before my 1921 visit, and took out the opening chapters with me, with the intention of continuing them. But as soon as they were confronted with the country they purported to describe, they seemed to wilt and go dead and I could do nothing with them. I used to look at them of an evening in my room at Dewas, and felt only distaste and despair. The gap between India remembered and India experienced was too wide. When I got back to England the gap narrowed, and I was able to resume . . . (*The Hill of Devi*, p. 155)

3 An attempt to look at *A Passage to India* as a portrayal of a particular period in the history of British India is made in Allen Greenberger's *The British Image of India: A Study in the Literature of Imperialism* (London, 1969).

4 *Abinger Harvest*, p. 24. The article was written in 1920 – the year preceding Forster's second visit to India; and it was published closely following *A Passage to India*, in January 1926, in *Atlantic Monthly*, vol. 137, pp. 30–7.

5 Edmund Candler (1874–1926), Journalist, teacher and writer, was educated at Cambridge; he lived in India for many years, teaching in Orissa, Bengal and the Punjab, and also working as a journalist. During the days of the Non-cooperation movement he was in the Punjab appointed to the post of the director of publicity to the Provincial Government. Apart from *Abdication* (London, 1922), Candler is also the author of another political novel about India, *Siri Ram: Revolutionist* (1912). In his 'unconventional autobiography', *Youth and the East* (1932) he reflects on his many contacts with India – with his Indian students, as well as with national leaders like Gandhi.

6 Hilton Brown was in the Indian Civil Service. Apart from *Dismiss* (London, 1923), he also wrote *Maya*, *The Civilian's South India*, and was a contributor to *Punch*, *Blackwood's Magazine*, *Cornhill Magazine* and *Madras Mail*, etc.

7 Candler, *Abdication*, p. 21.

8 Ibid., p. 277.

9 Brown, *Dismiss*, p. 36.

10 Ibid., p. 98.

11 Edward John Thompson (1886–1946), educational missionary, journalist, historian and writer, spent a number of years in India (1910–22), teaching in Bengal and also, at a later stage, as correspondent for the *Manchester Guardian*, Apart from his novels about India he also wrote *Krishna Kumari*, a play with an Indian theme, *A History of India*, *The Reconstruction of India*, and *You Have Lived Through All This: An Anatomy of the Age*, which is dedicated to Jawaharlal Nehru.

12 Thompson, *An Indian Day*, p. 278.

13 Thompson, *A Farewell to India*, p. 117.

14 Al Carthill was the pseudonym of John Perronet Thompson (1873–1935), who was in the Indian Civil Service for many years, holding important official posts such as chief secretary to the Punjab Government 1916–21, member of the Reforms, 1918–19, political secretary to the Government of India 1922–7, and chief commissioner of Delhi 1928–32. Apart from *The Lost Dominion*, he is also the author of *The Legacy of Liberalism* (1924) and *India, the White Paper* (1933).

15 Michael O'Dwyer (1864–1940) retired from the Indian Civil Service as lieutenant-governor of the Punjab. The part played by him in the circumstances surrounding the Amritsar Massacre has been referred to in the fourth chapter.

16 Carthill, *The Lost Dominion*, p. 49.

17 Ibid., p. 69.

18 Ibid., p. v.

19 O'Dwyer, *India As I Knew It: 1885–1925*, p. 453.

20 Ibid., p. 451.

21 It is worth noticing that while the titles – 'Abdication', 'Dismiss', 'An Indian Day', 'A Farewell to India', 'The Lost Dominion', 'India As I Knew It' – all point to a past significance, 'A Passage to India' suggests a connection with the future, and with further possibilities.

22 *A Passage to India*, ch. XIV, p. 143.

23 Ibid., ch. III, p. 30.
24 Ibid., ch. XXIX, p. 270.
25 Ibid., ch. V, p. 55.
26 Ibid., ch. XXIII, p. 216.
27 Ibid., pp. 216–17.
28 Ibid., pp. 217–18.
29 Ibid., ch. XXIII, pp. 218–19.
30 Ibid., ch. V, p. 53.
31 Ibid., p. 43.
32 Ibid., ch. III, p. 29.
33 In a long newspaper correspondence on this question which appeared soon
after *A Passage to India* was published, E. A. Horne of the Indian Educational
Service, who had spent 'the last fourteen years of [his] life in Chandrapore [Patna]
itself', criticised Forster's portrayal of Anglo-Indians as unreal – showing an
ignorance of actual Anglo-Indian life and manners. He observed that Forster's
Indian characters were real enough; as for the Anglo-Indians, he remarked:

Where have they come from? What planet do they inhabit? One rubs one's eyes.
They are not even good caricatures, for an artist must see his original clearly
before he can successfully caricature it. They are puppets, simulacra. The only
two of them that come alive at all are Ronny, the young and rapidly becoming
starched civilian, and the light-hearted Miss Derek . . .
   And why is this? Why are these people and these incidents so wildly
improbable and unreal? The explanation is a singular but a simple
one. Mr. Forster went out to India to see and to study, and to make friends of
Indians. He did not go out to India to see Anglo-Indians; and most of what he
knows about them, their ways and their catchwords, and has put into his book,
he has picked up from the stale gossip of Indians, just as the average Englishman
who goes out to India picks up most of what he knows about Indians from
other Englishmen. It is a curious revenge that the Indian enjoys in the
pages of Mr. Forster's novel which profess to deal with Anglo-Indian life and
manners; and some would say a just one. All the same, it is a thousand pities that
Mr. Forster did not see the real Anglo-India, for he would have written an
incomparably better and truer book; and we venture to suggest to him, next time
he goes to India: 'Try seeing Anglo-Indians'. (*New Statesman*, 16 August 1924, p.
514)

It was pointed out also, by W. E. Butler, another correspondent on the same
subject, that Forster's book did not show an appreciation of 'the devotion shown by
officials to the native individuals'; one particular instance of such 'devotion' was
cited by this correspondent, relating to an example of a colonel in charge of an
Indian native regiment, who had asked his wife to come out to help while the men
in his regiment, in camp, were dying of cholera. 'She went at once and took the
child. The tide turned and the epidemic declined, but the baby caught the cholera
and one morning as reveille sounded it died.' (Ibid., 28 August 1924, p. 568)
34 *A Passage to India*, ch. VII, pp. 65–6.
35 Ibid., ch. XXXVII, p. 335.
36 See Andrew Shonfield, 'The Politics of Forster's India', *Encounter*, XXX, no. 1,
January 1968, pp. 62–9.

37 Prior to 1923 the Indian Criminal Procedure discriminated between the Indian and European communities on the ground of racial distinctions, and outside the Presidency towns of Calcutta, Bombay and Madras the subordinate Indian magistrate had no jurisdiction over the Europeans living in his area. In 1921 (during the months when Forster was visiting India, and writing for *The Nation and the Athenaeum* about the acute racial differences) the question of the existing racial distinctions in the Criminal Procedure Code was discussed in the Legislative Assembly, and a committee was set up under the chairmanship of the late Tej Bahadur Sapru to inquire and report on the situation. As a result of the recommendations of this committee, the Criminal Procedure was amended in 1923 and then for the first time outside the Presidency towns Indians and Europeans could be tried equally, by an Indian, irrespective of his magisterial rank.

38 Cf. *A Passage to India*, ch. xx, p. 191. Another reference to the change in imperial policy is seen in ch. xxxiv, p. 306:

A few years ago . . . the Political Agent . . . had been a formidable figure, descending with all the thunders of Empire when it was most inconvenient, turning the policy inside out, requiring motor-cars and tiger-hunts, trees cut down that impeded the view from the guest House, cows milked in his presence, and generally arrogating the control of internal affairs. But there had been a change of policy in high quarters. Local thunders were no longer endorsed . . .

39 After his third visit to India in 1945, Forster said in a broadcast talk on the B.B.C. Home Service:

You cannot understand the modern Indians unless you realize that politics occupy them passionately and constantly, that artistic problems, and even social problems – yes, and even economic problems – are subsidiary. Their attitude is 'first we must find the correct political solution, and then we can deal with other matters'. I think the attitude is unsound, and used to say so; still, there it is, and they hold it much more vehemently than they did a quarter of a century ago. (See *Two Cheers for Democracy*, pp. 327–8.)

Asked what political influence *A Passage to India* had 'on the "Indian question" of the time', Forster is reported to have said: 'It had some political influence – it caused people to think of the link between India and Britain and to doubt if that link was altogether of a healthy nature . . .' (See K. Natwar-Singh (ed.), *E. M. Forster: A Tribute, With Selections from His Writings on India*, New York, 1964, p. xiii.)

40 *A Passage to India*, ch. xxvii, p. 261.

41 Aziz's character disappoints the Indian critic, Nirad C. Chaudhuri, who thinks that Forster ought to have chosen for his protagonist in the novel an Indian of the stature of Rammohun Roy or Bankim Chandra Chatterji, to represent the true spirit, strength of character and generosity of the Indians who were responsible for building modern India. 'Aziz and his friends', Chaudhuri writes, 'belong to the servile section and are all inverted toadies. With such material, a searching history of the Muslim destiny in India could have been written but not a novel on

Indo–British relations, for which it was essential to have a Hindu protagonist' ('Passage To and From India', *Encounter*, 11, June 1954, p. 22).

Chaudhuri's criticism might have been apt if Forster's intention behind the portrayal of Aziz was to present the image of a great Indian national figure, and to present him within the specific context of Indo-British relations. But Forster's intention was apparently more modest: he has tried (not limiting his study to the particular environment of British India) to look at Aziz as a modern, average, individual Indian, whose mental qualities may not be highly extraordinary, but are deeply interesting and attractive for him personally.

42 See *A Passage to India*, ch. XXIV, p. 226. Forster's portrayal of 'the untouchable' inspired the writing of the courageous and powerful Indian novel, *Untouchable* (London, 1935), which deals with the life of the outcaste Indians. The author, Mulk Raj Anand, writes about his debt to Forster: 'I could not have started off writing my first book, *Untouchable*, if I had not noticed your own sympathy for the outcastes of India in your famous book after I had stayed in the Sabarmati Ashram of Mahatma Gandhi'.

43 *A Passage to India*, ch. XXIV, p. 226.

44 Cf. Forster's comment elsewhere: 'Naked I came into this world, naked I shall go out of it! And a very good thing too, for it reminds me that I am naked under my shirt, whatever its colour' (*Two Cheers for Democracy*, p. 85).

45 See 'Author's Notes', *A Passage to India*, p. xxix. (The notes were specially written for the Everyman's Library edition, London, 1965.)

46 *A Passage to India*, ch. I, p. 10.

47 Ibid.

48 Ibid., ch. X, pp. 119–20.

49 Ibid., ch. XXXV, pp. 309–10.

50 Ibid., ch. XXXVI, p. 329.

51 Ibid., ch. XIV, pp. 142–3.

52 John Arlott, who followed George Orwell as the producer of literary programmes in the B.B.C.'s Eastern Service at that time, writes:

During the Second World War the B.B.C., within its Eastern Service, built up a programme-grouping called 'English to India' which was of a uniformly higher cultural and intellectual standard than any other section of British broadcasting until the creation of the Third Programme. It was not directly propagandist, but it sought, like much of the B.B.C.'s overseas output of the war period, to establish sympathy for Britain by its quality and integrity . . .

Forster was the one contributor the programme *had* to have if it was to command respect in India. He accepted that fact and became its only regular contributor throughout the war and for some three years afterwards.

He did not do these broadcasts for the usual reasons; he was not concerned with what he might earn from them, and he had neither the need nor the wish to create a reputation as a broadcaster . . . His strongest motive was his liking for the Indians . . . He was eager as *A Passage to India* would suggest to establish understanding, trust, and affection between Indians and people like himself. At a slightly lower level, he was anxious to show Indians that people like himself did exist in Britain . . . ('E. M. Forster at the Microphone', *Listener*, 2 January 1969, pp. 809)

53 'India Again', *Two Cheers for Democracy*, p. 328.

54 Ibid., p. 329.

55 'There is no one alive to-day of the stature of Tagore, or of Iqbal', Forster wrote in 1946; 'I have had the honour of meeting each of these great men once. Both are dead now, and their disappearance has impoverished the scene' (*Two Cheers for Democracy*, p. 333).

56 The publications of Mulk Raj Anand's *Untouchable*, Ahmed Ali's *Twilight in Delhi*, and Raja Rao's *The Serpent and the Rope*, were all due to Forster's help. (Cf. Natwar-Singh (ed.), *E. M. Forster: A Tribute*, pp. 32, 40, 45, 49.)

57 Forster has pointed out that 'the civilization, or blend of civilizations, which produced Aziz has been movingly evoked' in *Twilight in Delhi* (see 'Author's Notes', *A Passage to India*, Everyman's Library ed., p. xxx).

58 See Forster's preface in Anand, *Untouchable*, p. 7.

59 *Two Cheers for Democracy*, pp. 332–3.

60 Cf. ibid., p. 334.

61 'Since my last visit to India', Forster writes,

a film industry has sprung up. I believe it is the second largest in the world. It has its headquarters in Bombay. Its results are evident, and in the cities advertisements brighten the walls or hang down from the lamp-posts. They often take the form of a youth or a maiden. The maiden gazes before her at the traffic, the youth gazes down the nape of the maiden's neck; and thousands of passers-by see them and go in the evening for more. I went twice myself, but had no luck. (*Two Cheers for Democracy*, p. 333)

62 See *A Passage to India* (Everyman's Library ed., p. ix).

63 ibid.

Chapter 6

1 Some critics have attempted to read the novel as a definitive study in the Hindu way of life. The trend towards such an interpretation of *A Passage to India* started with Lionel Trilling's book which drew attention to the importance of the Hindu theme in the novel. Trilling says: 'The story is suffused with Hinduism. It is Mrs. Moore who carries the Hindu theme; it is Mrs. Moore, indeed, who is the story . . . the story is essentially concerned with Mrs. Moore's discovery that Christianity is not adequate' (*E. M. Forster*, London, 1962, pp. 131–2).

Glen O. Allen ('Structure, Symbol and Theme in E. M. Forster's *A Passage to India*', *PMLA*, LXX, no. 5, December 1955, pp. 934–54) has gone further in the pursuit of the Hindu theme, and has identified the three parts of the novel with the 'trichotomous division' of the Hindu attitude to life and doctrine of salvation: *Karma Marga* (the path of action), *Jnana Marga* (the path of knowledge) and *Bhakti Marga* (the path of devotion). He holds the view that 'Mosque' 'Caves' and 'Temple' – the three sections of the novel – are Forster's interpretations of the three Hindu *margas* (ways of life), and that Dr Aziz, Fielding and Professor Godbole represent these three ways, of action, knowledge, and devotion, respectively.

The three-part division of the novel has been connected by some other critics also with Hinduism's threefold division of the properties of creation into *sattva* (goodness), *rajas* (passion), and *tamas* (darkness). (See James McConkey, *The Novels of E. M. Forster*, New York, 1957, p. 145; and Wilfred Stone, *The Cave and the Mountain: A Study of E. M. Forster*, London, 1966, p. 312.)

While Trilling's view is reasonable as far as it goes, Glen O. Allen's interpretation is certainly not tenable. He misapplies the *Karma—Jnana—Bhakti—Marga* doctrine: in Hindu philosophy the three *margas* do not represent three exclusively different ways of life incorporating the isolated 'ingredients' of will, intellect and devotion. According to Allen, Forster portrays the three Hindu ways in the three parts of the novel in order to advocate that a wholesome way ought to be a combination of all the three 'in proportion'. But in Hindu philosophy it is in fact thought that a life lived according to any one of the three ways actually partakes of elements from the other two, and may lead to perfection of the entire self. Commenting on this point of the Hindu doctrine, Radhakrishnan writes (*Indian Philosophy*, vol. 1, rev. ed., London, 1929, pp. 553—4):

> It is true that in the finite life of the individual there seems to be some kind of antagonism between contemplation and action. This is only a sign of imperfection. When Krishna is asked about the particular method to be adopted, he clearly says that we need not worry about this question, since the different pathways are not ultimately distinct, but lead to the same goal, and are found together in the end though they cross and recross one another on the road. Man does not function in fractions. Progress is correlated and not dissociated development. Knowledge, feeling and will are different aspects of one movement of the soul.

It would also be inaccurate to identify Aziz, as Allen does in his essay, with 'the path of action', and Fielding with 'the path of knowledge'. Obviously, Aziz shows as much of the contemplative and emotional life as Fielding does of the active.

As for James McConkey's and Wilfred Stone's reference to the subject of *sattva—rajas—tamas*, both critics have only very vaguely alluded to this subject in Hindu philosophy without clarifying the actual nature of the correspondence that they suppose to be present between the three *gunas* (properties) and Forster's themes.

2 Apart from the account of a visit to a group of Buddhist caves in 1913 (see 'Indian Entries', *Encounter*, XVIII, no. 1, January 1962, pp. 26—7), Forster's published letters in *The Hill of Devi* and his accounts from diaries contain no notable references to his contact with the Buddhist element in the Indian tradition. The references to Buddha and his doctrines in *A Passage to India* are only incidental, and rather fanciful (whereas the Buddhist Lama is a main figure in *Kim* and Kipling's novel deeply evokes Buddhist thought); describing the Marabar caves Forster writes (*A Passage to India*, ch. XII, p. 130): 'Some saddhus did once settle in a cave, but they were smoked out, and even Buddha, who must have passed this way down to the Bo Tree of Gaya, shunned a renunciation more complete than his own, and has left no legend of struggle or victory in the Marabar'. A similar allusion to Buddhism, and to Jainism, is also seen in ch. XXIV, p. 232, where during Aziz's trial, the question whether the Marabar caves are Buddhist or Jain is disputed in the court. About Buddhism's virtual disappearance from India Forster wrote earlier, in 1920:

The glory is also gone from Boddh-Gaya, where Buddha obtained enlighten-ment, but a small temple exists, where he is adored by favour of the British Government in a half-hearted fashion. Boddh-Gaya is a sunken area; standing on its edge, one looks down on a tangle of paths and votive bells. No Indians worship there, for Buddhism has died out in India, in accordance with its own law. But pilgrims from Thibet sometimes light lamps so that the floor of the temple looks like a lake of fire and streams of hot air agitate the dirty banners above the image. Behind the temple is a neglected tree, descendant of the Bo Tree where Buddha sat and struggled with evil until 'the different regions of the sky grew clear, the moon shone forth, showers of flowers fell down from the sky upon the earth, and the night gleamed like a spotless maiden.'('Jehovah, Buddha, and the Greeks', *The Athenaeum*, 4 June 1920, p. 731)

With Buddhism virtually non-existent, the composite and complicated face of modern India is introduced to the reader in a single sentence in *A Passage to India*, such as: 'Hamidullah had called in on his way to a worrying committee of notables, nationalist in tendency, where Hindus, Moslems, two Sikhs, two Parsis, a Jain and a Native Christian tried to like one another more than came natural to them' (ch. IX, p. 111).

3 *A Passage to India*, ch. XXXIII, pp. 295–6.

4 *The Hill of Devi*, p. 68.

5 Ibid., p. 31. Forster writes: 'Their [the two Maharajahs] different tempera-ments converged in the adoration of Krishna, and they have between them helped to illuminate Indian religion for me'.

6 *Two Cheers for Democracy*, p. 299.

7 Ibid., p. 301.

8 *The Hill of Devi*, pp. 126–7.

9 Ibid., pp. 153–4.

10 Ibid., p. 87.

11 *The Hill of Devi*, p. 73. According to Hindu mythology, the tortoise is one of the ten different avatars of Lord Vishnu.

12 Ibid., p. 98.

13 Ibid., pp. 100–1.

14 Ibid., p. 101.

15 Ibid., p. 110.

16 Ibid., p. 112. In Hindu mythology Ganpati, the god with an elephant's head, is the son of Siva.

17 Ibid., p. 128. Hindu mythology ascribes a sacred place to the monkeys; the *Ramayan* depicts Hanuman, the 'Monkey-God', as Rama's devoted follower.

18 Ibid., p. 133.

19 Ibid., pp. 101–2.

20 Ibid., p. 105.

21 Ibid., pp. 105–6.

22 Ibid., p. 108.

23 Ibid., p. 109.

24 Ibid., p. 112.

25 Ibid., p. 106. See also p. 112, where, writing about the final day of the ceremony, Forster says: 'The expressions of most people were beautiful that day'.

26 Ibid., p. 106.

27 Ibid., p. 111.

28 Ibid., p. 107.

29 *A Passage to India*, ch. ii, pp. 20–2.

30 Ibid., ch. xxxiii, pp. 295–7.

31 Ibid., ch. viii, p. 104. Aziz's own personal superstition is seen when he does not 'fancy other people eating ham' (*A Passage to India*, ch. xiii, p. 133).

32 Ibid., ch. xxxv, p. 308.

33 Forster's sympathetic portrayal of Islam is seen also elsewhere (see 'The Mosque', *Anthenaeum*, 19 March 1920, pp. 367–8). He writes:

> It [the mosque] embodies no crisis, leads up through no gradation of nave and choir, and employs no hierarchy of priests. Equality before God – so doubtfully proclaimed by Christianity – lies at the very root of Islam . . . The Christian has a vague idea that God is inside the church, presumably near the east end. The Moslem, when his faith is pure, cherishes no such illusion, and, though he behaves in the sacred enclosure as tradition and propriety enjoin, attaches no sanctity to it beyond what is conferred by the presence of the devout'.

34 *A Passage to India*, ch. xii, p. 129. In the opening passage of the novel (ch. i, p. 9) the Ganges, near Chandrapore, is looked at realistically and with a touch of irony: 'Edged rather than washed by the river Ganges, it trails for a couple of miles along the bank, scarcely distinguishable from the rubbish it deposits so freely. There are no bathing-steps on the river front, as the Ganges happens not to be holy there . . .'

See also ch. ix, p. 109, where the Muslims talk scornfully about Hindu religious fairs, holy bathing, and idol worship:

> Mr. Syed Mohammed had visited religious fairs, at Allahabad and at Ujjain, and described them with biting scorn. At Allahabad there was flowing water, which carried impurities away, but at Ujjain the little river Sipra was banked up, and thousands of bathers deposited their germs in the pool. He spoke with disgust of the hot sun, the cow-dung and marigold flowers, and the encampment of saddhus, some of whom strode stark naked through the streets. Asked what was the name of the chief idol at Ujjain, he replied that he did not know, he had disdained to enquire, he really could not waste his time over such trivialities.

35 Ibid., ch. xxxv, p. 310.

36 Ibid., ch. xxiv, p. 220.

37 Ibid., ch. xviii, p. 176.

38 Ibid., ch. xxviii, p. 267. The Vedantic concept of Brahm as the one God behind the many is expostulated upon by the seers in *Brihadaranyaka-Upanishad*, 3 Adhyaya, 9 Brahmana (see *The Upanishads*, trans: F. Max Muller, Oxford, 1884, pt ii, pp. 139–42):

> Then Vidagdha Sakalya asked him: 'How many gods are there, O Yagnavalkya?' He replied . . . 'As many as . . . three and three hundred, three and three thousand'.
>
> 'Yes,' he said, and asked again: 'How many gods are there really, O Yagnavalkya?' 'Thirty-three,' he said.

'Yes,' he said, and asked again: 'How many gods are there really, O Yagnavalkya?' 'Three,' he said.
'Yes,' he said, and asked again: 'How many gods are there really, O Yagnavalkya?' 'Two,' he said.
'Yes,' he said, and asked again: 'How many gods are there really, O Yagnavalkya?' 'One and a half (adhyardha),' he said.
'Yes,' he said, and asked again: 'How many gods are there really, O Yagnavalkya?' 'One,' he said.
[Then, asked by Vidagdha Sakalya, Yagnavalkya names the various gods, and they talk about the one God.]
He asked: 'Who is the one god?'
Yagnavalkya replied: ' . . . He is Brahman . . .'

39 James McConkey (*The Novels of E. M. Forster*, pp. 159–60) says:

Granted the contemporary condition as Forster describes it, the way of Godbole is the only way: love, even though to exist it must maintain a detachment from the physical world and human relationships, offers the single upward path from the land of sterility and echoing evil. And Godbole, more than any other character in the novels, is, as we have seen the Forsterian voice itself.

'It is the Godbole vision we must understand', writes Wilfred Stone, 'if we are to understand the book' (*The Cave and the Mountain*, p. 334).
40 David Shusterman points out in a detailed study ('The Curious Case of Professor Godbole: *A Passage to India* Re-examined', *PMLA*, LXXVI, no. 4, September 1961, pp. 426–35) that Godbole's character shows the element of evil rather than good:

A close consideration of the novel will show that the role of Professor Godbole, though important, is important in a manner different from that which has been claimed: far from being an influence for good, he is an influence which is non-beneficial and, if not primarily and consciously evil, is at least in the direction of evil . . . One of Forster's main intentions is to show that Godbole, like other principal characters, is one of the baffled, unsatisfied children of the earth, attempting to penetrate into the mysteries of existence but never quite finding the true path to the ultimate knowledge, never reaching the passage to India . . . Godbole is truly, as his name implies [Greek, bolos, lump of earth], a lump of God's universe like all the others, and is only capable of occupying a minute portion of it . . .

41 From an account of the author's interview with Forster ('Call Me An Unbeliever: Interview with E. M. Forster', *The Statesman*, Calcutta, 23 September, 1968, p. 6). The name 'Godbole', a Marathi Surname, actually means 'sweet tongued'. According to information received from Forster's authorised biographer, P. N. Furbank, Forster had actually met and talked about Indian music with a Mr Godbole at an evening party held on 23 Februay 1913 by the Brahmo Samajists of Lahore (now a part of Pakistan). 'What a name!' – Forster remarked in a note on the back of his invitation card.
42 For Forster's acquaintance with Tilak's position in the Indian national

movement, see *Abinger Harvest*, p. 369.

43 Valentine Chirol's reports on India in *The Times* appeared in the book *Indian Unrest* (London, 1910). Forster's familiarity with Chirol's account is known by his reference in *The Hill of Devi* (pp. 47, 55) to the book and to the author, whom he describes as 'a travelling journalist of repute'.

44 See *Indian Unrest*, pp. 37–47.

45 *A Passage to India*, ch. VII, p. 71.

46 Ibid., p. 76.

47 *Indian Unrest*, p. 38.

48 *A Passage to India*, VII, p. 84.

49 *The Hill of Devi*, p. 133.

50 Ibid., p. 129.

51 Cf. *A Passage to India*, ch. XIII, p. 133: 'The Professor was not a very strict Hindu – he would take tea, fruit, soda-water, and sweets, whoever cooked them, and vegetables and rice if cooked by a Brahman; but not meat, not cakes lest they contained eggs, and he would not allow anyone else to eat beef: a slice of beef upon a distant plate would wreck his happiness'. In *The Hill of Devi*, Forster writes about the Maharajah's strong objection to anyone eating beef (p. 99), and also about the queer rules on food observed during Gokul Ashtami: 'For ten days nothing may be killed, not even an egg . . . But animals that have been killed already – i.e. tinned food – I may consume provided I come up to the New Palace to do so' (p. 103).

52 *A Passage to India*, XXXIII, p. 298.

53 Ibid.

54 It is natural, therefore, that when Gobole is looked at as an exponent of Hinduism he appears unconvincing. Nirad C. Chaudhuri, the Indian critic, writes: 'To those of us who are familiar with the teachings of the Hindu reformers of the 19th century, Godbole is not an exponent of Hinduism, he is a Clown', ('Passage To and From India', *Encounter*, II, no. 6, June 1954, p. 21).

55 *A Passage to India*, ch. XXXIV, p. 304.

56 Ibid., ch. XXXVII, pp. 332–3.

57 Ibid., ch. IX, p. 116.

58 'Religion is a living force to the Hindus, and can at certain moments fling down everything that is petty and temporary in their natures' (*A Passage to India*, ch. XXXVI, p. 316).

59 Ibid., ch. XXXI, p. 288.

60 Ibid., p. 287. The idea that the Hindu's mystical sense is more intense than the Muslim's is perhaps implied elsewhere in the novel. When, at the end of the story, Aziz and Fielding are riding together and Aziz, irritated at Fielding's curiosity about Krishna's birth ceremony, works up emotions about his own religion, he is shown to be lacking in depth:

A poem about Mecca – the Caaba of Union – the thorn-bushes where pilgrims die before they have seen the Friend – they flitted next; he thought of his wife; and then the whole semi-mystic, semi-sensuous overturn, so characteristic of his spiritual life, came to end like a landslip and rested in its due place, and he found himself riding in the jungle with his dear Cyril. (Ibid., XXXVII, p. 333).

61 Remarking about the account in the *Bhagavad Purana* Forster writes: 'If one can judge from a translation, and if one can condone silliness and prolixity, the

tenth book of the *Bhagavad Purana* must be a remarkable work. It has warmth and emotion and a sort of divine recklessness and a sort of crude human happiness' (*The Hill of Devi*, p. 118).

62 Ibid. The similarity between the two stories is pointed out also in *A Passage to India*, ch. XXXIII, p. 299.

63 *The Hill of Devi*, pp. 118–19.

64 See 'The Blue Boy', *Listener*, 14 March 1957, p. 444; and *A Presidential Address to the Cambridge Humanists – Summer 1959* (London, 1963).

65 'The Blue Boy', p. 444. Forster's account of Krishna's conversations with Arjuna (*Abinger Harvest*, pp. 380–2) as depicted in the *Bhagavad Gita*, has been discussed in chapter 1.

66 '*The Blue Boy*', p. 444.

67 Ibid. Forster's account is based on W. G. Archer's researches on the Krishna tradition in Indian painting and poetry published in *The Loves of Krishna* (London, 1957).

68 '*The Blue Boy*', p. 444.

69 In a passage which shows Forster's inclination towards Krishna he writes that he 'is indeed on nearer nodding terms with Krishna than with any other god. This is not saying much, for to what god does one venture to give a nod? Jehovah's awful one certainly invites no response. "Down on your knees!" is the more usual injunction. Krishna inclines to gaiety. Even if he kills a dragon he dances on its teeth, which St. Michael would not do' ('*The Blue Boy*', p. 444). But, asked whether he regarded himself as a 'believer' in Krishna, Forster firmly declared his position as 'non-believer' (cf. Appendix B).

70 *A Presidential Address to the Cambridge Humanists*, pp. 6–7. Forster's appreciation of the place of pleasure and fun ('what Christianity has shirked') in some aspects of Krishna worship is also suggested in the following excerpt, depicting Gokul Ashtami celebrations in *A Passage to India* (ch. XXXIII, p. 301):

Down in the sacred corridors, joy had seethed to jollity. It was their duty to play various games to amuse the newly born God, and to simulate his sports with the dairymaids of Brindaban . . . There is fun in heaven. God can play practical jokes upon Himself, draw chairs away from beneath His own posteriors, set His own turbans on fire, and steal His own petticoats when He bathes. By sacrificing good taste, this worship achieved what Christianity has shirked: the inclusion of merriment. All spirit as well as matter must participate in salvation, and if practical jokes are banned, the circle is incomplete.

71 Forster's account of his early curious impressions of the temples of Khajuraho has been referred to in chapter 1. In an early piece on the subject of the Hindu temple he wrote thus, expressing his conflicting reactions to the architecture in general:

The general deportment of the Temple is odious. It is unaccommodating, it rejects every human grace, its jokes are ill-bred, its fair ladies are fat, it ministers neither to the sense of beauty nor to the sense of time, and it is discontented with its own material. No one could love such a building. Yet no one can forget it. It remains in the mind when fairer types have faded, and sometimes seems to be the only type that has any significance. When we tire of being pleased and of being improved, and of the other gymnastics of the West, and care, or think we care, for Truth alone; then the Indian Temple exerts its power, and beckons down absurd or detestable vistas to an exit unknown to the Parthenon. We say 'here is truth,' and as soon as we have said the words the exit – if it was one, – closes, and we fly back to our old habits again. (*The Athenaeum*, 26 September 1919, p. 947)

72 Forster's later writings about Indian art and architecture, which like some of his earlier ones appeared in the form of reviews of a number of important books about the subject, contain valuable personal comments and independent interpretations of his own. Among these writings the most important are: (i) 'Indian Caves', *The Nation and the Athenaeum*, 11 July 1925, p. 462; (ii) 'The Art and Architecture of India', *Listener*, 10 September 1953, pp. 419–21; (iii) [Review of] *India: Paintings from Ajanta Caves* by H. Zwemmer, *Listener*, 12 August 1954, p. 253; unsigned (Forster's authorship identified by B. J. Kirkpatrick, *A Bibliography of E. M. Forster*, London, 1968, p. 152); (iv) 'The World Mountain', *Listener*, 2 December 1954, pp. 977–8; (v) 'Erotic Indian Sculpture', *Listener*, 12 March 1959, pp. 469–71. Further details of these articles will be found in the bibliography.

73 'Indian art is not the westerner's natural food', says Forster. 'It is desirable that he should eat of it, and it is disgraceful that the British, who have controlled the peninsula for over a hundred years, should have deterred him from eating, and should even have asserted that the food was rubbish or muck. All the same, little and often may be a sensible policy. It has worked in my own case. Each time I approach this great achievement of the human race I appreciate it longer . . .' (see 'The World Mountain').

74 On the subject of erotic sculptures in general, and of those at Khajuraho in particular, Forster writes (see 'Erotic Indian Sculpture').

Some of them are absurd and vulgar, but they are for the most part gracious and seductive, and this is the first point that has to be made about them. And they present sex as something pleasurable – that is an additional point that must be made. They are hedonistic. They are the complete antithesis of the House of Commons debate on the Wolfenden Report. In that debate sex was condoned, condemned, pitied, patronized, tolerated, deplored, justified, excommunicated, but never referred to as pleasant. The tacit rejection of pleasure, or the reduction of it to 'mere pleasure' falsifies all our public utterances on this subject, and many of our private comments.

All the same these Indian sculptures are puzzling. They must be unique. There seems nothing to which they can be compared. They are not comparable to the fertility symbols so frequent in India and elsewhere, and although they are heterosexual they show no interest in the propagation of the human race. They are not comparable to the grotesques on our medieval cathedrals, whose purpose is admonitory. They are not comparable to the indecencies in a lecher's cabinet, for they were destined for the exterior of a public building where human beings, whatever their age or caste, could see them as they went about their daily work. With what emotions were they viewed? They are a thousand years old, and it is difficult to say. Though the question can perhaps be approached by asking another question: with what emotion are the crucifixes viewed by those who pass by them daily in a Catholic town? Are the public displays of pleasure and of suffering equally potent? Or are they equally inoperative?

... I have only once seen sculptures of this type. They were in the Khajraho group of temples, and one of the things that struck me about them was their infrequency – their comparative infrequency. The Khajraho temples, symbolical of the world-mountain, are covered with sculptures all executed in the same style and with equal care, but the erotic ones are confined (as it were) to the exterior of the north-east transept. This is their locality and they do not stray from it. And I deduced from this that the temple-planners were not so much interested in the 'hot stuff' as in the stuff, hot, lukewarm and cold, that combines to build up the world-mountain.

75 The symbolism expressed in the temple architecture at Khajuraho is a characteristic feature of all Hindu temples. It is represented in even 'the simplest structures of Vedic times' (cf. Benjamin Rowland, *The Art and Architecture of India: Buddhist, Hindu, Jain*, London, 1953, p. 174).

76 *Listener*, 10 September 1953, p. 420. A contrast between Hinduism, and the congregational religions of Christianity, Buddhism and Islam is drawn also in 'The World Mountain'.

77 After visiting an exhibition of Indian art held at the Warburg Institute, London, Forster wrote in a letter (*Listener*, 5 December 1940, pp. 801–2):

The Hindu temple is not for community-worship. It is for the individual. Buddhism and Christianity have congregations, and monks and sermons, so they need large places to meet in. Hinduism doesn't, and however large and elaborate the Hindu temple is outside, the inner core of it is small, secret and dark. Today one hears of nothing but the community-spirit. It is boosted in season and out. I weary of it, and it was with relief and joy that I saw these great temples where the individual is at the last resort alone with his god, buried in the depths of the world-mountain. I came away feeling not only that Hindu art is a remarkable achievement – that I had always realised – but that it was an achievement that I might interpret in view of my own experiences and needs.

For you cannot imagine how much we over here are in need of inspiration, of spirituality, of something which will deliver us from the tyranny of the body-politic. Besides our war against totalitarianism, we have also an inner war, a struggle for truer values, a struggle of the individual towards the dark, secret place where he may find reality. I came away thinking, 'Yes, the people who built these temples, the people who planned Khajraho and Orissa and Madura – knew about that. They belonged to another civilization, but they knew, they knew that the community cannot satisfy the human spirit.'

Conclusion

1 The late Sir Akbar Hydari (cf. *The Hill of Devi*, p. 154) was an eminent nationalist, educationist and statesman of Hyderabad, who was a profound believer in Islam and also in Hindu and other cultures of India, and worked for Hindu – Moslem unity.

2 In November 1962 when the 'border-war' broke out between India and China Forster signed a strongly worded letter of protest against the Chinese attack,

which was in his view an attack on democracy and freedom in Asia. Calling for support for India the letter said: 'China's attack on India, a peaceful democracy and a member of the Commonwealth, a country engaged in a determined struggle to make a better life for its millions of citizens through freedom and independence, is a challenge to all of us . . .' (see *Spectator*, 30 November 1962, p. 865. The signatories of the letter, headed by Forster, also included Olaf Caroe, Barbara Ward and Guy Wint).

Bibliography

1. *A chronological list of Forster's writings about India, including his communications to the press about India and Indians*

1912   'Hymn Before Action', *Cambridge Magazine*, 10, no. 1 (summer 1920) 11–12; repr. *Abinger Harvest*, 1936.

1913   'Iron Horses in India', *Golden Hynde*, 1 (December 1913) 35–9. On railway travel in India.

1914   'Adrift in India: The Nine Gems of Ujjain', *New Weekly*, 1 (21 March 1914) 10; repr. *Abinger Harvest*.
'The Indian Mind', *New Weekly*, 1 (28 March 1914) 55. Review of *Reflections on the Problems of India* by A. S. Wadia.
'Adrift in India, 2: Advance, India!', *New Weekly*, 1 (11 April 1914) 106; repr. *Abinger Harvest*.
'Adrift in India, 3: In Rajasthan', *New Weekly*, 1 (16 May 1914) 269–70; repr. (omitting the first paragraph) as 'Adrift in India, 3; Jodhpur', *Abinger Harvest*.
'The Gods of India', *New Weekly*, 1 (30 May 1914) 338. Review of *The Gods of India*, by E. O. Martin.
'The Chitra', *New Weekly*, 1 (13 June 1914) 403. Review of *Chitra* by Rabindranath Tagore; repr. as 'Two Books by Tagore, I: Chitra', *Abinger Harvest*.
'The Age of Misery', *New Weekly*, II (27 June 1914) 52. Review of *Ancient India* by E. J. Rapson.
'Adrift in India, 4: The Suppliant', *New Weekly*, II (25 July 1914) 166; repr. *Abinger Harvest*.
'The Elder Tagore', *Daily News and Leader*, 11 November 1914. Review of *The Autobiography of Maharshi ('the Saint') Devendranath Tagore*, trans. S. Tagore and I. Devi.

1915   'The Indian Boom', *Daily News and Leader*, 2 February 1915. Review of *Svarnalata: Scenes from Hindu Village Life in Bengal* by T. N. Ganguli, trans. S. Tagore and I. Devi.
'A Great Anglo-Indian', *Daily News and Leader*, 29 March 1915. Review of *Studies in Literature and History* by Sir Alfred Lyall.
'The Mission of Hinduism', *Daily News and Leader*, 30 April 1915. Review of *Footfalls of Indian History* by Sister Nivedita (Margaret E. Noble); *Hinduism in Europe and America* by Elizabeth A. Reed.

1919 'Tagore as a Novelist', *The Athenaeum*, 1 August 1919, p. 687. Review of *The Home and the World* by Rabindranath Tagore; repr. as 'Two Books by Tagore, 2: *The Home and the World*', *Abinger Harvest*.
'The Temple', *The Athenaeum*, 26 September 1919, p. 947. Review of some official Indian Archaeological Publications.
('Sakuntala'), *The Athenaeum*, 28 November 1919, p. 1267. Review of the play *Sakuntala* by Kalidas (English version by Das Gupta and Laurence Binyon) at the Winter Garden Theatre, London; unsigned.

1920 'The Mosque', *The Athenaeum*, 19 March 1920, pp. 367–8. Review of *Moslem Architecture* by G. T. Riviora, trans. G. McN. Rushworth; repr. *Abinger Harvest*.
'The Golden Peak', *The Athenaeum*, 14 May 1920, pp. 631–2. Review of *Sakuntala* by Kalidas; a version for the English stage by Das Gupta and Laurence Binyon, with an introduction by Rabindranath Tagore.
'The Churning of the Ocean', *The Athenaeum*, 21 May 1920, pp. 667–8. Review of *The Ideals of Indian Art*, 2nd ed. by E. B. Havell; and *Chatterjee's Picture Albums*, volsı i–v.
'Jehovah, Buddha and the Greeks', *The Athenaeum*, 4 June 1920, pp. 730–1. Review of *Hellenism* by Norman Bentwich; and *Hellenism in Ancient India* by Gauranga Nath Bannerjee.
'Luso-India', *The Athenaeum*, 27 August 1920, p. 268. Review of *The Book of Duarte Barbosa*, vol. i; and *History of the Portuguese in Bengal* by J. J. A. Campos.
'Missionaries', *The Athenaeum*, 22 October 1920, pp. 545–7. Review of *In Unknown China* by S. Pollard; *The Rebuke of Islam* by W. H. T. Gairdner; *Women Workers of the Orient* by M. E. Burton; and *Character Building in Kashmir* by C. E. Tyndale-Biscoe.
[Review of] *The Diary of Ananda Ranga Pillai*, vol. vii, ed. H. Dodwell, *The Athenaeum*, 3 December 1920, p. 761; unsigned.
'The Poetry of Iqbal', *The Athenaeum*, 10 December 1920, pp. 803–4. Review of *The Secrets of Self* by Sheik Muhammed Iqbal, trans. from the Persian by R. A. Nicholson.

1922 'Reflections in India, 1: Too Late?' (By Our Indian Correspondent), *The Nation and the Athenaeum*, 21 January 1922, pp. 614–15; unsigned.
'Reflections in India, 2: The Prince's Progress' (By Our Indian Correspondent), *The Nation and the Athenaeum*, 28 January 1922, pp. 644–6; unsigned.
'The Emperor Babur', *The Nation and the Athenaeum*, 1 April 1922, pp. 21–2. Review of *The Memoirs of Babur*, Leyden and Erskine's translation, annotated and revised by Sir Lucas King; repr. *Abinger*

Harvest.

'The Mind of the Indian Native State' (By Our Indian Correspondent), *The Nation and the Athenaeum*, 29 April, 13 May 1922, pp. 146–7, 216–17; unsigned; repr. *Abinger Harvest.*

'India and the Turk' (From our Correspondent Lately in India), *The Nation and the Athenaeum*, 30 September 1922, pp. 844–5; signed F.

1923 'Pan', *Criterion*, 1 (July 1923) 402–8; repr. as 'Adrift in India, 5: Pan', *Abinger Harvest.*

1924 'The Birth of an Empire', *The Nation and the Athenaeum*, 26 April 1924, pp. 110–11. On the British Empire Exhibition at Wembley, with comments on the Indian section; repr. as 'Our Diversions, 2: The Birth of an Empire', *Abinger Harvest.*

'Eliza in Chains', *Cornhill Magazine*, n. s., LVI (May 1924) 598–609. Based on *Original Letters from India (1779–1815)* by Mrs Eliza Fay; repr. *Dial*, LXXVI (May 1924) 391–403.

A Passage to India (London, 1924).

'An Eighteenth-century Sailor', *The Nation and the Athenaeum*, 4 October 1924, p. 22. Review of *A History of the Indian Wars (1737)* by Clement Downing, ed. William Foster; signed E. M. F.

1925 'Indian Caves', *The Nation and the Athenaeum*, 11 July 1925, p. 462. Review of *My Pilgrimages to Ajanta and Bagh* by S. M. C. Dey.

Original Letters from India (1779–1815): Mrs. Fay, introductory and terminal notes by E. M. Forster (London, 1925).

1926 'Hickey's Last Party', *Calendar of Modern Letters*, II, February 1926. Review of *Memoirs of William Hickey*, vol. IV; repr. *Abinger Harvest.*

1927 Foreword to *Flowers and Elephants* by Constance Mary Evelyn Sitwell (London, 1927).

1935 Preface to Mulk Raj Anand's *Untouchable* (London, 1935).

1936 *Abinger Harvest* (London, 1936): including a selection of previously published articles on Indian subjects.

1937 [Letter to the Editor and appreciation of Sir Syed Ross Masood], *Urdu*, XVII (October 1937) 853–60; reprinted (omitting letter) as 'Syed Ross Masood', *Two Cheers for Democracy.*

'Sir Tukoji Rao Puar', *The Times*, 28 December 1937. Personal tribute.

1938 'Indians in England', *New Statesman and Nation*, 6 August 1938, pp. 311–12. Letter about ill-treatment of Indians in some London hotels.

1939 'Woodlanders on Devi', *New Statesman and Nation* (Literary Supplement), 6 May 1939, pp. 679–80.

1940   'The Individual and His God', *Listener*, 5 December 1940, pp. 801–2. Part of a broadcast talk in the Overseas Service on 22 November on the photographic exhibition of Indian art at the Warburg Institute, London.

1941   'Indian Broadcasting', *New Statesman and Nation*, 2 and 16 August 1941, pp. 112, 160. Letters.

1943   'An Indian on W. B. Yeats', *Listener*, 24 December 1942, p. 824. Review of *The Development of William Butler Yeats* by V. K. Narayana Menon (broadcast in the Indian Service). Introduction to *Literature and Authorship in India* by K. R. Shrinivasa Iyengar (London, 1943).

1944   'An Arnold in India', *Listener*, 12 October 1944, pp. 401–11. Broadcast talk in the Eastern Service; repr. as 'William Arnold', *Two Cheers for Democracy*.

1946   'India After Twenty-five Years' *Listener*, 31 January, 7 February 1946, pp. 133–34, 171–2. Broadcast talks in the Home Service; repr. as 'India Again', *Two Cheers for Democracy*. 'A Great Indian Philosopher', *Listener*, 23 May 1946, p. 686. Broadcast talk in the Home Service; repr. as 'Mohammed Iqbal', *Two Cheers for Democracy*.

1947   'Literature in India', *London Calling*, no. 416 (11 September 1947) 2. Part of broadcast talk in the Eastern Service.

1949   'Mahatma Gandhi' (Tribute by Forster), *Mahatma Gandhi; Essays and Reflections on his Life and Work, together with a New Memorial Section*, ed. S. Radhakrishnan (London, 1949).

1950   Foreword (with T. S. Eliot) to *Hali (a Play)* by G. V. Desani (London, 1950). 'The Tragic and the Comic View: A Novel of Changing India that Dramatizes Upheaval', *New York Times Book Review*, 26 March 1950, pp. 1, 30. Review of *The World is a Bridge* by Christine Weston. 'Bikaner', *Listener*, 22 June 1950, p. 1065. Review of *The Art and Architecture of Bikaner State* by Hermann Goetz. 'The Cambridge Chancellorship', *Spectator*, 10 November 1950, p. 468. Letter concerning the question of Jawaharlal Nehru's nomination.

1951   Introduction to *Maura* (a novel) by Huthi Singh (London, 1951). *Two Cheers for Democracy* (London, 1951): including a selection of previously published writings and broadcast talks on Indian subjects.

Foreword to *Zohra* (a novel) by Zeenuth Futehally (Bombay, 1951).

1953 'Lear in India', *Listener*, 26 March 1953, p. 519. Review of *Edward Lear's Indian Journal: Water-colours and Extracts*, ed. Ray Murphy.

'The Art and Architecture of India', *Listener*, 10 September 1953, pp. 419–21. Broadcast talk in the Third Programme on *The Art and Architecture of India: Buddhist, Hindu, and Jain* by Benjamin Rowland.

'The Birth of Krishna', *Observer*, 11 October 1953. Letter written on 28 August 1921; incorporated in *The Hill of Devi*.

The Hill of Devi (Being Letters from Dewas State Senior) (London, 1953).

1954 'East and West', *Observer*, 21 February 1954. Review of *Asia and Eastern Dominance* by K. M. Panikkar; and *The Men Who Ruled India, Vol. I, The Founders* by Philip Woodruff.

'Tidying India', *Listener*, 11 March 1954, pp. 435–6. Review of *My Public Life* by Sir Mirza Ismail.

[Review of] *India: Paintings from Ajanta Caves, Listener*, 12 August 1954, p. 253; unsigned.

'The World Mountain', *Listener*, 2 December 1954, pp. 977–8. Review of *The Art of India* by Stella Kramrisch.

1956 [Review of] *Indian Painting for the British: 1770–1880* by Mildred and W. G. Archer, *Listener*, 19 January 1956, p. 111; unsigned.

1957 'The Blue Boy', *Listener*, 14 March 1957, p. 444. Review of *The Loves of Krishna* by W. G. Archer.

'Light on Deoli', *Listener*, 5 December 1957, p. 951. Review of *The Twice Born* by G. Morris Carstairs.

1959 'Erotic Indian Sculpture', *Listener*, 12 March 1959, pp. 469, 471. Review of *Kama Kala* by Mulk Raj Anand.

'A Known Indian', *Observer*, 16 August 1959, p. 14. Review of *Passage to England* by Nirad C. Chaudhuri.

1960 'Descent to the Plains', *Observer*, 14 August 1960, p. 20. Review of *Gone Away* by Dom Moraes.

1962 'Indian Entries', *Encounter*, XVIII (January 1962) 20–7. Extracts from Forster's diary from 8 October 1912 to 2 April 1913; repr. as 'Indian Entries from a Diary', *Harper's Magazine*, February 1962, pp. 46–52, 55–6, with an introduction by Santha Rama Rau, pp. 46–7.

'Back India Appeal', *Spectator*, 30 November 1962, p. 856. Signed E. M. Forster, Olaf Caroe, Barbara Ward and Guy Wint on behalf of the United India Defence Fund.

2. *Select studies on Forster*

Ackerley, J. R., *E. M. Forster: A Portrait* (London, 1970).

Allen, Glen O., 'Structure, Symbol and Theme in E. M. Forster's *A Passage to India*', *PMLA*, LXX (December 1955) 934–54.

Beer, J. B. *The Achievement of E. M. Forster* (London, 1962).

Beer, J. B. and Das, G. K. *E. M. Forster: A Human Exploration* (London, 1979).

Bokhari, A. S., 'Homage à Monsieur Forster', *The Nation and the Athenaeum*, 4 August, 1928. (The article appeared anonymously.)

Bradbury, Malcolm (ed.), *Forster: A Collection of Critical Essays* (Twentieth Century Views, Englewood Cliffs, N.J., 1966).

Brander, Laurence, *E. M. Forster: A Critical Study* (London, 1968).

Burra, Peter, 'Introduction to *A Passage to India*' (Everyman's Library edition, London, 1965).

Chaudhuri, Nirad C., 'Passage To and From India', *Encounter*, II (June 1954).

Colmer, John, *A Passage to India* (Studies in Literature 30, London, 1967).

——*E. M. Forster, the Personal Voice* (London, 1975).

Crews, Frederick, *E. M. Forster: The Perils of Humanism* (Princeton, N. J., 1962).

Furbank, P. N., 'Tribute to Forster', *The Times* (Saturday Review), 28 December 1968.

——'The Personality of E. M. Forster', *Encounter*, XXXV (November 1970).

——*E. M. Forster: A Life,* vols. I & II (London, 1977–78).

Gardner, Philip (ed.), *E. M. Forster: The Critical Heritage* (London, 1973).

Godfrey, Denis, *E. M. Forster's Other Kingdom* (London, 1968).

Gowda, H. H. Anniah, *A Garland for E. M. Forster* (Mysore, 1969).

Gransden, K. W., *E. M. Forster* (Writers and Critics series, London, 1962).

Kettle, Arnold, *An Introduction to the English Novel*, vol. II (London, 1960).

Leavis, F. R., 'E. M. Forster', *The Common Pursuit* (London, 1952).

Levine, June Perry, *Creation and Criticism: 'A Passage to India'* (London, 1971).

Macaulay, Rose, *The Writings of E. M. Forster* (London, 1938).

Martin, John Sayre, *E.M. Forster, The Endless Journey* (London, 1976).

McConkey, James, *The Novels of E. M. Forster* (New York, 1957).

McDowell, Frederick P. W., *E. M. Forster* (Twayne's English Authors series, New York, 1969).

—— *E.M. Forster: An Annotated Bibliography of Writings about Him* (Illinois, 1976).

Mahood, M. M., 'Amritsar to Chandrapore: E. M. Forster & the Massacre', *Encounter*, ch. XLI (September 1973).

Meyers, Jeffrey, 'The Politics of *A Passage to India*', *Journal of Modern Literature*, 1 (3 March 1971).

Moody, Phillipa, *Forster: A Passage to India* (London, 1968).

Moore, Harry T., *E. M. Forster* (London, 1965).

Mortimer, Raymond, 'E. M. Forster: The Art of Being Individual', *The Sunday Times*, 29 December 1968.

Natwar-Singh, K. (ed.), *E. M. Forster: A Tribute* (with selections from his writings on India) (New York, 1964).

Perrott, Roy, 'The Quiet Revolutionary', *Observer* (Review), 5 January 1969.

Rama Rau, Santha, Introduction to 'Indian Entries' from a Diary by E. M. Forster, *Harper's Magazine*, February 1962.

Rutherford, A. (ed.), *Twentieth Century Interpretations of 'A Passage to India'* (Englewood Cliffs, N. J., 1970).

Shahane, V. A., *E. M. Forster: A Reassessment* (Delhi, 1962).

——*E. M. Forster: A Study in Double Vision* (Delhi, 1975).

—— *'A Passage to India': A Study* (Delhi, 1977).

Shahani, Ranjee G., 'Some British I Admire', *Asiatic Review*, July 1946.

Shonfield, Andrew, 'The Politics of Forster's India', *Encounter*, XXX (January 1968).

Shusterman, David, 'The Curious Case of Professor Godbole: *A Passage to India* Re-examined', *PMLA*, LXXVI (September 1961) 426–35.

Spencer, Michael, 'Hinduism in E. M. Forster's *A Passage to India*', *Journal of Asian Studies*, XXVII (February 1968).

Stallybrass, Oliver (ed.), *Aspects of E. M. Forster* (essays and recollections written for his ninetieth birthday) (London, 1969).

Stone, Wilfred, *The Cave and the Mountain: A Study of E. M. Forster* (London, 1966).

Thomson, George, *The Fiction of E. M. Forster* (Detroit, 1967).

Trilling, Lionel, *E. M. Forster* (London, 1944).

Warner, Rex, *E. M. Forster* (British Council pamphlet, supplement to *British Book News*) (London, 1950).

Woolf, Leonard, 'Arch Beyond Arch' (review of *A Passage to India*), *The Nation and the Athenaeum*, 14 June 1924.

Wright, Ralph, 'A Passage to India' (review), *New Statesman*, 21 June 1924.

3. *Some interviews with Forster*

1953   'The Art of Fiction: I, E. M. Forster' by P. N. Furbank and F. J. H. Haskell, *Paris Review*, I, no. 1 (spring 1953) 28–41.

1956   'Meet Mr. Forster', interview by Ela Sen, *Envoy* (London), July 1956.

1957   'A Conversation with E. M. Forster' by Angus Wilson, *Encounter*, IX (November 1957) 52–7.

1958   'E. M. Forster at Eighty' by Philip Toynbee, *Observer*, 28 December 1958.

1959   'E. M. Forster at Eighty' by K. W. Gransden, *Encounter*, XII (January 1959).
        'E. M. Forster on his Life and his Books' (an interview recorded for Television) by David Jones, *Listener*, 1 January 1959, pp. 11–12.
        'Recorded Interview with Mr. Forster' (recorded in Rome on 11 November 1959) by Patrick Smith. Script in possession of King's College, Cambridge.

1968   'Call Me An Unbeliever: Interview with E. M. Forster', by G. K. Das, *The Statesman* (Calcutta), 23 September 1968.

4. *Background studies*

Ackerley, J. R., *Hindu Holiday* (London, 1952).

Ali, Ahmed, *Twilight in Delhi* (London, 1940).

Anand, Mulk Raj, *Untouchable* (London, 1935).

——*Kama Kala* (some notes on the philosophical basis of Hindu erotic sculpture) (Geneva, 1958).

'An Englishwoman', 'Amritsar', *Blackwood's Magazine*, CCVII (April 1920).

Anonymous, 'Mem-Sahib's Point of View', *Cornhill Magazine*, XLVIII (May 1920).

Arberry, Arthur J., *The Koran Interpreted* (London, 1964).

Archer, W. G., *The Loves of Krishna* (London, 1957).

Aziz, K. K., *The Making of Pakistan: A Study in Nationalism* (London, 1967).

Banerjea, Surendranath, *A Nation in Making* (London, 1925).

Bennett, George (ed.), *The Concept of Empire: Burke to Attlee 1774–1947* (London, 1953).

Blunt, Edward, *The I.C.S.* (The Indian Civil Service), (London, 1931).

Blunt, Wilfrid S., *My Diaries*, Part 2 (1900–1914) (London, 1920).

Brown, Hilton, *Dismiss* (London, 1923).

Candler, Edmund, *Abdication* (London, 1922).

Carthill, Al (Thompson, John Perronet), *The Lost Dominion* (London, 1924).

Chirol, Sir Valentine, *Indian Unrest* (London, 1910).

Cornell, Louis L., *Kipling in India* (London, 1966).

Darling, Sir Malcolm *Apprentice to Power: India, 1904–1908* (London, 1966).

Forster, E. M. (writings in addition to those listed in Section 1)

——*Where Angels Fear to Tread* (London, 1905).

——*The Longest Journey* (London, 1907).

——*A Room With a View* (London, 1908).

——*Howards End* (London, 1910).

——*Egypt* (recommendations by a committee of the International Section of the Labour Research Department: notes by Forster) (London, 1920).

——*Alexandria: A History and a Guide* (Alexandria, 1922).

——*Pharos and Pharillon*(Richmond, 1923).

——*Aspects of the Novel* (London, 1927).

——*Goldsworthy Lowes Dickinson* (London, 1934).

——*England's Pleasant Land, A Pageant Play* (London, 1940).

——*Collected Short Stories* (London, 1948).

——*Marianne Thornton, 1797–1887: A Domestic Biography* (London, 1956).

——*A Presidential Address to the Cambridge Humanists, Summer 1959* (London, 1963).

——*Maurice* (London, 1971).

——*The Life to Come* (London, 1972).

——Some manuscripts in the possession of King's College, Cambridge: The Indian Diary; copyflow MSS. of *A Passage to India*; Commonplace Book; 'Three Countries – A Paper'.

Furneaux, Rupert, *Massacre at Amritsar* (London, 1963).

Gandhi, M. K., *An Autobiography: The Story of My Experiments with Truth*, trans. from Gujarati by Mahadev Desai (London, 1949).

——*The Collected Works of Mahatma Gandhi*, vol. xix (Delhi, 1966).

Gopal, S., *The Viceroyalty of Lord Irwin, 1926–1931* (Oxford, 1957).

Greenberger, Allen, *The British Image of India: A Study in the Literature of Imperialism* (London, 1969).

Gross, John (ed.), *Rudyard Kipling: the Man, his Work and his World* (London, 1972).

Hardinge of Penshurst, Lord, *My Indian Years* (London, 1948).

Havell, E. B., *The Ideals of Indian Art* (London, 1920).

Henn, T. R., *Kipling* (Writers and Critics series. London, 1967).

Howe, Susanne, *Novels of Empire* (New York, 1949).

Isherwood, Christopher (ed.), *Vedanta for the Western World* (London, 1963).

Iyer, Raghavan (ed.), *Utilitarianism and All That: the Political Theory of British Imperialism (St. Antony's Papers No. 8)* (London, 1960).

Khan, Syed Sirdar Ali, *The Earl of Reading* (London, 1924).

Kipling, Rudyard, *Kim* (London, 1901).

——*A Choice of Kipling's Verse*, ed. T. S. Eliot (London, 1941).

Lawrence, D. H., MSS. of Letters to Forster (1915–16, 1922, 1924) in the possession of King's College, Cambridge.

Low, D. A., 'The Government of India and the First Non-co-operation Movement–1920–22', *Journal of Asian Studies*, xxv (February 1966).

Max Muller, F. (trans.), *The Upanishads* (Oxford, 1884).

Meacham, Standish, *Henry Thornton of Clapham* (Cambridge, Mass., 1964).

Mehrotra, S. R., *India and the Commonwealth 1885–1929* (London, 1965).

Meyers, Jeffrey, *Fiction & the Colonial Experience* (Ipswich, 1973).

Moore, R. J., *Liberalism and Indian Politics, 1872–1922* (London, 1966).

Nagendra (ed.), *Indian Literature* (Agra, 1959).

Nehru, Jawaharlal, *The Discovery of India* (London, 1956).

O'Dwyer, Sir Michael, *India As I Knew It, 1885–1925* (London, 1925).

O'Malley, L. S. S., *The Indian Civil Service, 1601–1930* (London, 1931).

Parry, Benita, *Delusions and Discoveries* (London, 1972).

Philips, C. H. (ed.) *et al.*, *The Evolution of India and Pakistan, 1885 to 1947: Select Documents* (London, 1964).

Radhakrishnan, S. R., *Indian Philosophy*, vol. 1 (London, 1929).

——(ed.), *The Bhagavadgita*, with introductory essay, Sanskrit Text, English translation and notes (London, 1953).

——(ed.), *Mahatma Gandhi: Essays and Reflections on his Life and Work, together with a New Memorial Section* (London, 1949).

——(ed. with Moore, C. A.), *A Source Book in Indian Philosophy* (Princeton, N. J., 1967).

Rowland, Benjamin, *The Art and Architecture of India: Buddhist, Hindu, Jain* (London, 1953).

Sandison, Alan, *The Wheel of Empire* (London, 1967).

Singh, Bhupal, *A Survey of Anglo-Indian Fiction* (Oxford, 1934).

Singh, Madanjeet, *The Cave Paintings of Ajanta* (London, 1965).

Sitaramayya, Pattabhi, *The History of the Indian National Congress, I. 1885–1935* (Bombay, 1935).

Spear, Percival, *India, Pakistan and the West* (London, 1961).

Stokes, Eric, *The English Utilitarians and India* (Oxford, 1959).

Thompson, Edward John, *Atonement: A Play of Modern India* (London, 1924).

——*An Indian Day* (London, 1927).

——*A Farewell to India* (London, 1931).

Trevelyan, G. O., *The Competitionwallah* (London, 1864).

Waley, S. D., *Edwin Montagu: A Memoir and an Account of his Visits to India* (London, 1964).

Woodruff, Philip, *The Men Who Ruled India II: The Guardians* (London, 1965).

5. *Some official documents*

Imperial Gazetteer of India, vol. XI (Oxford, 1908).

Report on Indian Constitutional Reforms ('Montagu – Chelmsford Report') H. M. Stationery Office (London, 1918).

East India (Punjab Disturbances), 'Hunter Committee Report', Presented to Parliament, London, 1920.

Census of India, 1921, vol. XIII ('Central India Agency: Report and Tables') by the Superintendent of Census Operations (Calcutta, 1923).

East India (Progress and Report) H.M. Stationery Office (London, 1922).

The British Crown and the Indian States (An Outline sketch drawn up on behalf of the Standing Committee of the Chamber of Princes by the Directorate of the Chamber's special organization) (London, 1929).

The Constitution of India (Delhi, 1949).

Index